بِسْمِ اللهِ الرَّحْمَنِ الرَّحِيمِ

Hadith of the Prophet

Peace and Blessings be Upon Him

Sahih Al-Bukhari

Volume 1
Book 1 to 12

Copyright
K.F. National Library Cataloging-in-Publication Data
Edition. 2022
Editors/Writers Imam Ahmad and Noah Ibn Kathir

Other Great Books to Read

ISBN	9798774942602
ISBN	9798774942602
ISBN	9798517657411
ISBN	9798515913731
ISBN	9798515149253
ISBN	9798782321932
ISBN	9798782033439
ISBN	9781643542775
ISBN	9798418408044
ISBN	9781643544342
ISBN	9781727812718
ISBN	9781798285466
ISBN	9781643544328
ISBN	9781643544311
ISBN	9781643544236
ISBN	9781643544229
ISBN	9781643544212
ISBN	9781643544205

Content

VOLUME 1

Book 1, Revelation

Volume 1, Book 1, Number 1,

Narrated 'Umar bin Al-Khattab,

I heard Allah's Apostle saying, "The reward of deeds depends upon the intentions and every person will get the reward according to what he has intended. So whoever emigrated for worldly benefits or for a woman to marry, his emigration was for what he emigrated for."

Volume 1, Book 1, Number 2,

Narrated 'Aisha,

(the mother of the faithful believers) Al-Harith bin Hisham asked Allah's Apostle "O Allah's Apostle! How is the Divine Inspiration revealed to you?" Allah's Apostle replied, "Sometimes it is (revealed) like the ringing of a bell, this form of Inspiration is the hardest of all and then this state passes ' off after I have grasped what is inspired. Sometimes the Angel comes in the form of a man and talks to me and I grasp whatever he says." 'Aisha added, Verily I saw the Prophet being inspired Divinely on a very cold day and noticed the Sweat dropping from his forehead (as the Inspiration was over).

Volume 1, Book 1, Number 3,

Narrated 'Aisha,

(The mother of the faithful believers) The commencement of the Divine Inspiration to Allah's Apostle was in the form of good dreams which came true like bright day light, and then the love of seclusion was bestowed upon him. He used to go in seclusion in the cave of Hira where he used to worship (Allah alone) continuously for many days before his desire to see his family. He used to take with him the journey food for the stay and then come back to (his wife) Khadija to take his food likewise again till suddenly the Truth descended upon him while he was in the cave of Hira. The angel came to him and asked him to read. The Prophet replied, "I do not know how to read.

The Prophet added, "The angel caught me (forcefully) and pressed me so hard that I could not bear it any more. He then released me and again asked me to read and I replied, 'I do not know how to read.' Thereupon he caught me again and pressed me a second time till I could not bear it any more. He then released me and again asked me to read but again I replied, 'I do not know how to read (or what shall I read)?' Thereupon he caught me for the third time and pressed me, and then released me and said, 'Read in the name of your Lord, who has created (all that exists) has created man from a clot. Read! And your Lord is the Most Generous." (96.1, 96.2, 96.3) Then Allah's Apostle returned with the Inspiration and with his heart beating severely. Then he went to Khadija bint Khuwailid and said, "Cover me! Cover me!" They covered him till his fear was over and after that he told her everything that had happened and said, "I fear that something may happen to me." Khadija replied, "Never! By Allah, Allah will never disgrace you. You keep good relations with your Kith and kin, help the poor and the destitute, serve your guests generously and assist the deserving calamity-afflicted ones."

Khadija then accompanied him to her cousin Waraqa bin Naufal bin Asad bin 'Abdul 'Uzza, who, during the PreIslamic Period became a Christian and used to write the writing with Hebrew letters. He would write from the Gospel in Hebrew as much as Allah wished him to write. He was an old man and had lost his eyesight. Khadija said to Waraqa, "Listen to the story of your nephew, O my cousin!" Waraqa asked, "O my nephew! What have you seen?" Allah's Apostle described whatever he had seen. Waraqa said, "This is the same one who keeps the secrets (angel Gabriel) whom Allah had sent to Moses. I wish I were young and could live up to the time when your people would turn you out." Allah's Apostle asked, "Will they drive me out?" Waraqa replied in the affirmative and said, "Anyone (man) who came with something similar to what you have brought was treated with hostility; and if I should remain alive till the day when you will be turned out then I would support you strongly." But after a few days Waraqa died and the Divine Inspiration was also paused for a while.

Narrated Jabir bin 'Abdullah Al-Ansari while talking about the period of pause in revelation reporting the speech of the Prophet "While I was walking, all of a sudden I heard a voice from the sky. I looked up and saw the same angel who had visited me at the cave of Hira' sitting on a chair between the sky and the earth. I got afraid of him and came back home and said, 'Wrap me (in blankets).' And then Allah revealed the following Holy Verses (of Quran):

'O you (i.e. Muhammad)! wrapped up in garments!' Arise and warn (the people against Allah's Punishment),... up to 'and desert the idols.' (74.1-5) After this the revelation started coming strongly, frequently and regularly."

Volume 1, Book 1, Number 4:

Narrated Said bin Jubair:

Ibn 'Abbas in the explanation of the Statement of Allah. 'Move not your tongue concerning (the Quran) to make haste therewith." (75.16) Said "Allah's Apostle used to bear the revelation with great trouble and used to move his lips (quickly) with the Inspiration." Ibn 'Abbas moved his lips saying, "I am moving my lips in front of you as Allah's Apostle used to move his." Said moved his lips saying: "I am moving my lips, as I saw Ibn 'Abbas moving his." Ibn 'Abbas added, "So Allah revealed 'Move not your tongue concerning (the Qur'an) to make haste therewith. It is for us to collect it and to give you (O Muhammad) the ability to recite it (the Qur'an) (75.16-17) which means that Allah will make him (the Prophet) remember the portion of the Qur'an which was revealed at that time by heart and recite it. The Statement of Allah: And 'When we have recited it to you (O Muhammad through Gabriel) then you follow its (Qur'an) recital' (75.18) means 'listen to it and be silent.' Then it is for Us (Allah) to make It clear to you' (75.19) means 'Then it is (for Allah) to make you recite it (and its meaning will be clear by itself through your tongue). Afterwards, Allah's Apostle used to listen to Gabriel whenever he came and after his departure he used to recite it as Gabriel had recited it."

Volume 1, Book 1, Number 5:

Narrated Ibn 'Abbas:

Allah's Apostle was the most generous of all the people, and he used to reach the peak in generosity in the month of Ramadan when Gabriel met him. Gabriel used to meet him every night of Ramadan to teach him the Qur'an. Allah's Apostle was the most generous person, even more generous than the strong uncontrollable wind (in readiness and haste to do charitable deeds).

Volume 1, Book 1, Number 6:

Narrated 'Abdullah bin 'Abbas:

Abu Sufyan bin Harb informed me that Heraclius had sent a messenger to him while he had been accompanying a caravan from Quraish. They were merchants doing business in Sham (Syria, Palestine, Lebanon and Jordan), at the time when Allah's Apostle had truce with Abu Sufyan and Quraish infidels. So Abu Sufyan and his companions went to Heraclius at Ilya (Jerusalem). Heraclius called them in the court and he had all the senior Roman dignitaries around him. He called for his translator who, translating Heraclius's question said to them, "Who amongst you is closely related to that man who claims to be a Prophet?" Abu Sufyan replied, "I am the nearest relative to him (amongst the group)."

Heraclius said, "Bring him (Abu Sufyan) close to me and make his companions stand behind him." Abu Sufyan added, Heraclius told his translator to tell my companions that he wanted to put some questions to me regarding that man (The Prophet) and that if I told a lie they (my companions) should contradict me." Abu Sufyan added, "By Allah! Had I not been afraid of my companions labeling me a liar, I would not have spoken the truth about the Prophet. The first question he asked me about him was:

'What is his family status amongst you?'

I replied, 'He belongs to a good (noble) family amongst us.'

Heraclius further asked, 'Has anybody amongst you ever claimed the same (i.e. to be a Prophet) before him?'

I replied, 'No.'

He said, 'Was anybody amongst his ancestors a king?'

I replied, 'No.'

Heraclius asked, 'Do the nobles or the poor follow him?'

I replied, 'It is the poor who follow him.'

He said, 'Are his followers increasing decreasing (day by day)?'

I replied, 'They are increasing.'

He then asked, 'Does anybody amongst those who embrace his religion become displeased and re-nounce the religion afterwards?'

I replied, 'No.'

Heraclius said, 'Have you ever accused him of telling lies before his claim (to be a Prophet)?'

I replied, 'No. '

Heraclius said, 'Does he break his promises?'

I replied, 'No. We are at truce with him but we do not know what he will do in it.' I could not find opportunity to say anything against him except that.

Heraclius asked, 'Have you ever had a war with him?'

I replied, 'Yes.'

Then he said, 'What was the outcome of the battles?'

I replied, 'Sometimes he was victorious and sometimes we.'

Heraclius said, 'What does he order you to do?'

I said, 'He tells us to worship Allah and Allah alone and not to worship anything along with Him, and to renounce all that our ancestors had said. He orders us to pray, to speak the truth, to be chaste and to keep good relations with our Kith and kin.'

Heraclius asked the translator to convey to me the following, I asked you about his family and your reply was that he belonged to a very noble family. In fact all the Apostles come from noble fam-ilies amongst their respective peoples. I questioned you whether anybody else amongst you claimed such a thing, your reply was in the negative. If the answer had been in the affirmative, I would have thought that this man was following the previous man's statement. Then I asked you whether anyone of his ancestors was a king. Your reply was in the negative, and if it had been in the affirmative, I would have thought that this man wanted to take back his ancestral kingdom.

I further asked whether he was ever accused of telling lies before he said what he said, and your reply was in the negative. So I wondered how a person who does not tell a lie about others could ever tell a lie about Allah. I, then asked you whether the rich people followed him or the poor. You replied that it was the poor who followed him. And in fact all the Apostle have been followed by this very class of people. Then I asked you whether his followers were increasing or decreasing. You replied that they were increasing, and in fact this is the way of true faith, till it is complete in all respects. I further asked you whether there was anybody, who, after embracing his religion, became displeased and discarded his religion. Your reply was in the negative, and in fact this is (the sign of) true faith, when its delight enters the hearts and mixes with them completely. I asked you whether he had ever betrayed. You replied in the negative and likewise the Apostles never betray. Then I asked you what he ordered you to do. You replied that he ordered you to worship Allah and Allah alone and not to worship any thing along with Him and forbade you to worship idols and ordered you to pray, to speak the truth and to be chaste. If what you have said is true, he will very soon occupy this place underneath my feet and I knew it (from the scriptures) that he was going to appear but I did not know that he would be from you, and if I could reach him definitely, I would go immediately to meet him and if I were with him, I would certainly wash his feet.' Heraclius then asked for the letter addressed by Allah's Apostle

which was delivered by Dihya to the Governor of Busra, who forwarded it to Heraclius to read. The contents of the letter were as follows: "In the name of Allah the Beneficent, the Merciful (This letter is) from Muhammad the slave of Allah and His Apostle to Heraclius the ruler of Byzantine. Peace be upon him, who follows the right path. Furthermore I invite you to Islam, and if you become a Muslim you will be safe, and Allah will double your reward, and if you reject this invitation of Islam you will be committing a sin by misguiding your Arisiyin (peasants). (And I recite to you Allah's Statement:)

'O people of the scripture! Come to a word common to you and us that we worship none but Allah and that we associate nothing in worship with Him, and that none of us shall take others as Lords beside Allah. Then, if they turn away, say: Bear witness that we are Muslims (those who have surrendered to Allah).' (3:64).

Abu Sufyan then added, "When Heraclius had finished his speech and had read the letter, there was a great hue and cry in the Royal Court. So we were turned out of the court. I told my companions that the question of Ibn-Abi-Kabsha) (the Prophet Muhammad) has become so prominent that even the King of Bani Al-Asfar (Byzantine) is afraid of him. Then I started to become sure that he (the Prophet) would be the conqueror in the near future till I embraced Islam (i.e. Allah guided me to it)."

The sub narrator adds, "Ibn An-Natur was the Governor of Ilya' (Jerusalem) and Heraclius was the head of the Christians of Sham. Ibn An-Natur narrates that once while Heraclius was visiting ilya' (Jerusalem), he got up in the morning with a sad mood. Some of his priests asked him why he was in that mood? Heraclius was a foreteller and an astrologer. He replied, 'At night when I looked at the stars, I saw that the leader of those who practice circumcision had appeared (become the conqueror). Who are they who practice circumcision?' The people replied, 'Except the Jews nobody practices circumcision, so you should not be afraid of them (Jews).

'Just Issue orders to kill every Jew present in the country.'

While they were discussing it, a messenger sent by the king of Ghassan to convey the news of Allah's Apostle to Heraclius was brought in. Having heard the news, he (Heraclius) ordered the people to go and see whether the messenger of Ghassan was circumcised. The people, after seeing him, told Heraclius that he was circumcised. Heraclius then asked him about the Arabs. The messenger replied, 'Arabs also practice circumcision.'

(After hearing that) Heraclius remarked that sovereignty of the 'Arabs had appeared. Heraclius then wrote a letter to his friend in Rome who was as good as Heraclius in knowledge. Heraclius then left for Homs. (a town in Syrian and stayed there till he received the reply of his letter from his friend who agreed with him in his opinion about the emergence of the Prophet and the fact that he was a Prophet. On that Heraclius invited all the heads of the Byzantines to assemble in his palace at Homs. When they assembled, he ordered that all the doors of his palace be closed. Then he came out and said, 'O Byzantines! If success is your desire and if you seek right guidance and want your empire to remain then give a pledge of allegiance to this Prophet (i.e. embrace Islam).'

(On hearing the views of Heraclius) the people ran towards the gates of the palace like onagers but found the doors closed. Heraclius realized their hatred towards Islam and when he lost the hope of their embracing Islam, he ordered that they should be brought back in audience.

(When they returned) he said, 'What already said was just to test the strength of your conviction and I have seen it.' The people prostrated before him and became pleased with him, and this was the end of Heraclius's story (in connection with his faith).

Book 2: Belief

Volume 1, Book 2, Number 7:

Narrated Ibn 'Umar:

Allah's Apostle said: Islam is based on (the following) five (principles):

1. To testify that none has the right to be worshipped but Allah and Muhammad is Allah's Apostle.

2. To offer the (compulsory congregational) prayers dutifully and perfectly.

3. To pay Zakat (i.e. obligatory charity) .

4. To perform Hajj. (i.e. Pilgrimage to Mecca)

5. To observe fast during the month of Ramadan.

Volume 1, Book 2, Number 8:

Narrated Abu Huraira:

The Prophet said, "Faith (Belief) consists of more than sixty branches (i.e. parts). And Haya (This term "Haya" covers a large number of concepts which are to be taken together; amongst them are self respect, modesty, bashfulness, and scruple, etc.) is a part of faith."

Volume 1, Book 2, Number 9:

Narrated 'Abdullah bin 'Amr:

The Prophet said, "A Muslim is the one who avoids harming Muslims with his tongue and hands. And a Muhajir (emigrant) is the one who gives up (abandons) all what Allah has forbidden."

Volume 1, Book 2, Number 10:

Narrated Abu Musa:

Some people asked Allah's Apostle, "Whose Islam is the best? i.e. (Who is a very good Muslim)?" He replied, "One who avoids harming the Muslims with his tongue and hands."

Volume 1, Book 2, Number 11:

Narrated 'Abdullah bin 'Amr:

A man asked the Prophet , "What sort of deeds or (what qualities of) Islam are good?" The Prophet replied, 'To feed (the poor) and greet those whom you know and those whom you do not Know (See Hadith No. 27).

Volume 1, Book 2, Number 12,

Narrated Anas,

The Prophet said, "None of you will have faith till he wishes for his (Muslim) brother what he likes for himself."

Volume 1, Book 2, Number 13,

Narrated Abu Huraira,

"Allah's Apostle said, "By Him in Whose Hands my life is, none of you will have faith till he loves me more than his father and his children."

Volume 1, Book 2, Number 14,

Narrated Anas,

The Prophet said "None of you will have faith till he loves me more than his father, his children and all mankind."

Volume 1, Book 2, Number 15,

Narrated Anas,

The Prophet said, "Whoever possesses the following three qualities will have the sweetness (delight) of faith,

1. The one to whom Allah and His Apostle becomes dearer than anything else.

2. Who loves a person and he loves him only for Allah's sake.

3. Who hates to revert to Atheism (disbelief) as he hates to be thrown into the fire."

Volume 1, Book 2, Number 16,

Narrated Anas,

The Prophet said, "Love for the Ansar is a sign of faith and hatred for the Ansar is a sign of hypocrisy."

Volume 1, Book 2, Number 17:

Narrated 'Ubada bin As-Samit:

who took part in the battle of Badr and was a Naqib (a person heading a group of six persons), on the night of Al-'Aqaba pledge: Allah's Apostle said while a group of his companions were around him, "Swear allegiance to me for:

1. Not to join anything in worship along with Allah.

2. Not to steal.

3. Not to commit illegal sexual intercourse.

4. Not to kill your children.

5. Not to accuse an innocent person (to spread such an accusation among people).

6. Not to be disobedient (when ordered) to do good deed."

The Prophet added: "Whoever among you fulfills his pledge will be rewarded by Allah. And whoever indulges in any one of them (except the ascription of partners to Allah) and gets the punishment in this world, that punishment will be an expiation for that sin. And if one indulges in any of them, and Allah conceals his sin, it is up to Him to forgive or punish him (in the Hereafter)." 'Ubada bin As-Samit added: "So we swore allegiance for these." (points to Allah's Apostle)

Volume 1, Book 2, Number 18:

Narrated Abu Said Al-Khudri:

Allah's Apostle said, "A time will come that the best property of a Muslim will be sheep which he will take on the top of mountains and the places of rainfall (valleys) so as to flee with his religion from afflictions."

Volume 1, Book 2, Number 19:

Narrated 'Aisha:

Whenever Allah's Apostle ordered the Muslims to do something, he used to order them deeds which were easy for them to do, (according to their strength endurance). They said, "O Allah's Apostle! We are not like you. Allah has forgiven your past and future sins." So Allah's Apostle became angry and it was apparent on his face. He said, "I am the most Allah fearing, and know Allah better than all of you do."

Volume 1, Book 2, Number 20:

Narrated Anas:

The Prophet said, "Whoever possesses the following three qualities will taste the sweetness of faith:

1. The one to whom Allah and His Apostle become dearer than anything else.

2. Who loves a person and he loves him only for Allah's sake.

3. Who hates to revert to disbelief (Atheism) after Allah has brought (saved) him out from it, as he hates to be thrown in fire."

Volume 1, Book 2, Number 21:

Narrated Abu Said Al-Khudri:

The Prophet said, "When the people of Paradise will enter Paradise and the people of Hell will go to Hell, Allah will order those who have had faith equal to the weight of a grain of mustard seed to be taken out from Hell. So they will be taken out but (by then) they will be blackened (charred). Then they will be put in the river of Haya' (rain) or Hayat (life) (the Narrator is in doubt as to which is the right term), and they will revive like a grain that grows near the bank of a flood channel. Don't you see that it comes out yellow and twisted"

Volume 1, Book 2, Number 22:

Narrated Abu Said Al-Khudri:

Allah's Apostle said, "While I was sleeping I saw (in a dream) some people wearing shirts of which some were reaching up to the breasts only while others were even shorter than that. Umar bin Al-Khattab was shown wearing a shirt that he was dragging." The people asked, "How did you interpret it? (What is its interpretation) O Allah's Apostle?" He (the Prophet) replied, "It is the Religion."

Volume 1, Book 2, Number 23:

Narrated 'Abdullah (bin 'Umar):

Once Allah's Apostle passed by an Ansari (man) who was admonishing to his brother regarding Haya'. On that Allah's Apostle said, "Leave him as Haya' is a part of faith." (See Hadith No. 8)

Volume 1, Book 2, Number 24:

Narrated Ibn 'Umar:

Allah's Apostle said: "I have been ordered (by Allah) to fight against the people until they testify that none has the right to be worshipped but Allah and that Muhammad is Allah's Apostle, and offer the prayers perfectly and give the obligatory charity, so if they perform a that, then they save their lives an property from me except for Islamic laws and then their reckoning (accounts) will be done by Allah."

Volume 1, Book 2, Number 25:

Narrated Abu Huraira:

Allah's Apostle was asked, "What is the best deed?" He replied, "To believe in Allah and His Apostle (Muhammad). The questioner then asked, "What is the next (in goodness)? He replied, "To participate in Jihad (religious fighting) in Allah's Cause." The questioner again asked, "What is the next (in goodness)?" He replied, "To perform Hajj (Pilgrim age to Mecca) 'Mubrur, (which is accepted by Allah and is performed with the intention of seeking Allah's pleasure only and not to show off and without committing a sin and in accordance with the traditions of the Prophet)."

Volume 1, Book 2, Number 26:

Narrated Sa'd:

Allah's Apostle distributed (Zakat) amongst (a group of) people while I was sitting there but Allah's Apostle left a man whom I thought the best of the lot. I asked, "O Allah's Apostle! Why have you left that person? By Allah I regard him as a faithful believer." The Prophet commented: "Or merely a Muslim." I remained quiet for a while, but could not help repeating my question because of what I knew about him. And then asked Allah's Apostle, "Why have you left so and so? By Allah! He is a faithful believer." The Prophet again said, "Or merely a Muslim." And I could not help repeating my question because of what I knew about him. Then the Prophet said, "O Sa'd! I give to a person while another is dearer to me, for fear that he might be thrown on his face in the Fire by Allah."

Volume 1, Book 2, Number 27:

Narrated 'Abdullah bin 'Amr:

A person asked Allah's Apostle . "What (sort of) deeds in or (what qualities of) Islam are good?" He replied, "To feed (the poor) and greet those whom you know and those whom you don't know."

Volume 1, Book 2, Number 28:

Narrated Ibn 'Abbas:

The Prophet said: "I was shown the Hell-fire and that the majority of its dwellers were women who were ungrateful." It was asked, "Do they disbelieve in Allah?" (or are they ungrateful to Allah?) He replied, "They are ungrateful to their husbands and are ungrateful for the favors and the good (charitable deeds) done to them. If you have always been good (benevolent) to one of them and then she sees something in you (not of her liking), she will say, 'I have never received any good from you."

Volume 1, Book 2, Number 29.

Narrated Al-Ma'rur.

At Ar-Rabadha I met Abu Dhar who was wearing a cloak, and his slave, too, was wearing a similar one. I asked about the reason for it. He replied, "I abused a person by calling his mother with bad names." The Prophet said to me, 'O Abu Dhar! Did you abuse him by calling his mother with bad names You still have some characteristics of ignorance. Your slaves are your brothers and Allah has put them under your command. So whoever has a brother under his command should feed him of what he eats and dress him of what he wears. Do not ask them (slaves) to do things beyond their capacity (power) and if you do so, then help them.' "

Volume 1, Book 2, Number 30.

Narrated Al-Ahnaf bin Qais.

While I was going to help this man ('Ali Ibn Abi Talib), Abu Bakra met me and asked, "Where are you going?" I replied, "I am going to help that person." He said, "Go back for I have heard Allah's Apostle saying, 'When two Muslims fight (meet) each other with their swords, both the murderer as well as the murdered will go to the Hell-fire.' I said, 'O Allah's Apostle! It is all right for the murderer but what about the murdered one?' Allah's Apostle replied, "He surely had the intention to kill his companion."

Volume 1, Book 2, Number 31.

Narrated 'Abdullah.

When the following Verse was revealed: "It is those who believe and confuse not their belief with wrong (worshipping others besides Allah.)" (6.83), the companions of Allah's Apostle asked, "Who is amongst us who had not done injustice (wrong)?" Allah revealed: "No doubt, joining others in worship with Allah is a great injustice (wrong) indeed." (31.13)

Volume 1, Book 2, Number 32.

Narrated Abu Huraira.

The Prophet said, "The signs of a hypocrite are three.

1. Whenever he speaks, he tells a lie.

2. Whenever he promises, he always breaks it (his promise).

3. If you trust him, he proves to be dishonest. (If you keep something as a trust with him, he will not return it.)"

Volume 1, Book 2, Number 33:

Narrated 'Abdullah bin 'Amr:

The Prophet said, "Whoever has the following four (characteristics) will be a pure hypocrite and whoever has one of the following four characteristics will have one characteristic of hypocrisy unless and until he gives it up.

1. Whenever he is entrusted, he betrays.

2. Whenever he speaks, he tells a lie.

3. Whenever he makes a covenant, he proves treacherous.

4. Whenever he quarrels, he behaves in a very imprudent, evil and insulting manner."

Volume 1, Book 2, Number 34:

Narrated Abu Huraira:

Allah's Apostle said, "Whoever establishes the prayers on the night of Qadr out of sincere faith and hoping to attain Allah's rewards (not to show off) then all his past sins will be forgiven."

Volume 1, Book 2, Number 35:

Narrated Abu Huraira:

The Prophet said, "The person who participates in (Holy battles) in Allah's cause and nothing compels him to do so except belief in Allah and His Apostles, will be recompensed by Allah either with a reward, or booty (if he survives) or will be admitted to Paradise (if he is killed in the battle as a martyr). Had I not found it difficult for my followers, then I would not remain behind any sariya going for Jihad and I would have loved to be martyred in Allah's cause and then made alive, and then martyred and then made alive, and then again martyred in His cause."

Volume 1, Book 2, Number 36:

Narrated Abu Huraira:

Allah's Apostle said: "Whoever establishes prayers during the nights of Ramadan faithfully out of sincere faith and hoping to attain Allah's rewards (not for showing off), all his past sins will be forgiven."

Volume 1, Book 2, Number 37:

Narrated Abu Huraira:

Allah's Apostle said, "Whoever observes fasts during the month of Ramadan out of sincere faith, and hoping to attain Allah's rewards, then all his past sins will be forgiven."

Volume 1, Book 2, Number 38:

Narrated Abu Huraira:

The Prophet said, "Religion is very easy and whoever overburdens himself in his religion will not be able to continue in that way. So you should not be extremists, but try to be near to perfection and receive the good tidings that you will be rewarded; and gain strength by worshipping in the mornings, the nights." (See Fath-ul-Bari, Page 102, Vol 1).

Volume 1, Book 2, Number 39:

Narrated Al-Bara' (bin 'Azib):

When the Prophet came to Medina, he stayed first with his grandfathers or maternal uncles from Ansar. He offered his prayers facing Baitul-Maqdis (Jerusalem) for sixteen or seventeen months, but he wished that he could pray facing the Ka'ba (at Mecca). The first prayer which he offered facing the Ka'ba was the 'Asr prayer in the company of some people. Then one of those who had offered that prayer with him came out and passed by some people in a mosque who were bowing during their prayers (facing Jerusalem). He said addressing them, "By Allah, I testify that I have prayed with Allah's Apostle facing Mecca (Ka'ba).' Hearing that, those people changed their direction towards the Ka'ba immediately. Jews and the people of the scriptures used to be pleased to see the Prophet facing Jerusalem in prayers but when he changed his direction towards the Ka'ba, during the prayers, they disapproved of it.

Al-Bara' added, "Before we changed our direction towards the Ka'ba (Mecca) in prayers, some Muslims had died or had been killed and we did not know what to say about them (regarding their prayers.) Allah then revealed: And Allah would never make your faith (prayers) to be lost (i.e. the prayers of those Muslims were valid).' " (2.143).

Volume 1, Book 2, Number 40:

Narrated Abu Huraira:

Allah's Apostle said, "If any one of you improve (follows strictly) his Islamic religion then his good deeds will be rewarded ten times to seven hundred times for each good deed and a bad deed will be recorded as it is."

Volume 1, Book 2, Number 41:

Narrated 'Aisha:

Once the Prophet came while a woman was sitting with me. He said, "Who is she?" I replied, "She is so and so," and told him about her (excessive) praying. He said disapprovingly, "Do (good) deeds which is within your capacity (without being overtaxed) as Allah does not get tired (of giving rewards) but (surely) you will get tired and the best deed (act of Worship) in the sight of Allah is that which is done regularly."

Volume 1, Book 2, Number 42.

Narrated Anas.

The Prophet said, "Whoever said "None has the right to be worshipped but Allah and has in his heart good (faith) equal to the weight of a barley grain will be taken out of Hell. And whoever said. "None has the right to be worshipped but Allah and has in his heart good (faith) equal to the weight of a wheat grain will be taken out of Hell. And whoever said, "None has the right to be worshipped but Allah and has in his heart good (faith) equal to the weight of an atom will be taken out of Hell."

Volume 1, Book 2, Number 43.

Narrated 'Umar bin Al-Khattab.

Once a Jew said to me, "O the chief of believers! There is a verse in your Holy Book Which is read by all of you (Muslims), and had it been revealed to us, we would have taken that day (on which it was revealed as a day of celebration." 'Umar bin Al-Khattab asked, "Which is that verse?" The Jew replied, "This day I have perfected your religion For you, completed My favor upon you, And have chosen for you Islam as your religion." (5.3) 'Umar replied,"No doubt, we know when and where this verse was revealed to the Prophet. It was Friday and the Prophet was standing at 'Arafat (i.e. the Day of Hajj)"

Volume 1, Book 2, Number 44.

Narrated Talha bin 'Ubaidullah.

A man from Najd with unkempt hair came to Allah's Apostle and we heard his loud voice but could not understand what he was saying, till he came near and then we came to know that he was asking about Islam. Allah's Apostle said, "You have to offer prayers perfectly five times in a day and night (24 hours)." The man asked, "Is there any more (praying)?" Allah's Apostle replied, "No, but if you want to offer the Nawafil prayers (you can)." Allah's Apostle further said to him. "You have to observe fasts during the month of Ramad, an." The man asked, "Is there any more fasting?" Allah's Apostle replied, "No, but if you want to observe the Nawafil fasts (you can.)" Then Allah's Apostle further said to him, "You have to pay the Zakat (obligatory charity)." The man asked, "Is there any thing other than the Zakat for me to pay?" Allah's Apostle replied, "No, unless you want to give alms of your own." And then that man retreated saying, "By Allah! I will neither do less nor more than this."

Allah's Apostle said, "If what he said is true, then he will be successful (i.e. he will be granted Paradise)."

Volume 1, Book 2, Number 45:

Narrated Abu Huraira:

Allah's Apostle said, "(A believer) who accompanies the funeral procession of a Muslim out of sincere faith and hoping to attain Allah's reward and remains with it till the funeral prayer is offered and the burial ceremonies are over, he will return with a reward of two Qirats. Each Qirat is like the size of the (Mount) Uhud. He who offers the funeral prayer only and returns before the burial, will return with the reward of one Qirat only."

Volume 1, Book 2, Number 46:

Narrated 'Abdullah:

The Prophet said, "Abusing a Muslim is Fusuq (an evil doing) and killing him is Kufr (disbelief)." Narrated 'Ubada bin As-Samit: "Allah's Apostle went out to inform the people about the (date of the) night of decree (Al-Qadr) but there happened a quarrel between two Muslim men. The Prophet said, "I came out to inform you about (the date of) the night of Al-Qadr, but as so and so and so and so quarrelled, its knowledge was taken away (I forgot it) and maybe it was better for you. Now look for it in the 7th, the 9th and the 5th (of the last 10 nights of the month of Ramadan)."

Volume 1, Book 2, Number 47:

Narrated Abu Huraira:

One day while the Prophet was sitting in the company of some people, (The angel) Gabriel came and asked, "What is faith?" Allah's Apostle replied, 'Faith is to believe in Allah, His angels, (the) meeting with Him, His Apostles, and to believe in Resurrection." Then he further asked, "What is Islam?" Allah's Apostle replied, "To worship Allah Alone and none else, to offer prayers perfectly to pay the compulsory charity (Zakat) and to observe fasts during the month of Ramadan." Then he further asked, "What is Ihsan (perfection)?" Allah's Apostle replied, "To worship Allah as if you see Him, and if you cannot achieve this state of devotion then you must consider that He is looking at you." Then he further asked, "When will the Hour be established?" Allah's Apostle replied, 'The answerer has no better knowledge than the questioner. But I will inform you about its portents.

1. When a slave (lady) gives birth to her master.

2. When the shepherds of black camels start boasting and competing with others in the construction of higher buildings. And the Hour is one of five things which nobody knows except Allah.

The Prophet then recited: "Verily, with Allah (Alone) is the knowledge of the Hour--." (31. 34) Then that man (Gabriel) left and the Prophet asked his companions to call him back, but they could not see him. Then the Prophet said, "That was Gabriel who came to teach the people their religion." Abu 'Abdullah said: He (the Prophet) considered all that as a part of faith.

Volume 1, Book 2, Number 48:

Narrated 'Abdullah bin 'Abbas:

I was informed by Abu Sufyan that Heraclius said to him, "I asked you whether they (followers of Muhammad) were increasing or decreasing. You replied that they were increasing. And in fact, this is the way of true Faith till it is complete in all respects. I further asked you whether there was anybody, who, after embracing his (the Prophets) religion (Islam) became displeased and discarded it. You replied in the negative, and in fact, this is (a sign of) true faith. When its delight enters the heart and mixes with them completely, nobody can be displeased with it."

Volume 1, Book 2, Number 49:

Narrated An-Nu'man bin Bashir:

I heard Allah's Apostle saying, 'Both legal and illegal things are evident but in between them there are doubtful (suspicious) things and most of the people have no knowledge about them. So whoever saves himself from these suspicious things saves his religion and his honor. And whoever indulges in these suspicious things is like a shepherd who grazes (his animals) near the Hima (private pasture) of someone else and at any moment he is liable to get in it. (O people!) Beware! Every king has a Hima and the Hima of Allah on the earth is His illegal (forbidden) things. Beware! There is a piece of flesh in the body if it becomes good (reformed) the whole body becomes good but if it gets spoilt the whole body gets spoilt and that is the heart.

Volume 1, Book 2, Number 50:

Narrated Abu Jamra:

I used to sit with Ibn 'Abbas and he made me sit on his sitting place. He requested me to stay with him in order that he might give me a share from his property. So I stayed with him for two months. Once he told (me) that when the delegation of the tribe of 'Abdul Qais came to the Prophet, the Prophet asked them, "Who are the people (i.e. you)? (Or) who are the delegate?" They replied, "We are from the tribe of Rabi'a." Then the Prophet said to them, "Welcome! O people (or O delegation of 'Abdul Qais)! Neither will you have disgrace nor will you regret." They said, "O Allah's Apostle! We cannot come to you except in the sacred month and there is the infidel tribe of Mudar intervening between you and us. So please order us to do something good (religious deeds) so that we may inform our people whom we have left behind (at home), and that we may enter Paradise (by acting on them)." Then they asked about drinks (what is legal and what is illegal). The Prophet ordered them to do four things and forbade them from four things. He ordered them to believe in Allah Alone and asked them, "Do you know what is meant by believing in Allah Alone?" They replied, "Allah and His Apostle know better." Thereupon the Prophet said, "It means:

1. To testify that none has the right to be worshipped but Allah and Muhammad is Allah's Apostle.

2. To offer prayers perfectly

3. To pay the Zakat (obligatory charity)

4. To observe fast during the month of Ramadan.

5. And to pay Al-Khumus (one fifth of the booty to be given in Allah's Cause).

Then he forbade them four things, namely, Hantam, Dubba,' Naqir Ann Muzaffat or Muqaiyar; (These were the names of pots in which Alcoholic drinks were prepared) (The Prophet mentioned the container of wine and he meant the wine itself). The Prophet further said (to them): "Memorize them (these instructions) and convey them to the people whom you have left behind."

Volume 1, Book 2, Number 51:

Narrated 'Umar bin Al-Khattab:

Allah's Apostle said, "The reward of deeds depends upon the intention and every person will get the reward according to what he has intended. So whoever emigrated for Allah and His Apostle, then his emigration was for Allah and His Apostle. And whoever emigrated for worldly benefits or for a woman to marry, his emigration was for what he emigrated for."

Volume 1, Book 2, Number 52:

Narrated Abu Mas'ud:

The Prophet said, "If a man spends on his family (with the intention of having a reward from Allah) sincerely for Allah's sake then it is a (kind of) alms-giving in reward for him.

Volume 1, Book 2, Number 53:

Narrated Sa'd bin Abi Waqqas:

Allah's Apostle said, "You will be rewarded for whatever you spend for Allah's sake even if it were a morsel which you put in your wife's mouth."

Volume 1, Book 2, Number 54:

Narrated Jarir bin Abdullah:

I gave the pledge of allegiance to Allah's Apostle for the following:

1. offer prayers perfectly

2. pay the Zakat (obligatory charity)

3. and be sincere and true to every Muslim.

Volume 1, Book 2, Number 55:

Narrated Ziyad bin'Ilaqa:

I heard Jarir bin 'Abdullah (Praising Allah). On the day when Al-Mughira bin Shu'ba died, he (Jarir) got up (on the pulpit) and thanked and praised Allah and said, "Be afraid of Allah alone Who has none along with Him to be worshipped.(You should) be calm and quiet till the (new) chief comes to you and he will come to you soon. Ask Allah's forgiveness for your (late) chief because he himself loved to forgive others." Jarir added, "Amma badu (now then), I went to the Prophet and said, 'I give my pledge of allegiance to you for Islam." The Prophet conditioned (my pledge) for me to be sincere and true to every Muslim so I gave my pledge to him for this. By the Lord of this mosque! I am sincere and true to you (Muslims). Then Jarir asked for Allah's forgiveness and came down (from the pulpit).

Book 3: Knowledge

Volume 1, Book 3, Number 56:

Narrated Abu Huraira:

While the Prophet was saying something in a gathering, a Bedouin came and asked him, "When would the Hour (Doomsday) take place?" Allah's Apostle continued his talk, so some people said that Allah's Apostle had heard the question, but did not like what that Bedouin had asked. Some of them said that Alllah's Apostle had not heard it. When the Prophet finished his speech, he said, "Where is the questioner, who enquired about the Hour (Doomsday)?" The Bedouin said, "I am here, O Allah's Apostle ." Then the Prophet said, "When honesty is lost, then wait for the Hour (Doomsday)." The Bedouin said, "How will that be lost?" The Prophet said, "When the power or authority comes in the hands of unfit persons, then wait for the Hour (Doomsday.)"

Volume 1, Book 3, Number 57:

Narrated 'Abdullah bin 'Amr:

Once the Prophet remained behind us in a journey. He joined us while we were performing ablution for the prayer which was over-due. We were just passing wet hands over our feet (and not washing them properly) so the Prophet addressed us in a loud voice and said twice or thrice: "Save your heels from the fire."

Volume 1, Book 3, Number 58:

Narrated Ibn 'Umar:

Allah's Apostle said, "Amongst the trees, there is a tree, the leaves of which do not fall and is like a Muslim. Tell me the name of that tree." Everybody started thinking about the trees of the desert areas. And I thought of the date-palm tree but felt shy to answer the others then asked, "What is that tree, O Allah's Apostle ?" He replied, "It is the date-palm tree."

Volume 1, Book 3, Number 59:

Narrated Ibn 'Umar:

The Prophet said, "Amongst the trees, there is a tree, the leaves of which do not fall and is like a Muslim. Tell me the name of that tree." Everybody started thinking about the trees of the desert areas. And I thought of the date-palm tree. The others then asked, "Please inform us what is that tree, O Allah's Apostle?" He replied, "It is the date-palm tree."

Volume 1, Book 3, Number 60:

Narrated Ibn Umar:

same as above Hadith 59.

Volume 1, Book 3, Number 61:

Narrated Ibn Umar:

same as above Hadith 59.

Volume 1, Book 3, Number 62:

Narrated Ibn Umar:

same as above Hadith 59.

Volume 1, Book 3, Number 63:

Narrated Anas bin Malik:

While we were sitting with the Prophet in the mosque, a man came riding on a camel. He made his camel kneel down in the mosque, tied its foreleg and then said: "Who amongst you is Muhammad?" At that time the Prophet was sitting amongst us (his companions) leaning on his arm. We replied, "This white man reclining on his arm." The an then addressed him, "O Son of 'Abdul Muttalib."

The Prophet said, "I am here to answer your questions." The man said to the Prophet, "I want to ask you something and will be hard in questioning. So do not get angry." The Prophet said, "Ask whatever you want." The man said, "I ask you by your Lord, and the Lord of those who were before you, has Allah sent you as an Apostle to all the mankind?" The Prophet replied, "By Allah, yes." The man further said, "I ask you by Allah. Has Allah ordered you to offer five prayers in a day and night (24 hours).? He replied, "By Allah, Yes." The man further said, "I ask you by Allah! Has Allah ordered you to observe fasts during this month of the year (i.e. Ramadan)?" He replied, "By Allah, Yes." The man further said, "I ask you by Allah. Has Allah ordered you to take Zakat (obligatory charity) from our rich people and distribute it amongst our poor people?" The Prophet replied, "By Allah, yes." Thereupon that man said, "I have believed in all that with which you have been sent, and I have been sent by my people as a messenger, and I am Dimam bin Tha'laba from the brothers of Bani Sa'd bin Bakr."

Volume 1, Book 3, Number 64:

Narrated 'Abdullah bin Abbas:

Once Allah's Apostle gave a letter to a person and ordered him to go and deliver it to the Governor of Bahrain. (He did so) and the Governor of Bahrain sent it to Chousroes, who read that letter and then tore it to pieces. (The sub-narrator (Ibn Shihab) thinks that Ibn Al-Musaiyab said that Allah's Apostle invoked Allah against them (saying), "May Allah tear them into pieces, and disperse them all totally.)"

Volume 1, Book 3, Number 65:

Narrated Anas bin Malik:

Once the Prophet wrote a letter or had an idea of writing a letter. The Prophet was told that they (rulers) would not read letters unless they were sealed. So the Prophet got a silver ring made with "Muhammad Allah's Apostle" engraved on it. As if I were just observing its white glitter in the hand of the Prophet

Volume 1, Book 3, Number 66:

Narrated Abu Waqid Al-Laithi:

While Allah's Apostle was sitting in the mosque with some people, three men came. Two of them came in front of Allah's Apostle and the third one went away. The two persons kept on standing before Allah's Apostle for a while and then one of them found a place in the circle and sat there while the other sat behind the gathering, and the third one went away. When Allah's Apostle finished his preaching, he said, "Shall I tell you about these three persons? One of them be-took himself to Allah, so Allah took him into His grace and mercy and accommodated him, the second felt shy from Allah, so Allah sheltered Him in His mercy (and did not punish him), while the third turned his face from Allah and went away, so Allah turned His face from him likewise. "

Volume 1, Book 3, Number 67:

Narrated 'Abdur Rahman bin Abi Bakra's father:

Once the Prophet was riding his camel and a man was holding its rein. The Prophet asked, "What is the day today?" We kept quiet, thinking that he might give that day another name. He said, "Isn't it the day of Nahr (slaughtering of the animals of sacrifice)" We replied, "Yes." He further asked, "Which month is this?" We again kept quiet, thinking that he might give it another name. Then he said, "Isn't it the month of Dhul-Hijja?" We replied, "Yes." He said, "Verily! Your blood, property and honor are sacred to one another (i.e. Muslims) like the sanctity of this day of yours, in this month of yours and in this city of yours. It is incumbent upon those who are present to inform those who are absent because those who are absent might comprehend (what I have said) better than the present audience."

Volume 1, Book 3, Number 68:

Narrated Ibn Mas'ud:

The Prophet used to take care of us in preaching by selecting a suitable time, so that we might not get bored. (He abstained from pestering us with sermons and knowledge all the time).

Volume 1, Book 3, Number 69:

Narrated Anas bin Malik:

The Prophet said, "Facilitate things to people (concerning religious matters), and do not make it hard for them and give them good tidings and do not make them run away (from Islam)."

Volume 1, Book 3, Number 70:

Narrated Abu Wail:

'Abdullah used to give a religious talk to the people on every Thursday. Once a man said, "O Aba 'Abdur-Rahman! (By Allah) I wish if you could preach us daily." He replied, "The only thing which prevents me from doing so, is that I hate to bore you, and no doubt I take care of you in preaching by selecting a suitable time just as the Prophet used to do with us, for fear of making us bored."

Volume 1, Book 3, Number 71:

Narrated Muawiya:

I heard Allah's Apostle saying, "If Allah wants to do good to a person, He makes him comprehend the religion. I am just a distributor, but the grant is from Allah. (And remember) that this nation (true Muslims) will keep on following Allah's teachings strictly and they will not be harmed by any one going on a different path till Allah's order (Day of Judgment) is established."

Volume 1, Book 3, Number 72:

Narrated Ibn 'Umar:

We were with the Prophet and a spadix of date-palm tree was brought to him. On that he said, "Amongst the trees, there is a tree which resembles a Muslim." I wanted to say that it was the date-palm tree but as I was the youngest of all (of them) I kept quiet. And then the Prophet said, "It is the date-palm tree."

Volume 1, Book 3, Number 73:

Narrated 'Abdullah bin Mas'ud:

The Prophet said, "Do not wish to be like anyone except in two cases. (The first is) A person, whom Allah has given wealth and he spends it righteously; (the second is) the one whom Allah has given wisdom (the Holy Qur'an) and he acts according to it and teaches it to others." (Fateh-al-Bari page 177 Vol. 1)

Volume 1, Book 3, Number 74:

Narrated Ibn 'Abbas:

That he differed with Hur bin Qais bin Hisn Al-Fazari regarding the companion of (the Prophet) Moses. Ibn 'Abbas said that he was Khadir. Meanwhile, Ubai bin Ka'b passed by them and Ibn 'Abbas called him, saying "My friend (Hur) and I have differed regarding Moses' companion whom Moses, asked the way to meet. Have you heard the Prophet mentioning something about him? He said, "Yes. I heard Allah's Apostle saying, "While Moses was sitting in the company of some Israelites, a man came and asked him. "Do you know anyone who is more learned than you? Moses replied: "No." So Allah sent the Divine Inspiration to Moses: 'Yes, Our slave Khadir (is more learned than you.)' Moses asked (Allah) how to meet him (Khadir). So Allah made the fish as a sign for him and he was told that when the fish was lost, he should return (to the place where he had lost it) and there he would meet him (Al-Khadir). So Moses went on looking for the sign of the fish in the sea. The servant-boy of Moses said to him: Do you remember when we betook ourselves to the rock, I indeed forgot the fish, none but Satan made me forget to remember it. On that Moses said: 'That is what we have been seeking? (18.64) So they went back retracing their foot-steps, and found Khadir. (And) what happened further to them is narrated in the Holy Qur'an by Allah. (18.54 up to 18.82)

Volume 1, Book 3, Number 75:

Narrated Ibn 'Abbas:

Once the Prophet embraced me and said, "O Allah! Bestow on him the knowledge of the Book (Qur'an)."

Volume 1, Book 3, Number 76:

Narrated Ibn 'Abbas:

Once I came riding a she-ass and had (just) attained the age of puberty. Allah's Apostle was offering the prayer at Mina. There was no wall in front of him and I passed in front of some of the row while they were offering their prayers. There I let the she-ass loose to graze and entered the row, and nobody objected to it.

Volume 1, Book 3, Number 77:

Narrated Mahmud bin Rabi'a:

When I was a boy of five, I remember, the Prophet took water from a bucket (used far getting water out of a well) with his mouth and threw it on my face.

Volume 1, Book 3, Number 78:

Narrated Ibn 'Abbas:

that he differed with Hur bin Qais bin Hisn Al-Fazari regarding the companion of the Prophet Moses. Meanwhile, Ubai bin Ka'b passed by them and Ibn 'Abbas called him saying, "My friend (Hur) and I have differed regarding Moses' companion whom Moses asked the way to meet. Have you heard Allah's Apostle mentioning something about him? Ubai bin Ka'b said: "Yes, I heard the Prophet mentioning something about him (saying) while Moses was sitting in the company of some Israelites, a man came and asked him: "Do you know anyone who is more learned than you? Moses replied: "No." So Allah sent the Divine Inspiration to Moses: '--Yes, Our slave Khadir is more learned than you. Moses asked Allah how to meet him (Al-Khadir). So Allah made the fish a sign for him and he was told when the fish was lost, he should return (to the place where he had lost it) and there he would meet him (Al-Khadir). So Moses went on looking for the sign of the fish in the sea. The servant-boy of Moses said: 'Do you remember when we betook ourselves to the rock, I indeed forgot the fish, none but Satan made me forget to remember it. On that Moses said, 'That is what we have been seeking.' So they went back retracing their footsteps, and found Kha,dir. (and) what happened further about them is narrated in the Holy Qur'an by Allah." (18.54 up to 18.82)

Volume 1, Book 3, Number 79:

Narrated Abu Musa:

The Prophet said, "The example of guidance and knowledge with which Allah has sent me is like abundant rain falling on the earth, some of which was fertile soil that absorbed rain water and brought forth vegetation and grass in abundance. (And) another portion of it was hard and held the rain water and Allah benefited the people with it and they utilized it for drinking, making their animals drink from it and for irrigation of the land for cultivation. (And) a portion of it was barren which could neither hold the water nor bring forth vegetation (then that land gave no benefits). The first is the example of the person who comprehends Allah's religion and gets benefit (from the knowledge) which Allah has revealed through me (the Prophets and learns and then teaches others. The last example is that of a person who does not care for it and does not take Allah's guidance revealed through me (He is like that barren land.)"

Volume 1, Book 3, Number 80:

Narrated Anas:

Allah's Apostle said, "From among the portents of the Hour are (the following):

1. Religious knowledge will be taken away (by the death of Religious learned men).

2. (Religious) ignorance will prevail.

3. Drinking of Alcoholic drinks (will be very common).

4. There will be prevalence of open illegal sexual intercourse.

Volume 1, Book 3, Number 81:

Narrated Anas:

I will narrate to you a Hadith and none other than I will tell you about after it. I heard Allah's Apostle saying: From among the portents of the Hour are (the following):

1. Religious knowledge will decrease (by the death of religious learned men).

2. Religious ignorance will prevail.

3. There will be prevalence of open illegal sexual intercourse.

4. Women will increase in number and men will decrease in number so much so that fifty women will be looked after by one man.

Volume 1, Book 3, Number 82:

Narrated Ibn 'Umar:

Allah's Apostle said, "While I was sleeping, I saw that a cup full of milk was brought to me and I drank my fill till I noticed (the milk) its wetness coming out of my nails. Then I gave the remaining milk to 'Umar Ibn Al-Khattab" The companions of the Prophet asked, "What have you interpreted (about this dream)? "O Allah's Apostle ,!" he replied, "(It is religious) knowledge."

Volume 1, Book 3, Number 83:

Narrated 'Abdullah bin Amr bin Al 'Aas:

Allah's Apostle stopped (for a while near the Jimar) at Mina during his last Hajj for the people and they were asking him questions. A man came and said, "I forgot and got my head shaved before slaughtering the Hadi (sacrificing animal)." The Prophet said, "There is no harm, go and do the slaughtering now." Then another person came and said, "I forgot and slaughtered (the camel) before

Rami (throwing of the pebbles) at the Jamra." The Prophet said, "Do the Rami now and there is no harm."

The narrator added: So on that day, when the Prophet was asked about anything (as regards the ceremonies of Hajj) performed before or after its due time, his reply was: "Do it (now) and there is no harm."

Volume 1, Book 3, Number 84:

Narrated Ibn 'Abbas:

Somebody said to the Prophet (during his last Hajj), "I did the slaughtering before doing the Rami." The Prophet beckoned with his hand and said, "There is no harm in that." Then another person said, "I got my head shaved before offering the sacrifice." The Prophet beckoned with his hand saying, "There is no harm in that."

Volume 1, Book 3, Number 85:

Narrated Abu Huraira:

The Prophet said, "(Religious) knowledge will be taken away (by the death of religious scholars) ignorance (in religion) and afflictions will appear; and Harj will increase." It was asked, "What is Harj, O Allah's Apostle?" He replied by beckoning with his hand indicating "killing." (Fateh-al-Bari Page 192, Vol. 1)

Volume 1, Book 3, Number 86:

Narrated Asma:

I came to 'Aisha while she was praying, and said to her, "What has happened to the people?" She pointed out towards the sky. (I looked towards the mosque), and saw the people offering the prayer. Aisha said, "Subhan Allah." I said to her, "Is there a sign?" She nodded with her head meaning, "Yes." I, too, then stood (for the prayer of eclipse) till I became (nearly) unconscious and later on I poured water on my head. After the prayer, the Prophet praised and glorified Allah and then said,

"Just now at this place I have seen what I have never seen before, including Paradise and Hell. No doubt it has been inspired to me that you will be put to trials in your graves and these trials will be like the trials of Masiah-ad-Dajjal or nearly like it (the sub narrator is not sure which expression Asma' used). You will be asked, 'What do you know about this man (the Prophet Muhammad)?' Then the faithful believer (or Asma' said a similar word) will reply, 'He is Muhammad Allah's Apostle who had come to us with clear evidences and guidance and so we accepted his teachings and followed him. And he is Muhammad.' And he will repeat it thrice. Then the angels will say to him, 'Sleep in peace as we have come to know that you were a faithful believer.' On the other hand, a hypocrite or a doubtful person will reply, 'I do not know, but I heard the people saying something and so I said it.' (the same). "

Volume 1, Book 3, Number 87.

Narrated Abu Jamra.

I was an interpreter between the people and Ibn 'Abbas. Once Ibn 'Abbas said that a delegation of the tribe of Abdul Qais came to the Prophet who asked them, "Who are the people (i.e. you)? (Or) who are the delegates?" They replied, "We are from the tribe of Rabi'a." Then the Prophet said to them, "Welcome, O people (or said, "O delegation (of 'Abdul Qais).") Neither will you have disgrace nor will you regret." They said, "We have come to you from a distant place and there is the tribe of the infidels of Mudar intervening between you and us and we cannot come to you except in the sacred month. So please order us to do something good (religious deeds) and that we may also inform our people whom we have left behind (at home) and that we may enter Paradise (by acting on them.)" The Prophet ordered them to do four things, and forbade them from four things. He ordered them to believe in Allah Alone, the Honorable the Majestic and said to them, "Do you know what is meant by believing in Allah Alone?" They replied, "Allah and His Apostle know better." Thereupon the Prophet said, "(That means to testify that none has the right to be worshipped but Allah and that Muhammad is His Apostle, to offer prayers perfectly, to pay Zakat, to observe fasts during the month of Ramadan, (and) to pay Al-Khumus (one fifth of the booty to be given in Allah's cause)." Then he forbade them four things, namely Ad-Dubba.' Hantam, Muzaffat (and) An-Naqir or Muqaiyar(These were the names of pots in which alcoholic drinks used to be prepared). The Prophet further said, "Memorize them (these instructions) and tell them to the people whom you have left behind."

Volume 1, Book 3, Number 88.

Narrated 'Abdullah bin Abi Mulaika.

'Uqba bin Al-Harith said that he had married the daughter of Abi Ihab bin 'Aziz. Later on a woman came to him and said, "I have suckled (nursed) Uqba and the woman whom he married (his wife) at my breast." 'Uqba said to her, "Neither I knew that you have suckled (nursed) me nor did you tell me." Then he rode over to see Allah's Apostle at Medina, and asked him about it. Allah's Apostle said, "How can you keep her as a wife when it has been said (that she is your foster-sister)?" Then Uqba divorced her, and she married another man.

Volume 1, Book 3, Number 89.

Narrated 'Umar.

My Ansari neighbor from Bani Umaiya bin Zaid who used to live at 'Awali Al-Medina and used to visit the Prophet by turns. He used to go one day and I another day. When I went I used to bring the news of that day regarding the Divine Inspiration and other things, and when he went, he used to do the same for me. Once my Ansari friend, in his turn (on returning from the Prophet), knocked violently at my door and asked if I was there." I became horrified and came out to him. He said, "Today a great thing has happened." I then went to Hafsa and saw her weeping. I asked her, "Did Allah's Apostle divorce you all?" She replied, "I do not know." Then, I entered upon the Prophet and said while standing, "Have you divorced your wives?" The Prophet replied in the negative. On what I said, "Allahu-Akbar (Allah is Greater)." (See Hadith No. 119, Vol. 3 for details)

Volume 1, Book 3, Number 90ᴛ

Narrated Abu Mas'ud Al-Ansariᴛ

Once a man said to Allah's Apostle "O Allah's Apostleɪ I may not attend the (compulsory congregational) prayer because so and so (the Imam) prolongs the prayer when he leads us for it. The narrator added: "I never saw the Prophet more furious in giving advice than he was on that day. The Prophet said, "O peopleɪ Some of you make others dislike good deeds (the prayers). So whoever leads the people in prayer should shorten it because among them there are the sick the weak and the needy (having some jobs to do)."

Volume 1, Book 3, Number 91ᴛ

Narrated Zaid bin Khalid Al-Juhaniᴛ

A man asked the Prophet about the picking up of a "Luqata" (fallen lost thing). The Prophet replied, "Recognize and remember its tying material and its container, and make public announcement (about it) for one year, then utilize it but give it to its owner if he comes." Then the person asked about the lost camel. On that, the Prophet got angry and his cheeks or his Face became red and he said, "You have no concern with it as it has its water container, and its feet and it will reach water, and eat (the leaves) of trees till its owner finds it." The man then asked about the lost sheep. The Prophet replied, "It is either for you, for your brother (another person) or for the wolf."

Volume 1, Book 3, Number 92ᴛ

Narrated Abu Musaᴛ

The Prophet was asked about things which he did not like, but when the questioners insisted, the Prophet got angry. He then said to the people, "Ask me anything you like." A man asked, "Who is my father?" The Prophet replied, "Your father is Hudhafa." Then another man got up and said, "Who is my father, O Allah's Apostle ?" He replied, "Your father is Salim, Maula (the freed slave) of Shaiba." So when 'Umar saw that (the anger) on the face of the Prophet he said, "O Allah's Apostleɪ We repent to Allah (Our offending you)."

Volume 1, Book 3, Number 93:

Narrated Anas bin Malik:

One day Allah's Apostle came out (before the people) and 'Abdullah bin Hudhafa stood up and asked (him) "Who is my father?" The Prophet replied, "Your father is Hudhafa." The Prophet told them repeatedly (in anger) to ask him anything they liked. 'Umar knelt down before the Prophet and said thrice, "We accept Allah as (our) Lord and Islam as (our) religion and Muhammad as (our) Prophet." After that the Prophet became silent.

Volume 1, Book 3, Number 94:

Narrated Anas:

Whenever the Prophet asked permission to enter, he knocked the door thrice with greeting and whenever he spoke a sentence (said a thing) he used to repeat it thrice. (See Hadith No. 261, Vol. 8).

Volume 1, Book 3, Number 95:

Narrated Anas:

Whenever the Prophet spoke a sentence (said a thing), he used to repeat it thrice so that the people could understand it properly from him and whenever he asked permission to enter, (he knocked the door) thrice with greeting.

Volume 1, Book 3, Number 96:

Narrated 'Abdullah bin 'Amr:

Once Allah's Apostle remained behind us in a journey. He joined us while we were performing ablution for the 'Asr prayer which was over-due. We were just passing wet hands over our feet (not washing them properly) so the Prophet addressed us in a loud voice and said twice or thrice, "Save your heels from the fire."

Volume 1, Book 3, Number 97:

Narrated Abu Burda's father:

Allah's Apostle said "Three persons will have a double reward:

1. A Person from the people of the scriptures who believed in his prophet (Jesus or Moses) and then believed in the Prophet Muhammad (i .e. has embraced Islam).

2. A slave who discharges his duties to Allah and his master.

3. A master of a woman-slave who teaches her good manners and educates her in the best possible way (the religion) and manumits her and then marries her."

Volume 1, Book 3, Number 97g,

Narrated Ibn 'Abbas,

Once Allah's Apostle came out while Bilal was accompanying him. He went towards the women thinking that they had not heard him (i.e. his sermon). So he preached them and ordered them to pay alms. (Hearing that) the women started giving alms; some donated their ear-rings, some gave their rings and Bilal was collecting them in the corner of his garment.

Volume 1, Book 3, Number 98,

Narrated Abu Huraira,

I said, "O Allah's Apostle! Who will be the luckiest person, who will gain your intercession on the Day of Resurrection?" Allah's Apostle said, O Abu Huraira! "I have thought that none will ask me about it before you as I know your longing for the (learning of) Hadiths. The luckiest person who will have my intercession on the Day of Resurrection will be the one who said sincerely from the bottom of his heart "None has the right to be worshipped but Allah."

And 'Umar bin 'Abdul 'Aziz wrote to Abu Bakr bin Hazm, "Look for the knowledge of Hadith and get it written, as I am afraid that religious knowledge will vanish and the religious learned men will pass away (die). Do not accept anything save the Hadiths of the Prophet. Circulate knowledge and teach the ignorant, for knowledge does not vanish except when it is kept secretly (to oneself)."

Volume 1, Book 3, Number 99,

Narrated Abdullah Ibn Dinar,

also narrates the same (above-mentioned statement) as has been narrated by 'Umar bin 'Abdul 'Aziz up to "The religious scholar (learned men) will pass away (die)."

Volume 1, Book 3, Number 100,

Narrated 'Abdullah bin 'Amr bin Al' As,

I heard Allah's Apostle saying, "Allah does not take away the knowledge, by taking it away from (the hearts of) the people, but takes it away by the death of the religious learned men till when none of the (religious learned men) remains, people will take as their leaders ignorant persons who when consulted will give their verdict without knowledge. So they will go astray and will lead the people astray."

Volume 1, Book 3, Number 101:

Narrated Abu Said Al-Khudri:

Some women requested the Prophet to fix a day for them as the men were taking all his time. On that he promised them one day for religious lessons and commandments. Once during such a lesson the Prophet said, "A woman whose three children die will be shielded by them from the Hell fire." On that a woman asked, "If only two die?" He replied, "Even two (will shield her from the Hell-fire)."

Volume 1, Book 3, Number 102:

Narrated Abu Said Al-Khudri:

as above (the sub narrators are different). Abu Huraira qualified the three children referred to in the above mentioned Hadith as not having reached the age of committing sins (i.e. age of puberty) .

Volume 1, Book 3, Number 103:

Narrated Ibn Abu Mulaika:

Whenever 'Aisha (the wife of the Prophet) heard anything which she did not understand, she used to ask again till she understood it completely. Aisha said: "Once the Prophet said, "Whoever will be called to account (about his deeds on the Day of Resurrection) will surely be punished." I said, "Doesn't Allah say: "He surely will receive an easy reckoning." (84.8) The Prophet replied, "This means only the presentation of the accounts but whoever will be argued about his account, will certainly be ruined."

Volume 1, Book 3, Number 104:

Narrated Said:

Abu Shuraih said, "When 'Amr bin Said was sending the troops to Mecca (to fight 'Abdullah bin Az-Zubair) I said to him, 'O chief! Allow me to tell you what the Prophet said on the day following the conquests of Mecca. My ears heard and my heart comprehended, and I saw him with my own eyes, when he said it. He glorified and praised Allah and then said, "Allah and not the people has made Mecca a sanctuary. So anybody who has belief in Allah and the Last Day (i.e. a Muslim) should neither shed blood in it nor cut down its trees. If anybody argues that fighting is allowed in Mecca as Allah's Apostle did fight (in Mecca), tell him that Allah gave permission to His Apostle, but He did not give it to you. The Prophet added: Allah allowed me only for a few hours on that day (of the conquest) and today (now) its sanctity is the same (valid) as it was before. So it is incumbent upon those who are present to convey it (this information) to those who are absent." Abu- Shuraih was asked, "What did 'Amr reply?" He said 'Amr said, "O Abu Shuraih! I know better than you (in this respect). Mecca does not give protection to one who disobeys (Allah) or runs after committing murder, or theft (and takes refuge in Mecca).

Volume 1, Book 3, Number 105:

Narrated Abu Bakra:

The Prophet said. No doubt your blood, property, the sub-narrator Muhammad thought that Abu Bakra had also mentioned and your honor (chastity), are sacred to one another as is the sanctity of this day of yours in this month of yours. It is incumbent on those who are present to inform those who are absent." (Muhammad the Subnarrator used to say, "Allah's Apostle told the truth.") The Prophet repeated twice: "No doubt! Haven't I conveyed Allah's message to you.

Volume 1, Book 3, Number 106:

Narrated 'Ali:

The Prophet said, "Do not tell a lie against me for whoever tells a lie against me (intentionally) then he will surely enter the Hell-fire."

Volume 1, Book 3, Number 107:

Narrated 'Abdullah bin Az-Zubair:

I said to my father, 'I do not hear from you any narration (Hadith) of Allah s Apostle as I hear (his narrations) from so and so?" Az-Zubair replied. I was always with him (the Prophet) and I heard him saying "Whoever tells a lie against me (intentionally) then (surely) let him occupy, his seat in Hell-fire.

Volume 1, Book 3, Number 108:

Narrated Anas:

The fact which stops me from narrating a great number of Hadiths to you is that the Prophet said: "Whoever tells a lie against me intentionally, then (surely) let him occupy his seat in Hell-fire."

Volume 1, Book 3, Number 109:

Narrated Salama:

I heard the Prophet saying, "Whoever (intentionally) ascribes to me what I have not said then (surely) let him occupy his seat in Hell-fire."

Volume 1, Book 3, Number 110:

Narrated Abu Huraira:

The Prophet said, "Name yourselves with my name (use my name) but do not name yourselves with my Kunya name (i.e. Abu-l Qasim). And whoever sees me in a dream then surely he has seen me for Satan cannot impersonate me. And whoever tells a lie against me (intentionally), then (surely) let him occupy his seat in Hell-fire."

Volume 1, Book 3, Number 111:

Narrated Ash-Sha'bi:

Abu Juhaifa said, "I asked Ali, 'Have you got any book (which has been revealed to the Prophet apart from the Qur'an)?' 'Ali replied, 'No, except Allah's Book or the power of understanding which has been bestowed (by Allah) upon a Muslim or what is (written) in this sheet of paper (with me).' Abu Juhaifa said, "I asked, 'What is (written) in this sheet of paper?' Ali replied, it deals with The Diyya (compensation (blood money) paid by the killer to the relatives of the victim), the ransom for the releasing of the captives from the hands of the enemies, and the law that no Muslim should be killed in Qisas (equality in punishment) for the killing of (a disbeliever).

Volume 1, Book 3, Number 112:

Narrated Abu Huraira:

In the year of the Conquest of Mecca, the tribe of Khuza'a killed a man from the tribe of Bani Laith in revenge for a killed person, belonging to them. They informed the Prophet about it. So he rode his Rahila (she-camel for riding) and addressed the people saying, "Allah held back the killing from Mecca. (The sub-narrator is in doubt whether the Prophet said "elephant or killing," as the Arabic words standing for these words have great similarity in shape), but He (Allah) let His Apostle and the believers over power the infidels of Mecca. Beware! (Mecca is a sanctuary) Verily! Fighting in Mecca was not permitted for anyone before me nor will it be permitted for anyone after me. It (war) in it was made legal for me for few hours or so on that day. No doubt it is at this moment a sanctuary, it is not allowed to uproot its thorny shrubs or to uproot its trees or to pick up its Luqatt (fallen things) except by a person who will look for its owner (announce it publicly). And if somebody is killed, then his closest relative has the right to choose one of the two-- the blood money (Diyya) or retaliation having the killer killed. In the meantime a man from Yemen came and said, "O Allah's Apostle! Get that written for me." The Prophet ordered his companions to write that for him. Then a man from Quraish said, "Except Al-Iqhkhir (a type of grass that has good smell) O Allah's Apostle, as we use it in our houses and graves." The Prophet said, "Except Al-Idhkhiri.e. Al-Idhkhir is allowed to be plucked."

Volume 1, Book 3, Number 113.

Narrated Abu Huraira.

There is none among the companions of the Prophet who has narrated more Hadiths than I except 'Abdallah bin Amr (bin Al-'As) who used to write them and I never did the same.

Volume 1, Book 3, Number 114.

Narrated 'Ubaidullah bin 'Abdullah.

Ibn 'Abbas said, "When the ailment of the Prophet became worse, he said, 'Bring for me (writing) paper and I will write for you a statement after which you will not go astray.' But 'Umar said, 'The Prophet is seriously ill, and we have got Allah's Book with us and that is sufficient for us.' But the companions of the Prophet differed about this and there was a hue and cry. On that the Prophet said to them, 'Go away (and leave me alone). It is not right that you should quarrel in front of me." Ibn 'Abbas came out saying, "It was most unfortunate (a great disaster) that Allah's Apostle was prevented from writing that statement for them because of their disagreement and noise. (Note: It is apparent from this Hadith that Ibn 'Abbes had witnessed the event and came out saying this statement. The truth is not so, for Ibn 'Abbas used to say this statement on narrating the Hadith and he had not witnessed the event personally. See Fath Al-Bari Vol. 1, p.220 footnote.) (See Hadith No. 228, Vol. 4).

Volume 1, Book 3, Number 115.

Narrated Um Salama.

One night Allah's Apostle got up and said, "Subhan Allah! How many afflictions have been descended tonight and how many treasures have been disclosed! Go and wake the sleeping lady occupants of these dwellings (his wives) up (for prayers). A well-dressed (soul) in this world may be naked in the Hereafter. "

Volume 1, Book 3, Number 116.

Narrated 'Abdullah bin 'Umar.

Once the Prophet led us in the 'Isha' prayer during the last days of his life and after finishing it (the prayer) (with Taslim) he said: "Do you realize (the importance of) this night?" Nobody present on the surface of the earth tonight will be living after the completion of one hundred years from this night."

Volume 1, Book 3, Number 117.

Narrated Ibn 'Abbas.

I stayed overnight in the house of my aunt Maimuna bint Al-Harith (the wife of the Prophet)
while the Prophet was there with her during her night turn. The Prophet offered the 'Isha' prayer (in
the mosque), returned home and after having prayed four Rakat, he slept. Later on he got up at night
and then asked whether the boy (or he used a similar word) had slept? Then he got up for the prayer
and I stood up by his left side but he made me stand to his right and offered five Rakat followed by
two more Rakat. Then he slept and I heard him snoring and then (after a while) he left for the (Fajr)
prayer.

Volume 1, Book 3, Number 118:

Narrated Abu Huraira:

People say that I have narrated many Hadiths (The Prophet's narrations). Had it not been for two
verses in the Qur'an, I would not have narrated a single Hadith, and the verses are:

"Verily those who conceal the clear sign and the guidance which We have sent down . . . (up to)
Most Merciful." (2:159-160). And no doubt our Muhajir (emigrant) brothers used to be busy in the
market with their business (bargains) and our Ansari brothers used to be busy with their property
(agriculture). But I (Abu Huraira) used to stick to Allah's Apostle contented with what will fill my
stomach and I used to attend that which they used not to attend and I used to memorize that which
they used not to memorize.

Volume 1, Book 3, Number 119:

Narrated Abu Huraira:

I said to Allah's Apostle "I hear many narrations (Hadiths) from you but I forget them." Allah's
Apostle said, "Spread your Rida' (garment)." I did accordingly and then he moved his hands as if
filling them with something (and emptied them in my Rida') and then said, "Take and wrap this sheet
over your body." I did it and after that I never forgot any thing.

Volume 1, Book 3, Number 120:

Narrated Ibrahim bin Al-Mundhir:

Ibn Abi Fudaik narrated the same as above (Hadith...119) but added that the Prophet had moved
his hands as if filling them with something and then he emptied them in the Rida' of Abu Huraira.

Volume 1, Book 3, Number 121:

Narrated Abu Huraira:

I have memorized two kinds of knowledge from Allah's Apostle . I have propagated one of them to
you and if I propagated the second, then my pharynx (throat) would be cut (i.e. killed).

Volume 1, Book 3, Number 122:

Narrated Jarir:

The Prophet said to me during Hajjat-al-Wida': Let the people keep quiet and listen. Then he said (addressing the people), "Do not (become infidels) revert to disbelief after me by striking the necks (cutting the throats) of one another (killing each other)."

Volume 1, Book 3, Number 123:

Narrated Said bin Jubair:

I said to Ibn 'Abbas, "Nauf-Al-Bakali claims that Moses (the companion of Khadir) was not the Moses of Bani Israel but he was another Moses." Ibn 'Abbas remarked that the enemy of Allah (Nauf) was a liar.

Volume 1, Book 3, Number 124:

Narrated Ubai bin Ka'b:

The Prophet said, "Once the Prophet Moses stood up and addressed Bani Israel. He was asked, "Who is the most learned man amongst the people. He said, "I am the most learned." Allah admonished Moses as he did not attribute absolute knowledge to Him (Allah). So Allah inspired to him "At the junction of the two seas there is a slave amongst my slaves who is more learned than you." Moses said, "O my Lord! How can I meet him?" Allah said: Take a fish in a large basket (and proceed) and you will find him at the place where you will lose the fish. So Moses set out along with his (servant) boy, Yusha' bin Nuin and carried a fish in a large basket till they reached a rock, where they laid their heads (i.e. lay down) and slept. The fish came out of the basket and it took its way into the sea as in a tunnel. So it was an amazing thing for both Moses and his (servant) boy. They proceeded for the rest of that night and the following day. When the day broke, Moses said to his (servant) boy: "Bring us our early meal. No doubt, we have suffered much fatigue in this journey." Moses did not get tired till he passed the place about which he was told. There the (servant) boy told Moses, "Do you remember when we betook ourselves to the rock, I indeed forgot the fish." Moses remarked, "That is what we have been seeking. So they went back retracing their foot-steps, till they reached the rock. There they saw a man covered with a garment (or covering himself with his own garment). Moses greeted him. Al-Khadir replied saying, "How do people greet each other in your land?" Moses said, "I am Moses." He asked, "The Moses of Bani Israel?" Moses replied in the affirmative and added, "May I follow you so that you teach me of that knowledge which you have been taught." Al-Khadir replied, "Verily! You will not be able to remain patient with me, O Moses! I have some of the knowledge of Allah which He has taught me and which you do not know, while you have some knowledge which Allah has taught you which I do not know." Moses said, "Allah willing, you will find me patient and I will not disobey you in aught. So both of them set out walking along the sea-shore, as they did not have a boat. In the meantime a boat passed by them and they requested the crew of the boat to take them on board. The crew recognized Al-Khadir and took them on board without fare. Then a sparrow came and stood on the edge of the boat and dipped its beak once or twice in the sea. Al-Khadir said: "O Moses! My knowledge and your knowledge have not decreased Allah's knowledge except as much as this sparrow has decreased the water of the sea with its beak." Al-Khadir went to one of the planks of the boat and plucked it out. Moses said, "These people gave us a free lift but you have broken their boat and scuttled it so as to drown its people." Al-Khadir replied, "Didn't I tell you that you will not be able to remain patient with me." Moses said, "Call me not to account for what I forgot." The first (excuse) of Moses was that he had forgotten. Then they proceeded further and found a boy playing with other boys. Al-Khadir took hold of the boy's head from the top and plucked it out with his hands (i.e. killed him). Moses said, "Have you killed an innocent soul who has killed none." Al-Kha,dir replied, "Did I not tell you that you cannot remain patient with me?" Then they both proceeded till when they came to the people of a town, they asked them for food, but they refused to entertain them. Then they found there a wall on the point of collapsing. Al-Khadir repaired it with his own hands. Moses said, "If you had wished, surely you could have taken wages for it." Al-Khadir replied, "This is the parting between you and me." The Prophet added, "May Allah be Merciful to Moses! Would that he could have been more patient to learn more about his story with Al-Khadir. "

Volume 1, Book 3, Number 125:

Narrated Abu Musa:

A man came to the Prophet and asked, "O Allah's Apostle! What kind of fighting is in Allah's cause? (I ask this), for some of us fight because of being enraged and angry and some for the sake of his pride and haughtiness." The Prophet raised his head (as the questioner was standing) and said, "He who fights so that Allah's Word (Islam) should be superior, then he fights in Allah's cause."

Volume 1, Book 3, Number 126:

Narrated 'Abdullah bin 'Amar:

I saw the Prophet near the Jamra and the people were asking him questions (about religious problems). A man asked, "O Allah's Apostle! I have slaughtered the Hadi (animal) before doing the Rami." The Prophet replied, "Do the Rami (now) and there is no harm." Another person asked, "O Allah's Apostle! I got my head shaved before slaughtering the animal." The Prophet replied, "Do the slaughtering (now) and there is no harm." So on that day, when the Prophet was asked about anything as regards the ceremonies of Hajj performed before or after its due time his reply was, "Do it (now) and there is no harm."

Volume 1, Book 3, Number 127:

Narrated 'Abdullah:

While I was going with the Prophet through the ruins of Medina and he was reclining on a date-palm leaf stalk, some Jews passed by. Some of them said to the others: Ask him (the Prophet) about the spirit. Some of them said that they should not ask him that question as he might give a reply which would displease them. But some of them insisted on asking, and so one of them stood up and asked, "O Aba-l-Qasim ! What is the spirit?" The Prophet remained quiet. I thought he was being inspired Divinely. So I stayed till that state of the Prophet (while being inspired) was over. The Prophet then said, "And they ask you (O Muhammad) concerning the spirit --Say: The spirit -- its knowledge is with my Lord. And of knowledge you (mankind) have been given only a little)." (17.85)

Volume 1, Book 3, Number 128:

Narrated Aswad:

Ibn Az-Zubair said to me, "Aisha used to tell you secretly a number of things. What did she tell you about the Ka'ba?" I replied, "She told me that once the Prophet said, 'O 'Aisha! Had not your people been still close to the pre-Islamic period of ignorance (infidelity)! I would have dismantled the Ka'ba and would have made two doors in it; one for entrance and the other for exit." Later on Ibn Az-Zubair did the same.

Volume 1, Book 3, Number 129:

Narrated Abu At-Tufail:

the above mentioned Statement of 'Ali.

Volume 1, Book 3, Number 130:

Narrated Anas bin Malik:

"Once Mu'adh was along with Allah's Apostle as a companion rider. Allah's Apostle said, "O Mu'adh bin Jabal." Mu'adh replied, "Labbaik and Sa'daik. O Allah's Apostle!" Again the Prophet said, "O Mu'adh!" Mu'adh said thrice, "Labbaik and Sa'daik, O Allah's Apostle!" Allah's Apostle said, "There is none who testifies sincerely that none has the right to be worshipped but Allah and Muhammad is his Apostle, except that Allah, will save him from the Hell-fire." Mu'adh said, "O Allah's Apostle ! Should I not inform the people about it so that they may have glad tidings?" He replied, "When the people hear about it, they will solely depend on it." Then Mu'adh narrated the above-mentioned Hadith just before his death, being afraid of committing sin (by not telling the knowledge).

Volume 1, Book 3, Number 131:

Narrated Anas:

I was informed that the Prophet had said to Mu'adh, "Whosoever will meet Allah without associating anything in worship with Him will go to Paradise." Mu'adh asked the Prophet, "Should I not inform the people of this good news?" The Prophet replied, "No, I am afraid, lest they should depend upon it (absolutely)."

Volume 1, Book 3, Number 132:

Narrated Um Salama:

Um-Sulaim came to Allah's Apostle and said, "Verily, Allah is not shy of (telling you) the truth. Is it necessary for a woman to take a bath after she has a wet dream (nocturnal sexual discharge?) The Prophet replied, "Yes, if she notices a discharge." Um Salama, then covered her face and asked, "O Allah's Apostle! Does a woman get a discharge?" He replied, "Yes, let your right hand be in dust (An Arabic expression you say to a person when you contradict his statement meaning "you will not achieve goodness"), and that is why the son resembles his mother."

Volume 1, Book 3, Number 133:

Narrated 'Abdullah bin 'Umar:

Once Allah's Apostle said, "Amongst the trees there is a tree, the leaves of which do not fall and is like a Muslim, tell me the name of that tree." Everybody started thinking about the trees of the desert areas and I thought of the date-palm tree but felt shy (to answer). The others asked, "O Allah's Apostle! inform us of it." He replied, "it is the date-palm tree." I told my father what had come to my mind and on that he said, "Had you said it I would have preferred it to such and such a thing that I might possess."

Volume 1, Book 3, Number 134:

Narrated 'Ali:

I used to get the emotional urethral discharge frequently so I requested Al-Miqdad to ask the Prophet about it. Al-Miqdad asked him and he replied, "One has to perform ablution (after it)." (See Hadith No. 269).

Volume 1, Book 3, Number 135:

Narrated Nafi:

'Abdullah bin 'Umar said: "A man got up in the mosque and said: O Allah's Apostle 'At which place you order us that we should assume the Ihram?' Allah's Apostle replied, 'The residents of Medina should assure the Ihram from Dhil-Hulaifa, the people of Syria from Al-Ju,hfa and the people of Najd from Qarn." Ibn 'Umar further said, "The people consider that Allah's Apostle had also said, 'The residents of Yemen should assume Ihram from Yalamlam.' " Ibn 'Umar used to say, "I do not: remember whether Allah's Apostle had said the last statement or not?"

Volume 1, Book 3, Number 136:

Narrated Ibn 'Umar:

A man asked the Prophet : "What (kinds of clothes) should a Muhrim (a Muslim intending to perform 'Umra or Hajj) wear? He replied, "He should not wear a shirt, a turban, trousers, a head cloak or garment scented with saffron or Wars (kinds of perfumes). And if he has n slippers, then he can use Khuffs (leather socks) but the socks should be cut short so as to make the ankles bare." (See Hadith No. 615, Vol. 2).

Book 4: Ablutions (Wudu')

Volume 1, Book 4, Number 137:

Narrated Abu Huraira:

Allah's Apostle said, "The prayer of a person who does ,Hadath (passes, urine, stool or wind) is not accepted till he performs (repeats) the ablution." A person from Hadaramout asked Abu Huraira, "What is 'Hadath'?" Abu Huraira replied, " 'Hadath' means the passing of wind from the anus."

Volume 1, Book 4, Number 138:

Narrated Nu'am Al-Mujmir:

Once I went up the roof of the mosque, along with Abu Huraira. He perform ablution and said, "I heard the Prophet saying, "On the Day of Resurrection, my followers will be called "Al-Ghurr-ul-Muhajjalun" from the trace of ablution and whoever can increase the area of his radiance should do so (i.e. by performing ablution regularly).' "

Volume 1, Book 4, Number 139:

Narrated 'Abbas bin Tamim:

My uncle asked Allah's Apostle about a person who imagined to have passed wind during the prayer. Allah' Apostle replied: "He should not leave his prayers unless he hears sound or smells something."

Volume 1, Book 4, Number 140:

Narrated Kuraib:

Ibn 'Abbas said, "The Prophet slept till he snored and then prayed (or probably lay till his breath sounds were heard and then got up and prayed)." Ibn 'Abbas added: "I stayed overnight in the house of my aunt, Maimuna, the Prophet slept for a part of the night, (See Fateh-al-Bari page 249, Vol. 1), and late in the night, he got up and performed ablution from a hanging water skin, a light (perfect) ablution and stood up for the prayer. I, too, performed a similar ablution, then I went and stood on his left. He drew me to his right and prayed as much as Allah wished, and again lay and slept till his breath sounds were heard. Later on the Mua'dhdhin (callmaker for the prayer) came to him and informed him that it was time for Prayer. The Prophet went with him for the prayer without performing a new ablution." (Sufyan said to 'Amr that some people said, "The eyes of Allah's Apostle sleep but his heart does not sleep." 'Amr replied, "I heard 'Ubaid bin 'Umar saying that the dreams of Prophets were Divine Inspiration, and then he recited the verse: 'I (Abraham) see in a dream, (O my son) that I offer you in sacrifice (to Allah)." (37.102) (See Hadith No. 183)

Volume 1, Book 4, Number 141:

Narrated Usama bin Zaid:

Allah's Apostle proceeded from 'Arafat till when he reached the mountain pass, he dismounted, urinated and then performed ablution but not a perfect one. I said to him, ("Is it the time for) the prayer, O Allah's Apostle?" He said, "The (place of) prayer is ahead of you." He rode till when he reached Al-Muzdalifa, he dismounted and performed ablution and a perfect one. The (call for) Iqama was pronounced and he led the Maghrib prayer. Then everybody made his camel kneel down at its place. Then the Iqama was pronounced for the 'Isha' prayer which the Prophet led and no prayer was offered in between the two . prayers ('Isha' and Maghrib).

Volume 1, Book 4, Number 142:

Narrated 'Ata' bin Yasar:

Ibn 'Abbas performed ablution and washed his face (in the following way): He ladled out a handful of water, rinsed his mouth and washed his nose with it by putting in water and then blowing it out. He then, took another handful (of water) and did like this (gesturing) joining both hands, and washed his face, took another handful of water and washed his right forearm. He again took another handful of water and washed his left forearm, and passed wet hands over his head and took another handful of water and poured it over his right foot (up to his ankles) and washed it thoroughly and similarly took another handful of water and washed thoroughly his left foot (up to the ankles) and said, "I saw Allah's Apostle performing ablution in this way."

Volume 1, Book 4, Number 143:

Narrated Ibn 'Abbas:

The Prophet said, "If anyone of you on having sexual relations with his wife said (and he must say it before starting) 'In the name of Allah. O Allah! Protect us from Satan and also protect what you bestow upon us (i.e. the coming offspring) from Satan, and if it is destined that they should have a child then, Satan will never be able to harm that offspring."

Volume 1, Book 4, Number 144:

Narrated Anas:

Whenever the Prophet went to answer the call of nature, he used to say, "Allah-umma inni a'udhu bika minal khubuthi wal khaba'ith i.e. O Allah, I seek Refuge with You from all offensive and wicked things (evil deeds and evil spirits)."

Volume 1, Book 4, Number 145:

Narrated Ibn 'Abbas:

Once the Prophet entered a lavatory and I placed water for his ablution. He asked, "Who placed it?" He was informed accordingly and so he said, "O Allah! Make him (Ibn 'Abbas) a learned scholar in religion (Islam)."

Volume 1, Book 4, Number 146:

Narrated Abu Aiyub Al-Ansari:

Allah's Apostle said, "If anyone of you goes to an open space for answering the call of nature he should neither face nor turn his back towards the Qibla; he should either face the east or the west."

Volume 1, Book 4, Number 147:

Narrated 'Abdullah bin 'Umar:

People say, "Whenever you sit for answering the call of nature, you should not face the Qibla or Bait-ulMaqdis (Jerusalem)." I told them. "Once I went up the roof of our house and I saw Allah's Apostle answering the call of nature while sitting on two bricks facing Bait-ul-Maqdis (Jerusalem) (but there was a screen covering him. ' (FatehAl-Bari, Page 258, Vol. 1).

Volume 1, Book 4, Number 148:

Narrated 'Aisha:

The wives of the Prophet used to go to Al-Manasi, a vast open place (near Baqia at Medina) to answer the call of nature at night. 'Umar used to say to the Prophet "Let your wives be veiled," but Allah's Apostle did not do so. One night Sauda bint Zam'a the wife of the Prophet went out at 'Isha' time and she was a tall lady. 'Umar addressed her and said, "I have recognized you, O Sauda." He said so, as he desired eagerly that the verses of Al-Hijab (the observing of veils by the Muslim women) may be revealed. So Allah revealed the verses of "Al-Hijab" (A complete body cover excluding the eyes).

Volume 1, Book 4, Number 149:

Narrated 'Aisha:

The Prophet said to his wives, "You are allowed to go out to answer the call of nature. "

Volume 1, Book 4, Number 150:

Narrated 'Abdullah bin 'Umar:

I went up to the roof of Hafsa's house for some job and I saw Allah's Apostle answering the call of nature facing Sham (Syria, Jordan, Palestine and Lebanon regarded as one country) with his back towards the Qibla. (See Hadith No. 147).

Volume 1, Book 4, Number 151:

Narrated 'Abdullah bin 'Umar:

Once I went up the roof of our house and saw Allah's Apostle answering the call of nature while sitting over two bricks facing Bait-ul-Maqdis (Jerusalem). (See Hadith No. 147).

Volume 1, Book 4, Number 152:

Narrated Anas bin Malik:

Whenever Allah's Apostle went to answer the call of nature, I along with another boy used to accompany him with a tumbler full of water. (Hisham commented, "So that he might wash his private parts with it.)"

Volume 1, Book 4, Number 153:

Narrated Anas:

Whenever Allah's Apostle went to answer the call of nature, I along with another boy from us used to go behind him with a tumbler full of water.

Volume 1, Book 4, Number 154:

Narrated Anas bin Malik:

Whenever Allah's Apostle went to answer the call of nature, I along with another boy used to carry a tumbler full of water (for cleaning the private parts) and an 'Anza (spear-headed stuck).

Volume 1, Book 4, Number 155:

Narrated Abu Qatada:

Allah's Apostle said, "Whenever anyone of you drinks water, he should not breathe in the drinking utensil, and whenever anyone of you goes to a lavatory, he should neither touch his penis nor clean his private parts with his right hand."

Volume 1, Book 4, Number 156:

Narrated Abu Qatada:

The Prophet said, "Whenever anyone of you makes water he should not hold his penis or clean his private parts with his right hand. (And while drinking) one should not breathe in the drinking utensil ."

Volume 1, Book 4, Number 157:

Narrated Abu Huraira:

I followed the Prophet while he was going out to answer the call of nature. He used not to look this way or that. So, when I approached near him he said to me, "Fetch for me some stones for ' cleaning the privates parts (or said something similar), and do not bring a bone or a piece of dung." So I brought the stones in the corner of my garment and placed them by his side and I then went away from him. When he finished (from answering the call of nature) he used, them .

Volume 1, Book 4, Number 158:

Narrated 'Abdullah:

The Prophet went out to answer the call of nature and asked me to bring three stones. I found two stones and searched for the third but could not find it. So took a dried piece of dung and brought it to him. He took the two stones and threw away the dung and said, "This is a filthy thing."

Volume 1, Book 4, Number 159:

Narrated Ibn 'Abbas:

The Prophet performed ablution by washing the body parts only once.

Volume 1, Book 4, Number 160:

Narrated 'Abdullah bin Zaid:

The Prophet performed ablution by washing the body parts twice.

Volume 1, Book 4, Number 161:

Narrated Humran:

(the slave of 'Uthman) I saw 'Uthman bin 'Affan asking for a tumbler of water (and when it was brought) he poured water over his hands and washed them thrice and then put his right hand in the water container and rinsed his mouth, washed his nose by putting water in it and then blowing it out. then he washed his face and forearrlns up to the elbows thrice, passed his wet hands over his head and washed his feet up to the ankles thrice. Then he said, "Allah's Apostle said 'If anyone Performs ablution like that of mine and offers a two-rak'at prayer during which he does not think of anything else (not related to the present prayer) then his past sins will be forgiven.' " After performing the ablution 'Uthman said, "I am going to tell you a Hadith which I would not have told you, had I not been compelled by a certain Holy Verse (the sub narrator 'Urwa said: This verse is: "Verily, those who conceal the clear signs and the guidance which we have sent down...)" (2:159). I heard the Prophet saying, 'If a man performs ablution perfectly and then offers the compulsory congregational prayer, Allah will forgive his sins committed between that (prayer) and the (next) prayer till he offers it.

Volume 1, Book 4, Number 162:

Narrated Abu Huraira:

The Prophet said, "Whoever performs ablution should clean his nose with water by putting the water in it and then blowing it out, and whoever cleans his private parts with stones should do it with odd number of stones."

Volume 1, Book 4, Number 163:

Narrated Abu Huraira:

Allah's Apostle said, "If anyone of you performs ablution he should put water in his nose and then blow it out and whoever cleans his private parts with stones should do so with odd numbers. And whoever wakes up from his sleep should wash his hands before putting them in the water for ablution, because nobody knows where his hands were during sleep."

Volume 1, Book 4, Number 164:

Narrated 'Abdullah bin 'Amr:

The Prophet remained behind us on a journey. He joined us while we were performing ablution for the 'Asr prayer which was over-due and we were just passing wet hands over our feet (not washing them thoroughly) so he addressed us in a loud voice saying twice orthriae, "Save your heels from the fire."

Volume 1, Book 4, Number 165:

Narrated Humran:

(the freed slave of 'Uthman bin 'Affan) I saw 'Uthman bin 'Affan asking (for a tumbler of water) to perform ablution (and when it was brought) he poured water from it over his hands and washed them thrice and then put his right hand in the water container and rinsed his mouth and washed his nose by putting water in it and then blowing it out. Then he washed his face thrice and (then) fore-arms up to the elbows thrice, then passed his wet hands over his head and then washed each foot thrice. After that 'Uthman said, "I saw the Prophet performing ablution like this of mine, and he said, 'If anyone performs ablution like that of mine and offers a two-rak'at prayer during which he does not think of anything else (not related to the present prayer) then his past sins will be forgiven. '

Volume 1, Book 4, Number 166:

Narrated Muhammad Ibn Ziyad:

I heard Abu Huraira saying as he passed by us while the people were performing ablution from a utensil containing water, "Perform ablution perfectly and thoroughly for Abul-Qasim (the Prophet) said, 'Save your heels from the Hell-fire.' "

Volume 1, Book 4, Number 167:

Narrated 'Ubaid Ibn Juraij:

I asked 'Abdullah bin 'Umar, "O Abu 'Abdur-Rahman! I saw you doing four things which I never saw being done by anyone of you companions?" 'Abdullah bin 'Umar said, "What are those, O Ibn Juraij?" I said, "I never saw you touching any corner of the Ka'ba except these (two) facing south (Yemen) and I saw you wearing shoes made of tanned leather and dyeing your hair with Hinna; (a kind of dye). I also noticed that whenever you were in Mecca, the people assume l,hram on seeing the new moon crescent (1st of Dhul-Hijja) while you did not assume the Ihlal (Ihram)--(Ihram is also called Ihlal which means 'Loud calling' because a Muhrim has to recite Talbiya aloud when assuming the state of Ihram)--till the 8th of Dhul-Hijja (Day of Tarwiya). 'Abdullah replied, "Regarding the corners of Ka'ba, I never saw Allah's Apostle touching except those facing south (Yemen) and re-garding the tanned leather shoes, no doubt I saw Allah's Apostle wearing non-hairy shoes and he used to perform ablution while wearing the shoes (i.e. wash his feet and then put on the shoes). So I love to wear similar shoes. And about the dyeing of hair with Hinna; no doubt I saw Allah's Apostle dyeing his hair with it and that is why I like to dye (my hair with it). Regarding Ihlal, I did not see Al-lah's Apostle assuming Ihlal till he set out for Hajj (on the 8th of Dhul-Hijja)."

Volume 1, Book 4, Number 168:

Narrated Um-'Atiya:

that the Prophet at the time of washing his deceased daughter had said to them, "Start from the right side beginning with those parts which are washed in ablution."

Volume 1, Book 4, Number 169.

Narrated 'Aisha.

The Prophet used to like to start from the right side on wearing shoes, combing his hair and cleaning or washing himself and on doing anything else.

Volume 1, Book 4, Number 170.

Narrated Anas bin Malik.

saw Allah's Apostle when the 'Asr prayer was due and the people searched for water to perform ablution but they could not find it. Later on (a pot full of) water for ablution was brought to Allah's Apostle . He put his hand in that pot and ordered the people to perform ablution from it. I saw the water springing out from underneath his fingers till all of them performed the ablution (it was one of the miracles of the Prophet).

Volume 1, Book 4, Number 171.

Narrated Ibn Sirrn.

I said to 'Ablda, "I have some of the hair of the Prophet which I got from Anas or from his family." 'Abida replied. "No doubt if I had a single hair of that it would have been dearer to me than the whole world and whatever is in it."

Volume 1, Book 4, Number 172.

Narrated Anas.

When Allah's Apostle got his head shaved, Abu- Talha was the first to take some of his hair.

Volume 1, Book 4, Number 173.

Narrated Abu Huraira.

Allah's Apostle said, "If a dog drinks from the utensil of anyone of you it is essential to wash it seven times."

Volume 1, Book 4, Number 174.

Narrated Abu Huraira.

The Prophet said, "A man saw a dog eating mud from (the severity of) thirst. So, that man took a shoe (and filled it) with water and kept on pouring the water for the dog till it quenched its thirst. So Allah approved of his deed and made him to enter Paradise." And narrated Hamza bin 'Abdullah. My father said. "During the lifetime of Allah's Apostle, the dogs used to urinate, and pass through the mosques (come and go), nevertheless they never used to sprinkle water on it (urine of the dog.)"

Volume 1, Book 4, Number 175:

Narrated 'Adi bin Hatim:

I asked the Prophet (about the hunting dogs) and he replied, "If you let loose (with Allah's name) your tamed dog after a game and it hunts it, you may eat it, but if the dog eats of (that game) then do not eat it because the dog has hunted it for itself." I further said, "Sometimes I send my dog for hunting and find another dog with it. He said, "Do not eat the game for you have mentioned Allah's name only on sending your dog and not the other dog."

Volume 1, Book 4, Number 176:

Narrated Abu Huraira:

Allah's Apostle said, "A person is considered in prayer as long as he is waiting for the prayer in the mosque as long as he does not do Hadath." A non-Arab man asked, "O Abii Huraira! What is Hadath?" I replied, "It is the passing of wind (from the anus) (that is one of the types of Hadath)."

Volume 1, Book 4, Number 177:

Narrated 'Abbas bin Tamim:

My uncle said: The Prophet said, "One should not leave his prayer unless he hears sound or smells something."

Volume 1, Book 4, Number 178:

Narrated 'Ali:

I used to get emotional urethral discharges frequently and felt shy to ask Allah's Apostle about it. So I requested Al-Miqdad bin Al-Aswad to ask (the Prophet) about it. Al-Miqdad asked him and he replied, "On has to perform ablution (after it)."

Volume 1, Book 4, Number 179:

Narrated Zaid bin Khalid:

I asked 'Uthman bin 'Affan about a person who engaged in intercourse but did no discharge. 'Uthman replied, "He should perform ablution like the one for ar ordinary prayer but he must wash his penis." 'Uthman added, "I heard it from Allah's Apostle." I asked 'Ali Az-Zubair, Talha and Ubai bin

Ka'b about it and they, too, gave the same reply. (This order was cancelled later on and taking a bath became necessary for such cases).

Volume 1, Book 4, Number 180:

Narrated Abu Said Al-Khud:

Allah's Apostle sent for a Ansari man who came with water dropping from his head. The Prophet said, "Perhaps we have forced you to hurry up, haven't we?" The Ansari replied, "Yes." Allah's Apostle further said, "If you are forced to hurry up (during intercourse) or you do not discharge then ablution is due on you (This order was cancelled later on, i.e. one has to take a bath).

Volume 1, Book 4, Number 181:

Narrated Usama bin Zaid:

"When Allah's Apostle departed from 'Arafat, he turned towards a mountain pass where he answered the call of nature. (After he had finished) I poured water and he performed ablution and then I said to him, "O Allah's Apostle! Will you offer the prayer?" He replied, "The Musalla (place of the prayer) is ahead of you (in Al-Muzdalifa)."

Volume 1, Book 4, Number 182:

Narrated Al-Mughira bin Shu'ba:

I was in the company of Allah's Apostle on one of the journeys and he went out to answer the call of nature (and after he finished) I poured water and he performed ablution; he washed his face, forearms and passed his wet hand over his head and over the two Khuff, (leather socks).

Volume 1, Book 4, Number 183:

Narrated 'Abdullah bin 'Abbas:

that he stayed overnight in the house of Maimuna the wife of the Prophet, his aunt. He added : I lay on the bed (cushion transversally) while Allah's Apostle and his wife lay in the length-wise direction of the cushion. Allah's Apostle slept till the middle of the night, either a bit before or a bit after it and then woke up, rubbing the traces of sleep off his face with his hands. He then, recited the last ten verses of Sura Al-Imran, got up and went to a hanging water-skin. He then Performed the ablution from it and it was a perfect ablution, and then stood up to offer the prayer. I, too, got up and did as the Prophet had done. Then I went and stood by his side. He placed his right hand on my head and caught my right ear and twisted it. He prayed two Rakat then two Rakat and two Rakat and then two Rakat and then two Rakat and then two Rakat (separately six times), and finally one Rak'a (the Witr).

Then he lay down again in the bed till the Mu'adhdhin came to him where upon the Prophet got up, offered a two light Rakat prayer and went out and led the Fajr prayer

Volume 1, Book 4, Number 184:

Narrated Asma' bint Abu Bakr:

I came to 'Aisha the wife of the Prophet during the solar eclipse. The people were standing and offering the prayer and she was also praying. I asked her, "What is wrong with the people?" She beckoned with her hand towards the sky and said, "Subhan Allah." I asked her, "Is there a sign?" She pointed out, "Yes." So I, too, stood for the prayer till I fell unconscious and later on I poured water on my head. After the prayer, Allah's Apostle praised and glorified Allah and said, "Just now I have seen something which I never saw before at this place of mine, including Paradise and Hell. I have been inspired (and have understood) that you will be put to trials in your graves and these trials will be like the trials of Ad-Dajjal, or nearly like it (the sub narrator is not sure of what Asma' said). Angels will come to every one of you and ask, 'What do you know about this man?' A believer will reply, 'He is Muhammad, Allah's Apostle , and he came to us with self-evident truth and guidance. So we accepted his teaching, believed and followed him.' Then the angels will say to him to sleep in peace as they have come to know that he was a believer. On the other hand a hypocrite or a doubtful person will reply, 'I do not know but heard the people saying something and so I said the same.' "

Volume 1, Book 4, Number 185:

Narrated Yahya Al-Mazini:

A person asked 'Abdullah bin Zaid who was the grandfather of 'Amr bin Yahya, "Can you show me how Allah's Apostle used to perform ablution?" 'Abdullah bin Zaid replied in the affirmative and asked for water. He poured it on his hands and washed them twice, then he rinsed his mouth thrice and washed his nose with water thrice by putting water in it and blowing it out. He washed his face thrice and after that he washed his forearms up to the elbows twice and then passed his wet hands over his head from its front to its back and vice versa (beginning from the front and taking them to the back of his head up to the nape of the neck and then brought them to the front again from where he had started) and washed his feet (up to the ankles).

Volume 1, Book 4, Number 186:

Narrated 'Amr:

My father saw 'Amr bin Abi Hasan asking 'Abdullah bin Zaid about the ablution of the Prophet. 'Abdullah bin Zaid asked for earthen-ware pot containing water and in front of them performed ablution like that of the Prophet . He poured water from the pot over his hand and washed his hands thrice and then he put his hands in the pot and rinsed his mouth and washed his nose by putting water in it and then blowing it out with three handfuls of water. Again he put his hand in the water and washed his face thrice and washed his forearms up to the elbows twice; and then put his hands in the water and then passed them over his head by bringing them to the front and then to the rear of the head once, and then he washed his feet up to the ankles.

Volume 1, Book 4, Number 187:

Narrated Abu Juhaifa:

Allah's Apostle came to us at noon and water for ablution was brought to him. After he had performed ablution, the remaining water was taken by the people and they started smearing their bodies with it (as a blessed thing). The Prophet offered two Rakat of the Zuhr prayer and then two Rakat of the 'Asr prayer while an 'Anza (spear-headed stick) was there (as a Sutra) in front of him. Abu Musa said: The Prophet asked for a tumbler containing water and washed both his hands and face in it and then threw a mouthful of water in the tumbler and said to both of us (Abu Musa and Bilal), "Drink from the tumbler and pour some of its water on your faces and chests."

Volume 1, Book 4, Number 188:

Narrated Ibn Shihab:

Mahmud bin Ar-Rabi' who was the person on whose face the Prophet had ejected a mouthful of water from his family's well while he was a boy, and 'Urwa (on the authority of Al-Miswar and others) who testified each other, said, "Whenever the Prophet , performed ablution, his companions were nearly fighting for the remains of the water."

Volume 1, Book 4, Number 189:

Narrated As-Sa'ib bin Yazid:

My aunt took me to the Prophet and said, "O Allah's Apostle! This son of my sister has got a disease in his legs." So he passed his hands on my head and prayed for Allah's blessings for me; then he performed ablution and I drank from the remaining water. I stood behind him and saw the seal of Prophethood between his shoulders, and it was like the "Zir-al-Hijla" (means the button of a small tent, but some said 'egg of a partridge.' etc.)

Volume 1, Book 4, Number 190:

Narrated 'Amr bin Yahya:

(on the authority of his father) 'Abdullah bin Zaid poured water on his hands from a utensil containing water and washed them and then with one handful of water he rinsed his mouth and cleaned his nose by putting water in it and then blowing it out. He repeated it thrice. He, then, washed his hands and forearms up to the elbows twice and passed wet hands over his head, both forwards and backwards, and washed his feet up to the ankles and said, "This is the ablution of Allah's Apostle."

Volume 1, Book 4, Number 191:

Narrated Amr bin Yahya:

My father said, "I saw Amr bin Abi Hasan asking 'Abdullah bin Zaid about the ablution of the Prophet. Abdullah bin Zaid asked for an earthenware pot containing water and performed ablution in front of them. He poured water over his hands and washed them thrice. Then he put his (right) hand in the pot and rinsed his mouth and washed his nose by putting water in it and then blowing it out thrice with three handfuls of water Again he put his hand in the water and washed his face thrice. After that he put his hand in the pot and washed his forearms up to the elbows twice and then again put his hand in the water and passed wet hands over his head by bringing them to the front and then to the back and once more he put his hand in the pot and washed his feet (up to the ankles.)"

Volume 1, Book 4, Number 192:

Narrated Wuhaib: that he (the Prophet in narration 191 above) had passed his wet hands

Volume 1, Book 4, Number 193:

Narrated Jabir:

Allah's Apostle came to visit me while I was sick and unconscious. He performed ablution and sprinkled the remaining water on me and I became conscious and said, "O Allah's Apostle! To whom will my inheritance go as I have neither ascendants nor descendants?" Then the Divine verses regarding Fara'id (inheritance) were revealed.

Volume 1, Book 4, Number 194:

Narrated Anas:

It was the time for prayer, and those whose houses were near got up and went to their people (to perform ablution), and there remained some people (sitting). Then a painted stove pot (Mikhdab) containing water was brought to Allah's Apostles The pot was small, not broad enough for one to spread one's hand in; yet all the people performed ablution. (The sub narrator said, "We asked Anas, 'How many persons were you?' Anas replied 'We were eighty or more"). (It was one of the miracles of Allah's Apostle).

Volume 1, Book 4, Number 195:

Narrated Abu Musa:

Once the Prophet asked for a tumbler containing water. He washed his hands and face in it and also threw a mouthful of water in it.

Volume 1, Book 4, Number 196:

Narrated 'Abdullah bin Zaid:

Once Allah's Apostle came to us and we brought out water for him in a brass pot. He performed ablution thus: He washed his face thrice, and his forearms to the elbows twice, then passed his wet hands lightly over the head from front to rear and brought them to front again and washed his feet (up to the ankles).

Volume 1, Book 4, Number 197:

Narrated 'Aisha:

When the ailment of the Prophet became aggravated and his disease became severe, he asked his wives to permit him to be nursed (treated) in my house. So they gave him the permission. Then the Prophet came (to my house) with the support of two men, and his legs were dragging on the ground, between 'Abbas, and another man." 'Ubaid-Ullah (the sub narrator) said, "I informed 'Abdullah bin 'Abbas of what 'Aisha said. Ibn 'Abbas said: 'Do you know who was the other man?' I replied in the negative. Ibn 'Abbas said, 'He was 'Ali (bin Abi Talib)." 'Aisha further said, "When the Prophet came to my house and his sickness became aggravated he ordered us to pour seven skins full of water on him, so that he might give some advice to the people. So he was seated in a Mikhdab (brass tub) belonging to Hafsa, the wife of the Prophet. Then, all of us started pouring water on him from the water skins till he beckoned to us to stop and that we have done (what he wanted us to do). After that he went out to the people."

Volume 1, Book 4, Number 198:

Narrated 'Amr bin Yahya:

(on the authority of his father) My uncle used to perform ablution extravagantly and once he asked 'Abdullah bin Zaid to tell him how he had seen the Prophet performing ablution. He asked for an earthen-ware pot containing water, and poured water from it on his hands and washed them thrice, and then put his hand in the earthen-ware pot and rinsed his mouth and washed his nose by putting water in it and then blowing it Out thrice with one handful of water; he again put his hand in the water and took a handful of water and washed his face thrice, then washed his hands up to the elbows twice, and took water with his hand, and passed it over his head from front to back and then from back to front, and then washed his feet (up to the ankles) and said, "I saw the Prophet performing ablution in that way."

Volume 1, Book 4, Number 199:

Narrated Thabit:

Anas said, "The Prophet asked for water and a tumbler with a broad base and no so deep, containing a small quantity of water, was brought to him whereby he put his fingers in it." Anas further said, ' noticed the water springing out from amongst his fingers." Anas added, ' estimated that the people who performed ablution with it numbered between seventy to eighty."

Volume 1, Book 4, Number 200:

Narrated Anas:

The Prophet used to take a bath with one Saor up to five Mudds (1 Sa'= Mudds) of water and used to perform ablution with one Mudd of water.

Volume 1, Book 4, Number 201:

Narrated 'Abdullah bin 'Umar:

Sa'd bin Abi Waqqas said, "The Prophet passed wet hands over his Khuffs." 'Abdullah bin 'Umar asked Umar about it. 'Umar replied in the affirmative and added, "Whenever Sa'd narrates a Hadith from the Prophet, there is no need to ask anyone else about it."

Volume 1, Book 4, Number 202:

Narrated Al-Mughlra bin Shu'ba:

Once Allah's Apostle went out to answer the call of nature and I followed him with a tumbler containing water, and when he finished, I poured water and he performed ablution and passed wet hands over his Khuffs.

Volume 1, Book 4, Number 203:

Narrated Ja'far bin 'Amr bin Umaiya Ad-Damri:

My father said, "I saw the Prophet passing wet hands over his Khuffs."

Volume 1, Book 4, Number 204:

Narrated Ja'far bin 'Amr:

My father said, "I saw the Prophet passing wet hands over his turban and Khuffs (leather socks)."

Volume 1, Book 4, Number 205:

Narrated 'Urwa bin Al-Mughira:

My father said, "Once I was in the company of the Prophet on a journey and I dashed to take off his Khuffs. He ordered me to leave them as he had put them after performing ablution. So he passed wet hands or them.

Volume 1, Book 4, Number 206:

Narrated 'Abdullah bin 'Abbas:

Allah's Apostle ate a piece of cooked mutton from the shoulder region and prayed without repeating ablution.

Volume 1, Book 4, Number 207:

Narrated Ja'far bin 'Amr bin Umaiya:

My father said, "I saw Allah's Apostle taking a piece of (cooked) mutton from the shoulder region and then he was called for prayer. He put his knife down and prayed without repeating ablution."

Volume 1, Book 4, Number 208:

Narrated Suwaid bin Al-Nu'man:

In the year of the conquest of Khaibar I went with Allah's Apostle till we reached Sahba,' a place near Khaibar, where Allah's Apostle offered the 'Asr prayer and asked for food. Nothing but Sawrq was brought. He ordered it to be moistened with water. He and all of us ate it and the Prophet got up for the evening prayer (Maghrib prayer), rinsed his mouth with water and we did the same, and he then prayed without repeating the ablution.

Volume 1, Book 4, Number 209:

Narrated Maimuna:

The Prophet ate (a piece of) mutton from the shoulder region and then prayed without repeating the ablution.

Volume 1, Book 4, Number 210:

Narrated Ibn 'Abbas:

Allah's Apostle drank milk, rinsed his mouth and said, "It has fat."

Volume 1, Book 4, Number 211:

Narrated 'Aisha:

Allah's Apostle said, "If anyone of you feels drowsy while praying he should go to bed (sleep) till his slumber is over because in praying while drowsy one does not know whether one is asking for forgiveness or for a bad thing for oneself."

Volume 1, Book 4, Number 212:

Narrated Anas:

The Prophet said, "If anyone of you feels drowsy while praying, he should sleep till he understands what he is saying (reciting)."

Volume 1, Book 4, Number 213:

Narrated 'Amr bin 'Amir:

Anas said, "The Prophet used to perform ablution for every prayer." I asked Anas, "What you used to do?' Anas replied, "We used to pray with the same ablution until we break it with Hadath."

Volume 1, Book 4, Number 214:

Narrated Suwaid bin Nu'man:

In the year of the conquest of Khaibar I went with Allah's Apostle till we reached As-Sahba' where Allah's Apostle led the 'Asr prayer and asked for the food. Nothing but Sawiq was brought and we ate it and drank (water). The Prophet got up for the (Maghrib) Prayer, rinsed his mouth with water and then led the prayer without repeating the ablution.

Volume 1, Book 4, Number 215:

Narrated Ibn 'Abbas:

Once the Prophet, while passing through one of the grave-yards of Medina or Mecca heard the voices of two persons who were being tortured in their graves. The Prophet said, "These two persons are being tortured not for a major sin (to avoid)." The Prophet then added, "Yes! (they are being tortured for a major sin). Indeed, one of them never saved himself from being soiled with his urine while the other used to go about with calumnies (to make enmiy between friends). The Prophet then asked for a green leaf of a date-palm tree, broke it into two pieces and put one on each grave. On being asked why he had done so, he replied, "I hope that their torture might be lessened, till these get dried."

Volume 1, Book 4, Number 216:

Narrated Anas bin Malik:

Whenever the Prophet went to answer the call of nature, I used to bring water with which he used to clean his private parts.

Volume 1, Book 4, Number 217:

Narrated Ibn 'Abbas:

The Prophet once passed by two graves and said, "These two persons are being tortured not for a major sin (to avoid). One of them never saved himself from being soiled with his urine, while the other used to go about with calumnies(to make enmity between friends)." The Prophet then took a green leaf of a date-palm tree, split it into (pieces) and fixed one on each grave. They said, "O Allah's Apostle! Why have you done so?" He replied, "I hope that their punishment might be lessened till these (the pieces of the leaf) become dry." (See the foot-note of Hadith 215).

Volume 1, Book 4, Number 218:

Narrated Anas bin Malik:

The Prophet saw a Bedouin making water in the mosque and told the people not to disturb him. When he finished, the Prophet asked for some water and poured it over (the urine).

Volume 1, Book 4, Number 219:

Narrated Abu Huraira:

A Bedouin stood up and started making water in the mosque. The people caught him but the Prophet ordered them to leave him and to pour a bucket or a tumbler of water over the place where he had passed the urine. The Prophet then said, "You have been sent to make things easy and not to make them difficult."

Volume 1, Book 4, Number 220:

Narrated Anas bin Malik:

The Prophet said as above (219).

Volume 1, Book 4, Number 221:

Narrated Anas bin Malik:

A Bedouin came and passed urine in one corner of the mosque. The people shouted at him but the Prophet stopped them till he finished urinating. The Prophet ordered them to spill a bucket of water over that place and they did so.

Volume 1, Book 4, Number 222:

Narrated 'Aisha:

(the mother of faithful believers) A child was brought to Allah's Apostle and it urinated on the garment of the Prophet. The Prophet asked for water and poured it over the soiled place.

Volume 1, Book 4, Number 223:

Narrated Um Qais bint Mihsin:

I brought my young son, who had not started eating (ordinary food) to Allah's Apostle who took him and made him sit in his lap. The child urinated on the garment of the Prophet, so he asked for water and poured it over the soiled (area) and did not wash it.

Volume 1, Book 4, Number 224:

Narrated Hudhaifa:

Once the Prophet went to the dumps of some people and passed urine while standing. He then asked for water and so I brought it to him and he performed ablution.

Volume 1, Book 4, Number 225:

Narrated Hudhaifa':

The Prophet and I walked till we reached the dumps of some people. He stood, as any one of you stands, behind a wall and urinated. I went away, but he beckoned me to come. So I approached him and stood near his back till he finished.

Volume 1, Book 4, Number 226:

Narrated Abu Wail:

Abu Musa Al-Ash'ari used to lay great stress on the question of urination and he used to say, "If anyone from Bani Israel happened to soil his clothes with urine, he used to cut that portion away." Hearing that, Hudhaifa said to Abu Wail, "I wish he (Abu Musa) didn't (lay great stress on that matter)." Hudhaifa added, "Allah's Apostle went to the dumps of some people and urinated while standing."

Volume 1, Book 4, Number 227:

Narrated Asma':

A woman came to the Prophet and said, "If anyone of us gets menses in her clothes then what should she do?" He replied, "She should (take hold of the soiled place), rub it and put it in the water and rub it in order to remove the traces of blood and then pour water over it. Then she can pray in it."

Volume 1, Book 4, Number 228:

Narrated 'Aisha:

Fatima bint Abi Hubaish came to the Prophet and said, "O Allah's Apostle I get persistent bleeding from the uterus and do not become clean. Shall I give up my prayers?" Allah's Apostle replied, "No, because it is from a blood vessel and not the menses. So when your real menses begins give up your prayers and when it has finished wash off the blood (take a bath) and offer your prayers." Hisham (the sub narrator) narrated that his father had also said, (the Prophet told her): "Perform ablution for every prayer till the time of the next period comes."

Volume 1, Book 4, Number 229:

Narrated 'Aisha:

I used to wash the traces of Janaba (semen) from the clothes of the Prophet and he used to go for prayers while traces of water were still on it (water spots were still visible).

Volume 1, Book 4, Number 230:

Narrated 'Aisha:

as above (229).

Volume 1, Book 4, Number 231:

Narrated Sulaiman bin Yasar:

I asked 'Aisha about the clothes soiled with semen. She replied, "I used to wash it off the clothes of Allah's Apostle and he would go for the prayer while water spots were still visible. "

Volume 1, Book 4, Number 232:

Narrated 'Amr bin Maimun:

I heard Sulaiman bin Yasar talking about the clothes soiled with semen. He said that 'Aisha had said, "I used to wash it off the clothes of Allah's Apostle and he would go for the prayers while water spots were still visible on them.

Volume 1, Book 4, Number 233:

Narrated 'Aisha:

I used to wash the semen off the clothes of the Prophet and even then I used to notice one or more spots on them.

Volume 1, Book 4, Number 234:

Narrated Abu Qilaba:

Anas said, "Some people of 'Ukl or 'Uraina tribe came to Medina and its climate did not suit them. So the Prophet ordered them to go to the herd of (Milch) camels and to drink their milk and urine (as a medicine). So they went as directed and after they became healthy, they killed the shepherd of the Prophet and drove away all the camels. The news reached the Prophet early in the morning and he sent (men) in their pursuit and they were captured and brought at noon. He then ordered to cut their hands and feet (and it was done), and their eyes were branded with heated pieces of iron, They were put in 'Al-Harra' and when they asked for water, no water was given to them." Abu Qilaba said, "Those people committed theft and murder, became infidels after embracing Islam and fought against Allah and His Apostle ."

Volume 1, Book 4, Number 235:

Narrated Anas:

Prior to the construction of the mosque, the Prophet offered the prayers at sheep-folds.

Volume 1, Book 4, Number 236:

Narrated Maimuna:

Allah's Apostle was asked regarding ghee (cooking butter) in which a mouse had fallen. He said, "Take out the mouse and throw away the ghee around it and use the rest."

Volume 1, Book 4, Number 237:

Narrated Maimuna:

The Prophet was asked regarding ghee in which a mouse had fallen. He said, "Take out the mouse and throw away the ghee around it (and use the rest.)"

Volume 1, Book 4, Number 238:

Narrated Abu Huraira:

The Prophet said, "A wound which a Muslim receives in Allah's cause will appear on the Day of Resurrection as it was at the time of infliction; blood will be flowing from the wound and its color will be that of the blood but will smell like musk."

Volume 1, Book 4, Number 239:

Narrated Abu Huraira:

Allah's Apostle said, "We (Muslims) are the last (people to come in the world) but (will be) the foremost (on the Day of Resurrection)." The same narrator told that the Prophet had said, "You should not pass urine in stagnant water which is not flowing then (you may need to) wash in it."

Volume 1, Book 4, Number 240:

Narrated 'Abdullah:

While Allah's Apostle was prostrating (as stated below).

Volume 1, Book 4, Number 241:

Narrated 'Abdullah bin Mas'ud:

Once the Prophet was offering prayers at the Ka'ba. Abu Jahl was sitting with some of his companions. One of them said to the others, "Who amongst you will bring the abdominal contents (intestines, etc.) of a camel of Bani so and so and put it on the back of Muhammad, when he prostrates?" The most unfortunate of them got up and brought it. He waited till the Prophet prostrated and then placed it on his back between his shoulders. I was watching but could not do any thing. I wish I had some people with me to hold out against them. They started laughing and falling on one another. Allah's Apostle was in prostration and he did not lift his head up till Fatima (Prophet's daughter) came and threw that (camel's abdominal contents) away from his back. He raised his head and said thrice, "O Allah! Punish Quraish." So it was hard for Abu Jahl and his companions when the Prophet invoked Allah against them as they had a conviction that the prayers and invocations were accepted in this city (Mecca). The Prophet said, "O Allah! Punish Abu Jahl, 'Utba bin Rabi'a, Shaiba bin Rabi'a, Al-

Walid bin 'Utba, Umaiya bin Khalaf, and 'Uqba bin Al Mu'it (and he mentioned the seventh whose name I cannot recall). By Allah in Whose Hands my life is, I saw the dead bodies of those persons who were counted by Allah's Apostle in the Qalib (one of the wells) of Badr.

Volume 1, Book 4, Number 242:

Narrated Anas:

The Prophet once spat in his clothes.

Volume 1, Book 4, Number 243:

Narrated Aisha:

The Prophet said, "All drinks that produce intoxication are Haram (forbidden to drink).

Volume 1, Book 4, Number 244:

Narrated Abu Hazim:

Sahl bin Sa'd As-Sa'idi, was asked by the people, "With what was the wound of the Prophet treated? Sahl replied, "None remains among the people living who knows that better than I. 'Ah used to bring water in his shield and Fatima used to wash the blood off his face. Then straw mat was burnt and the wound was filled with it."

Volume 1, Book 4, Number 245:

Narrated Abu Burda:

My father said, "I came to the Prophet and saw him carrying a Siwak in his hand and cleansing his teeth, saying, 'U' U'," as if he was retching while the Siwak was in his mouth."

Volume 1, Book 4, Number 246:

Narrated Hudhaifa:

Whenever the Prophet got up at night, he used to clean his mouth with Siwak.

Volume 1, Book 4, Number 247:

Narrated Al-Bara 'bin 'Azib:

The Prophet said to me, "Whenever you go to bed perform ablution like that for the prayer, lie or your right side and say, "Allahumma aslamtu wajhi ilaika, wa fauwadtu amri ilaika, wa alja'tu Zahri ilaika raghbatan wa rahbatan ilaika. La Malja' wa la manja minka illa ilaika. Allahumma amantu bikitabika-l-ladhi anzalta wa bina-biyika-l ladhi arsalta" (O Allah! I surrender to You and entrust all my affairs to You and depend upon You for Your Blessings both with hope and fear of You. There is no fleeing from You, and there is no place of protection and safety except with You O Allah! I believe in Your Book (the Qur'an) which You have revealed and in Your Prophet (Muhammad) whom You have sent). Then if you die on that very night, you will die with faith (i.e. or the religion of Islam). Let the aforesaid words be your last utterance (before sleep)." I repeated it before the Prophet and when I reached "Allahumma amantu bikitabika-l-ladhi anzalta (O Allah I believe in Your Book which You have revealed)." I said, "Wa-rasulika (and your Apostle)." The Prophet said, "No, (but say): 'Wanabiyika-l-ladhi arsalta (Your Prophet whom You have sent), instead."

Book 5: Bathing (Ghusl)

Volume 1, Book 5, Number 248:

Narrated 'Aisha:

Whenever the Prophet took a bath after Janaba he started by washing his hands and then performed ablution like that for the prayer. After that he would put his fingers in water and move the roots of his hair with them, and then pour three handfuls of water over his head and then pour water all over his body.

Volume 1, Book 5, Number 249:

Narrated Maimuna:

(the wife of the Prophet) Allah's Apostle performed ablution like that for the prayer but did not wash his feet. He washed off the discharge from his private parts and then poured water over his body. He withdrew his feet from that place (the place where he took the bath) and then washed them. And that was his way of taking the bath of Janaba.

Volume 1, Book 5, Number 250:

Narrated 'Aisha:

The Prophet and I used to take a bath from a single pot called 'Faraq'.

Volume 1, Book 5, Number 251:

Narrated Abu Salama:

'Aisha's brother and I went to 'Aisha and he asked her about the bath of the Prophet. She brought a pot containing about a Sa' of water and took a bath and poured it over her head and at what time there was a screen between her and us.

Volume 1, Book 5, Number 252:

Narrated Abu Ja'far:

While I and my father were with Jabir bin 'Abdullah, some People asked him about taking a bath He replied, "A Sa' of water is sufficient for you." A man said, "A Sa' is not sufficient for me." Jabir said, "A Sa was sufficient for one who had more hair than you and was better than you (meaning the Prophet)." And then Jabir (put on) his garment and led the prayer.

Volume 1, Book 5, Number 253ᵢ

Narrated Ibn 'Abbasᵢ

The Prophet and Maimuna used to take a bath from a single pot.

Volume 1, Book 5, Number 254ᵢ

Narrated Jubair bin Mutimᵢ

Allah's Apostle said, "As for me, I pour water three times on my head." And he pointed with both his hands.

Volume 1, Book 5, Number 255ᵢ

Narrated Jabir bin 'Abdullahᵢ

The Prophet used to pour water three times on his head.

Volume 1, Book 5, Number 256ᵢ

Narrated Abu Ja'farᵢ

Jabir bin Abdullah said to me, "Your cousin (Hasan bin Muhammad bin Al-Hanafiya) came to me and asked about the bath of Janaba. I replied, 'The Prophet uses to take three handfuls of water, pour them on his head and then pour more water over his body.' Al-Hasan said to me, 'I am a hairy man.' I replied, 'The Prophet had more hair than you'. "

Volume 1, Book 5, Number 257ᵢ

Narrated Maimunaᵢ

I placed water for the bath of the Prophet. He washed his hands twice or thrice and then poured water on his left hand and washed his private parts. He rubbed his hands over the earth (and cleaned them), rinsed his mouth, washed his nose by putting water in it and blowing it out, washed his face and both forearms and then poured water over his body. Then he withdrew from that place and washed his feet.

Volume 1, Book 5, Number 258ᵢ

Narrated 'Aishaᵢ

Whenever the Prophet took the bath of Janaba (sexual relation or wet dream) he asked for the Hilab or some other scent. He used to take it in his hand, rub it first over the right side of his head and then over the left and then rub the middle of his head with both hands.

Volume 1, Book 5, Number 259:

Narrated Maimuna:

I placed water for the bath of the Prophet and he poured water with his right hand on his left and washed them. Then he washed his private parts and rubbed his hands on the ground, washed them with water, rinsed his mouth and washed his nose by putting water in it and blowing it out, washed his face and poured water on his head. He withdrew from that place and washed his feet. A piece of cloth (towel) was given to him but he did not use it.

Volume 1, Book 5, Number 260:

Narrated Maimuna:

The Prophet took the bath of Janaba. (sexual relation or wet dream). He first cleaned his private parts with his hand, and then rubbed it(that hand) on the wall (earth) and washed it. Then he performed ablution like that for the prayer, and after the bath he washed his feet.

Volume 1, Book 5, Number 261:

Narrated Aisha:

The Prophet and I used to take a bath from a single pot of water and our hands used to go in the pot after each other in turn.

Volume 1, Book 5, Number 262:

Narrated 'Aisha:

Whenever Allah's Apostle took a bath of Janaba, he washed his hands first.

Volume 1, Book 5, Number 263:

Narrated 'Aisha:

The Prophet and I used to take a bath from a single pot of water after Janaba.

Volume 1, Book 5, Number 264:

Narrated Anas bin Malik:

the Prophet and one of his wives used to take a bath from a single pot of water. (Shu'ba added to Anas's Statement "After the Janaba")

Volume 1, Book 5, Number 265:

Narrated Maimuna:

I placed water for the bath of Allah's Apostle and he poured water over his hands and washed them twice or thrice; then he poured water with his right hand over his left and washed his private parts (with his left hand). He rubbed his hand over the earth and rinsed his mouth and washed his nose by putting water in it and blowing it out. After that he washed his face, both fore arms and head thrice and then poured water over his body. He withdrew from that place and washed his feet.

Volume 1, Book 5, Number 266:

Narrated Maimuna bint Al-Harith:

I placed water for the bath of Allah's Apostle and put a screen. He poured water over his hands, and washed them once or twice. (The subnarrator added that he did not remember if she had said thrice or not). Then he poured water with his right hand over his left one and washed his private parts. He rubbed his hand over the earth or the wall and washed it. He rinsed his mouth and washed his nose by putting water in it and blowing it out. He washed his face, forearms and head. He poured water over his body and then withdrew from that place and washed his feet. I presented him a piece of cloth (towel) and he pointed with his hand (that he does not want it) and did not take it.

Volume 1, Book 5, Number 267:

Narrated Muhammad bin Al-Muntathir:

on the authority of his father that he had asked 'Aisha (about the Hadith of Ibn 'Umar). She said, "May Allah be Merciful to Abu 'Abdur-Rahman. I used to put scent on Allah's Apostle and he used to go round his wives, and in the morning he assumed the Ihram, and the fragrance of scent was still coming out from his body."

Volume 1, Book 5, Number 268:

Narrated Qatada:

Anas bin Malik said, "The Prophet used to visit all his wives in a round, during the day and night and they were eleven in number." I asked Anas, "Had the Prophet the strength for it?" Anas replied, "We used to say that the Prophet was given the strength of thirty (men)." And Sa'id said on the authority of Qatada that Anas had told him about nine wives only (not eleven).

Volume 1, Book 5, Number 269:

Narrated 'Ali:

I used to get emotional urethral discharge frequently. Being the son-in-law of the Prophet I requested a man to ask him about it. So the man asked the Prophet about it. The Prophet replied, "Perform ablution after washing your organ (penis)."

Volume 1, Book 5, Number 270:

Narrated Muhammad bin Al-Muntathir:

on the authority of his father that he had asked 'Aisha about the saying of Ibn 'Umar(i.e. he did not like to be a Muhrim while the smell of scent was still coming from his body). 'Aisha said, "I scented Allah's Apostle and he went round (had sexual intercourse with) all his wives, and in the morning he was Muhrim (after taking a bath)."

Volume 1, Book 5, Number 271:

Narrated 'Aisha:

It is as if I am just looking at the glitter of scent in the parting of the Prophet's head hair while he was a Muhrim.

Volume 1, Book 5, Number 272:

Narrated Hisham bin 'Urwa:

(on the authority of his father) 'Aisha said, "Whenever Allah's Apostle took the bath of Janaba, he cleaned his hands and performed ablution like that for prayer and then took a bath and rubbed his hair, till he felt that the whole skin of the head had become wet, then he would pour water thrice and wash the rest of the body." 'Aisha further said, "I and Allah's Apostle used to take a bath from a single water container, from which we took water simultaneously."

Volume 1, Book 5, Number 273:

Narrated Maimuna:

Water was placed for the ablution of Allah's Apostle after Janaba. He poured water with his right hand over his left twice or thrice and then washed his private parts and rubbed his hand on the earth or on a wall twice or thrice and then rinsed his mouth, washed his nose by putting water in it and then blowing it out arid then washed his face and forearms and poured water over his head and washed his body. Then he shifted from that place and washed his feet. I brought a piece of cloth, but he did not take it and removed the traces of water from his body with his hand."

Volume 1, Book 5, Number 274.

Narrated Abu Huraira.

Once the call (Iqama) for the prayer was announced and the rows were straightened. Allah's Apostle came out; and when he stood up at his Musalla, he remembered that he was Junub. Then he ordered us to stay at our places and went to take a bath and then returned with water dropping from his head. He said, "Allahu-Akbar", and we all offered the prayer with him.

Volume 1, Book 5, Number 275.

Narrated Maimuna.

I placed water for the bath of the Prophet and screened him with a garment. He poured water over his hands and washed them. After that he poured water with his right hand over his left and washed his private parts, rubbed his hands with earth and washed them, rinsed his mouth, washed his nose by putting water in it and then blowing it out and then washed his face and forearms. He poured water over his head and body. He then shifted from that place and washed his feet. I gave him a piece of cloth but he did not take it and came out removing the water (from his body) with both his hands.

Volume 1, Book 5, Number 276.

Narrated Aisha.

Whenever any one of us was Junub, she poured water over her head thrice with both her hands and then rubbed the right side of her head with one hand and rubbed the left side of the head with the other hand.

Volume 1, Book 5, Number 277.

Narrated Abu Huraira.

The Prophet said, 'The (people of) Bani Israel used to take bath naked (all together) looking at each other. The Prophet Moses used to take a bath alone. They said, 'By Allah! Nothing prevents Moses from taking a bath with us except that he has a scrotal hernia.' So once Moses went out to take a bath and put his clothes over a stone and then that stone ran away with his clothes. Moses followed that stone saying, "My clothes, O stone! My clothes, O stone! till the people of Bani Israel saw him and said, 'By Allah, Moses has got no defect in his body. Moses took his clothes and began to beat the stone." Abu Huraira added, "By Allah! There are still six or seven marks present on the stone from that excessive beating."

Narrated Abu Huraira. The Prophet said, "When the Prophet Job (Aiyub) was taking a bath naked, golden locusts began to fall on him. Job started collecting them in his clothes. His Lord addressed him, 'O Job! Haven't I given you enough so that you are not in need of them.' Job replied, 'Yes!' By Your Honor (power)! But I cannot dispense with Your Blessings.' "

Volume 1, Book 5, Number 278:

Narrated Um Hani bint Abi Talib:

I went to Allah's Apostle in the year of the conquest of Mecca and found him taking a bath while Fatima was screening him. The Prophet asked, "Who is it?" I replied, "I am Um-Hani."

Volume 1, Book 5, Number 279:

Narrated Maimuna:

I screened the Prophet while he was taking a bath of Janaba. He washed his hands, poured water from his right hand over his left and washed his private parts. Then he rubbed his hand over a wall or the earth, and performed ablution similar to that for the prayer but did not wash his feet. Then he poured water over his body, shifted from that place, and washed his feet.

Volume 1, Book 5, Number 280:

Narrated Um-Salama:

(the mother of the believers) Um Sulaim, the wife of Abu Talha, came to Allah's Apostle and said, "O Allah's Apostle! Verily Allah is not shy of (telling you) the truth. Is it necessary for a woman to take a bath after she has a wet dream (nocturnal sexual discharge)?" Allah's Apostle replied, "Yes, if she notices a discharge."

Volume 1, Book 5, Number 281:

Narrated Abu Huraira:

The Prophet came across me in one of the streets of Medina and at that time I was Junub. So I slipped away from him and went to take a bath. On my return the Prophet said, "O Abu Huraira! Where have you been?" I replied, "I was Junub, so I disliked to sit in your company." The Prophet said, "Subhan Allah! A believer never becomes impure."

Volume 1, Book 5, Number 282:

Narrated Anas bin Malik:

The Prophet used to visit all his wives in one night and he had nine wives at that time.

Volume 1, Book 5, Number 283:

Narrated Abu Huraira:

Allah's Apostle came across me and I was Junub He took my hand and I went along with him till he sat down I slipped away, went home and took a bath. When I came back. he was still sitting there. He then said to me, "O Abu Huraira! Where have you been?' I told him about it The Prophet said, "Subhan Allah! O Abu Huraira! A believer never becomes impure."

Volume 1, Book 5, Number 284:

Narrated Abu Salama :

I asked 'Aisha "Did the Prophet use to sleep while he was Junub?" She replied, "Yes, but he used to perform ablution (before going to bed).

Volume 1, Book 5, Number 285:

Narrated 'Umar bin Al-Khattab:

I asked Allah's Apostle "Can any one of us sleep while he is Junub?" He replied, "Yes, if he performs ablution, he can sleep while he is Junub."

Volume 1, Book 5, Number 286:

Narrated 'Aisha:

Whenever the Prophet intended to sleep while he was Junub, he used to wash his private parts and perform ablution like that for the prayer.

Volume 1, Book 5, Number 287:

Narrated 'Abdullah:

'Umar asked the Prophet "Can anyone of us sleep while he is Junub?" He replied, "Yes, if he performs ablution."

Volume 1, Book 5, Number 288:

Narrated 'Abdullah bin 'Umar:

Umar bin Al-Khattab told Allah's Apostle, "I became Junub at night." Allah's Apostle replied, "Perform ablution after washing your private parts and then sleep."

Volume 1, Book 5, Number 289:

Narrated Hisham:

as the following Hadith 290.

Volume 1, Book 5, Number 290:

Narrated Abu Huraira:

The Prophet said, "When a man sits in between the four parts of a woman and did the sexual intercourse with her, bath becomes compulsory."

Volume 1, Book 5, Number 291:

Narrated Zaid bin Khalid AjJuhani:

I asked 'Uthman bin 'Affan about a man who engaged in the sexual intercourse with his wife but did not discharge. 'Uthman replied, "He should perform ablution like that for the prayer after washing his private parts." 'Uthman added, "I heard that from Allah's Apostle." I asked 'Ali bin Abi Talib, Az-Zubair bin Al-'Awwam, Talha bin 'Ubaidullah and Ubai bin Ka'b and a gave the same reply. (Abu Aiylub said that he had heard that from Allah's Apostle) (This order was cancelled later on so one has to take a bath. See, Hadith No. 180).

Volume 1, Book 5, Number 292:

Narrated Ubai bin Ka'b:

I asked Allah's Apostle about a man who engages in sexual intercourse with his wife but does not discharge. He replied, "He should wash the parts which comes in contact with the private parts of the woman, perform ablution and then pray." (Abu 'Abdullah said, "Taking a bath is safer and is the last order.")

Book 6: Menstrual Periods

Volume 1, Book 6, Number 293:

Narrated Al-Qasim:

'Aisha said, "We set out with the sole intention of performing Hajj and when we reached Sarif, (a place six miles from Mecca) I got my menses. Allah's Apostle came to me while I was weeping. He said 'What is the matter with you? Have you got your menses?' I replied, 'Yes.' He said, 'This is a thing which Allah has ordained for the daughters of Adam. So do what all the pilgrims do with the exception of the Taw-af (Circumambulation) round the Ka'ba." 'Aisha added, "Allah's Apostle sacrificed cows on behalf of his wives."

Volume 1, Book 6, Number 294:

Narrated 'Aisha:

While in menses, I used to comb the hair of Allah's Apostle .

Volume 1, Book 6, Number 295:

Narrated 'Urwa:

A person asked me, "Can a woman in menses serve me? And can a Junub woman come close to me?" I replied, "All this is easy for me. All of them can serve me, and there is no harm for any other person to do the same. 'Aisha told me that she used to comb the hair of Allah's Apostle while she was in her menses, and he was in Itikaf (in the mosque). He would bring his head near her in her room and she would comb his hair, while she used to be in her menses."

Volume 1, Book 6, Number 296:

Narrated 'Aisha:

The Prophet used to lean on my lap and recite Qur'an while I was in menses.

Volume 1, Book 6, Number 297:

Narrated Um Salama:

While I was laying with the Prophet under a single woolen sheet, I got the menses. I slipped away and put on the clothes for menses. He said, "Have you got "Nifas" (menses)?" I replied, "Yes." He then called me and made me lie with him under the same sheet.

Volume 1, Book 6, Number 298:

Narrated 'Aisha:

The Prophet and I used to take a bath from a single pot while we were Junub. During the menses, he used to order me to put on an Izar (dress worn below the waist) and used to fondle me. While in Itikaf, he used to bring his head near me and I would wash it while I used to be in my periods (menses).

Volume 1, Book 6, Number 299:

Narrated 'Abdur-Rahman bin Al-Aswad:

(on the authority of his father) 'Aisha said: "Whenever Allah's Apostle wanted to fondle anyone of us during her periods (menses), he used to order her to put on an Izar and start fondling her." 'Aisha added, "None of you could control his sexual desires as the Prophet could."

Volume 1, Book 6, Number 300:

Narrated Maimuna:

When ever Allah's Apostle wanted to fondle any of his wives during the periods (menses), he used to ask her to wear an Izar.

Volume 1, Book 6, Number 301:

Narrated Abu Said Al-Khudri:

Once Allah's Apostle went out to the Musalla (to offer the prayer) o 'Id-al-Adha or Al-Fitr prayer. Then he passed by the women and said, "O women! Give alms, as I have seen that the majority of the dwellers of Hell-fire were you (women)." They asked, "Why is it so, O Allah's Apostle ?" He replied, "You curse frequently and are ungrateful to your husbands. I have not seen anyone more deficient in intelligence and religion than you. A cautious sensible man could be led astray by some of you." The women asked, "O Allah's Apostle! What is deficient in our intelligence and religion?" He said, "Is not the evidence of two women equal to the witness of one man?" They replied in the affirmative. He said, "This is the deficiency in her intelligence. Isn't it true that a woman can neither pray nor fast during her menses?" The women replied in the affirmative. He said, "This is the deficiency in her religion."

Volume 1, Book 6, Number 302:

Narrated 'Aisha:

We set out with the Prophet for Hajj and when we reached Sarif I got my menses. When the Prophet came to me, I was weeping. He asked, "Why are you weeping?" I said, "I wish if I had not performed Hajj this year." He asked, "May be that you got your menses?" I replied, "Yes." He then said, "This is the thing which Allah has ordained for all the daughters of Adam. So do what all the pilgrims do except that you do not perform the Tawaf round the Ka'ba till you are clean."

Volume 1, Book 6, Number 303:

Narrated 'Aisha:

Fatima bint Abi Hubaish said to Allah's Apostle, "O Allah's Apostle! I do not become clean (from bleeding). Shall I give up my prayers?" Allah's Apostle replied: "No, because it is from a blood vessel and not the menses. So when the real menses begins give up your prayers and when it (the period) has finished wash the blood off your body (take a bath) and offer your prayers."

Volume 1, Book 6, Number 304:

Narrated Asma' bint Abi Bakr:

A woman asked Allah's Apostle, "O Allah's Apostle! What should we do, if the blood of menses falls on our clothes?" Allah's Apostle replied, "If the blood of menses falls on the garment of anyone of you, she must take hold of the blood spot, rub it, and wash it with water and then pray in (with it)."

Volume 1, Book 6, Number 305:

Narrated 'Aisha:

Whenever anyone of us got her menses, she, on becoming clean, used to take hold of the blood spot and rub the blood off her garment, and pour water over it and wash that portion thoroughly and sprinkle water over the rest of the garment. After that she would pray in (with) it.

Volume 1, Book 6, Number 306:

Narrated 'Aisha:

Once one of the wives of the Prophet did Itikaf along with him and she was getting bleeding in between her periods. She used to see the blood (from her private parts) and she would perhaps put a dish under her for the blood. (The sub-narrator 'Ikrima added, 'Aisha once saw the liquid of safflower and said, "It looks like what so and so used to have.")

Volume 1, Book 6, Number 307:

Narrated 'Aisha:

"One of the wives of Allah's Apostle joined him in I'tikaf and she noticed blood and yellowish discharge (from her private parts) and put a dish under her when she prayed."

Volume 1, Book 6, Number 308:

Narrated 'Aisha:

One of the mothers of the faithful believers (i.e. the wives of the Prophet) did I'tikaf while she was having bleeding in between her periods.

Volume 1, Book 6, Number 309:

Narrated 'Aisha:

None of us had more than a single garment and we used to have our menses while wearing it. Whenever it got soiled with blood of menses we used to apply saliva to the blood spot and rub off the blood with our nails.

Volume 1, Book 6, Number 310:

Narrated Um-'Atiya:

We were forbidden to mourn for a dead person for more than three days except in the case of a husband for whom mourning was allowed for four months and ten days. (During that time) we were not allowed to put ko,hl (Antimony eye power) in our eyes or to use perfumes or to put on colored clothes except a dress made of 'Asb (a kind of Yemen cloth, very coarse and rough). We were allowed very light perfumes at the time of taking a bath after menses and also we were forbidden to go with the funeral procession .

Volume 1, Book 6, Number 311:

Narrated 'Aisha:

A woman asked the Prophet about the bath which is take after finishing from the menses. The Prophet told her what to do and said, "Purify yourself with a piece of cloth scented with musk." The woman asked, "How shall I purify myself with it" He said, "Subhan Allah! Purify yourself (with it)." I pulled her to myself and said, "Rub the place soiled with blood with it."

Volume 1, Book 6, Number 312:

Narrated 'Aisha:

An Ansari woman asked the Prophet how to take a bath after finishing from the menses. He replied, "Take a piece a cloth perfumed with musk and clean the private parts with it thrice." The Prophet felt shy and turned his face. So pulled her to me and told her what the Prophet meant.

Volume 1, Book 6, Number 313:

Narrated 'Aisha:

In the last Hajj of Allah's Apostle I assume the Ihram for Hajj along with Allah Apostle. I was one of those who intended Tamattu' (to perform Hajj an 'Umra) and did not take the Hadi (animal for sacrifice) with me. I got my menses and was not clean till the night of 'Arafa I said, "O Allah's Apostle! It is the night of the day of 'Arafat and I intended to perform the Hajj Tamattu' with 'Umra Allah's Apostle told me to undo my hair and comb it and to postpone the 'Umra. I did the same and completed the Hajj. On the night of Al-Hasba (i.e. place outside Mecca where the pilgrims go after finishing all the ceremonies Hajj at Mina) he (the Prophet ordered 'Abdur Rahman ('Aisha's brother) to take me to At-Tan'im to assume the Ihram for'Umra in lieu of that of Hajj-atTamattu' which I had intended to perform.

Volume 1, Book 6, Number 314:

Narrated 'Aisha:

On the 1st of Dhul-Hijja we set out with the intention of performing Hajj. Allah's Apostle said, "Any one who likes to assume the Ihram for 'Umra he can do so. Had I not brought the Hadi with me, I would have assumed the Ihram for 'Umra. "Some of us assumed the Ihram for 'Umra while the others assumed the Ihram for Hajj. I was one of those who assumed the Ihram for 'Umra. I got menses and kept on menstruating until the day of 'Arafat and complained of that to the Prophet . He told me to postpone my 'Umra, undo and comb my hair, and to assure the Ihram of Hajj and I did so. On the right of Hasba, he sent my brother 'Abdur-Rahman bin Abi Bakr with me to At-Tah'im, where I assumed the Ihram for'Umra in lieu of the previous one. Hisham said, "For that ('Umra) no Hadi, fasting or alms were required.

Volume 1, Book 6, Number 315:

Narrated Anas bin Malik:

The Prophet said, "At every womb Allah appoints an angel who says, 'O Lord! A drop of semen, O Lord! A clot. O Lord! A little lump of flesh." Then if Allah wishes (to complete) its creation, the angel asks, (O Lord!) Will it be a male or female, a wretched or a blessed, and how much will his provision be? And what will his age be?' So all that is written while the child is still in the mother's womb."

Volume 1, Book 6, Number 316:

Narrated 'Urwa:

'Aisha said, "We set out with the Prophet in his last Hajj. Some of us intended to perform 'Umra while others Hajj. When we reached Mecca, Allah's Apostle said, 'Those who had assumed the Ihram for'Umra and had not brought the Hadi should finish his Ihram and whoever had assumed the Ihram for 'Umra and brought the Hadi should not finish the Ihram till he has slaughtered his Hadi and whoever had assumed the Ihram for Hajj should complete his Hajj." 'Aisha further said, "I got my periods (menses) and kept on menstruating till the day of 'Arafat, and I had assumed the Ihram for 'Umra only (Tamattu'). The Prophet ordered me to undo and comb my head hair and assume the Ihram for Hajj only and leave the 'Umra. I did the same till I completed the Hajj. Then the Prophet sent 'Abdur Rahman bin Abi Bakr with me and ordered me to perform 'Umra from At-Tan'im in lieu of the missed 'Umra."

Volume 1, Book 6, Number 317:

Narrated 'Aisha:

Fatima bint Abi Hubaish used to have bleeding in between the periods, so she asked the Prophet about it . He replied, "The bleeding is from a blood vessel and not the menses. So give up the prayers when the (real) menses begin and when it has finished, take a bath and start praying."

Volume 1, Book 6, Number 318:

Narrated Mu'adha:

A woman asked 'Aisha, "Should I offer the prayers that which I did not offer because of menses" 'Aisha said, "Are you from the Huraura' (a town in Iraq?) We were with the Prophet and used to get our periods but he never ordered us to offer them (the Prayers missed during menses)." 'Aisha perhaps said, "We did not offer them."

Volume 1, Book 6, Number 319:

Narrated Zainab bint Abi Salama:

Um-Salama said, "I got my menses while I was lying with the Prophet under a woolen sheet. So I slipped away, took the clothes for menses and put them on. Allah's Apostle said, 'Have you got your menses?' I replied, 'Yes.' Then he called me and took me with him under the woolen sheet." Um Salama further said, "The Prophet used to kiss me while he was fasting. The Prophet and I used to take the bath of Janaba from a single pot."

Volume 1, Book 6, Number 320:

Narrated Um Salama:

While I was lying with the Prophet under a woolen sheet, I got my menses. I slipped away and put on the clothes for menses. The Prophet said, "Have you got your menses?" I replied, "Yes." He called me and I slept with him under the woolen sheet.

Volume 1, Book 6, Number 321:

Narrated Aiyub:

Hafsa said, 'We used to forbid our young women to go out for the two 'Id prayers. A woman came and stayed at the palace of Bani Khalaf and she narrated about her sister whose husband took part in twelve holy battles along with the Prophet and her sister was with her husband in six (out of these twelve). She (the woman's sister) said, "We used to treat the wounded, look after the patients and once I asked the Prophet, 'Is there any harm for any of us to stay at home if she doesn't have a veil?' He said, 'She should cover herself with the veil of her companion and should participate in the good deeds and in the religious gathering of the Muslims.' When Um 'Atiya came I asked her whether she had heard it from the Prophet. She replied, "Yes. May my father be sacrificed for him (the Prophet)! (Whenever she mentioned the Prophet she used to say, 'May my father be sacrificed for him) I have heard the Prophet saying, 'The unmarried young virgins and the mature girl who stay often screened or the young unmarried virgins who often stay screened and the menstruating women should come out and participate in the good deeds as well as the religious gathering of the faithful believers but the menstruating women should keep away from the Musalla (praying place).' " Hafsa asked Um 'Atiya surprisingly, "Do you say the menstruating women?" She replied, "Doesn't a menstruating woman attend 'Arafat (Hajj) and such and such (other deeds)?"

Volume 1, Book 6, Number 322:

Narrated 'Aisha:

Fatima bint Abi Hubaish asked the Prophet, "I got persistent bleeding (in between the periods) and do not become clean. Shall I give up prayers?" He replied, "No, this is from a blood vessel. Give up the prayers only for the days on which you usually get the menses and then take a bath and offer your prayers."

Volume 1, Book 6, Number 323:

Narrated Um 'Atiya:

We never considered yellowish discharge as a thing of importance (as menses).

Volume 1, Book 6, Number 324:

Narrated 'Aisha:

(the wife of the Prophet) Um Habiba got bleeding in between the periods for seven years. She asked Allah's Apostle about it. He ordered her to take a bath (after the termination of actual periods) and added that it was (from) a blood vessel. So she used to take a bath for every prayer.

Volume 1, Book 6, Number 325:

Narrated 'Aisha:

(the wife of the Prophet) I told Allah's Apostle that Safiya bint Huyai had got her menses. He said, "She will probably delay us. Did she perform Tawaf (Al-Ifada) with you?" We replied, "Yes." On that the Prophet told her to depart.

Volume 1, Book 6, Number 326:

Narrated Ibn 'Abbas:

A woman is al lowed to leave (go back home) if she gets menses (after Tawaf-AlIfada). Ibn 'Umar formerly used to say that she should not leave but later on I heard him saying, "She may leave, since Allah's Apostle gave them the permission to leave (after Tawaf-AlIfada."

Volume 1, Book 6, Number 327:

Narrated 'Aisha:

The Prophet said to me, "Give up the prayer when your menses begin and when it has finished, wash the blood off your body (take a bath) and start praying."

Volume 1, Book 6, Number 328:

Narrated Samura bin Jundab:

The Prophet offered the funeral prayer for the dead body of a woman who died of (during) delivery (i.e. child birth) and he stood by the middle of her body.

Volume 1, Book 6, Number 329:

Narrated Maimuna:

(the wife of the Prophet) During my menses, I never prayed, but used to sit on the mat beside the mosque of Allah's Apostle. He used to offer the prayer on his sheet and in prostration some of his clothes used to touch me."

Book 7: Rubbing hands and feet with dust (Tayammum)

Volume 1, Book 7, Number 330:

Narrated 'Aisha:

(the wife of the Prophet) We set out with Allahs Apostle on one of his journeys till we reached Al-Baida' or Dhatul-Jaish, a necklace of mine was broken (and lost). Allah's Apostle stayed there to search for it, and so did the people along with him. There was no water at that place, so the people went to Abu- Bakr As-Siddiq and said, "Don't you see what 'Aisha has done? She has made Allah's Apostle and the people stay where there is no water and they have no water with them." Abu Bakr came while Allah's Apostle was sleeping with his head on my thigh, He said, to me: "You have detained Allah's Apostle and the people where there is no water and they have no water with them.

So he admonished me and said what Allah wished him to say and hit me on my flank with his hand. Nothing prevented me from moving (because of pain) but the position of Allah's Apostle on my thigh. Allah's Apostle got up when dawn broke and there was no water. So Allah revealed the Divine Verses of Tayammum. So they all performed Tayammum. Usaid bin Hudair said, "O the family of Abu Bakr! This is not the first blessing of yours." Then the camel on which I was riding was caused to move from its place and the necklace was found beneath it.

Volume 1, Book 7, Number 331:

Narrated Jabir bin 'Abdullah:

The Prophet said, "I have been given five things which were not given to any one else before me.

1. Allah made me victorious by awe, (by His frightening my enemies) for a distance of one month's journey.

2. The earth has been made for me (and for my followers) a place for praying and a thing to perform Tayammum, therefore anyone of my followers can pray wherever the time of a prayer is due.

3. The booty has been made Halal (lawful) for me yet it was not lawful for anyone else before me.

4. I have been given the right of intercession (on the Day of Resurrection).

5. Every Prophet used to be sent to his nation only but I have been sent to all mankind.

Volume 1, Book 7, Number 332:

Narrated 'Urwa's father:

Aisha said, "I borrowed a necklace from Asma' and it was lost. So Allah's Apostle sent a man to search for it and he found it. Then the time of the prayer became due and there was no water. They prayed (without ablution) and informed Allah's Apostle about it, so the verse of Tayammum was revealed." Usaid bin Hudair said to 'Aisha, "May Allah reward you. By Allah, whenever anything happened which you did not like, Allah brought good for you and for the Muslims in that."

Al-Jurf and the time for the 'Asr prayer became due while he was at Marbad-AnNa'am (sheepfold), so he (performed Tayammum) and prayed there and then entered Medina when the sun was still high but he did not repeat that prayer.

Volume 1, Book 7, Number 333:

Narrated Abu Juhaim Al-Ansari:

The Prophet came from the direction of Bir Jamal. A man met him and greeted him. But he did not return back the greeting till he went to a (mud) wall and smeared his hands and his face with its dust (performed Tayammum) and then returned back the greeting.

Volume 1, Book 7, Number 334:

Narrated 'Abdur Rahman bin Abza:

A man came to 'Umar bin Al-Khattab and said, "I became Junub but no water was available." 'Ammar bin Yasir said to 'Umar, "Do you remember that you and I (became Junub while both of us) were together on a journey and you didn't pray but I rolled myself on the ground and prayed? I informed the Prophet about it and he said, 'It would have been sufficient for you to do like this.' The Prophet then stroked lightly the earth with his hands and then blew off the dust and passed his hands over his face and hands."

Volume 1, Book 7, Number 335:

Narrated Said bin 'Abdur Rahman bin Abza:

(on the authority of his father who said) 'Ammar said so (the above Statement). And Shu'ba stroked lightly the earth with his hands and brought them close to his mouth (blew off the dust) and passed them over his face and then the backs of his hands. 'Ammar said, "Ablution (meaning Tayammum here) is sufficient for a Muslim if water is not available."

Volume 1, Book 7, Number 336:

Narrated 'Abdur Rahman bin Abza:

that while he was in the company of 'Umar, 'Ammar said to 'Umar, "We were in a detachment and became Junub and I blew the dust off my hands (performed the rolling over the earth and prayed.)"

Volume 1, Book 7, Number 337:

Narrated 'Abdur Rahman bin Abza:

'Ammar said to 'Umar "I rolled myself in the dust and came to the Prophet who said, 'Passing dusted hands over the face and the backs of the hands is sufficient for you.' "

Volume 1, Book 7, Number 338:

Narrated 'Ammar:

as above.

Volume 1, Book 7, Number 339:

Narrated 'Ammar:

The Prophet stroked the earth with his hands and then passed them over his face and the backs of his hands (while demonstrating Tayammum).

Volume 1, Book 7, Number 340:

Narrated 'Imran:

Once we were traveling with the Prophet and we carried on traveling till the last part of the night and then we (halted at a place) and slept (deeply). There is nothing sweeter than sleep for a traveler in the last part of the night. So it was only the heat of the sun that made us to wake up and the first to wake up was so and so, then so and so and then so and so (the narrator 'Auf said that Abu Raja' had told him their names but he had forgotten them) and the fourth person to wake up was 'Umar bin Al-Khattab. And whenever the Prophet used to sleep, nobody would wake up him till he himself used to get up as we did not know what was happening (being revealed) to him in his sleep. So, 'Umar got up and saw the condition of the people, and he was a strict man, so he said, "Allahu Akbar" and raised his voice with Takbir, and kept on saying loudly till the Prophet got up because of it. When he got up, the people informed him about what had happened to them. He said, "There is no harm (or it will not be harmful). Depart!" So they departed from that place, and after covering some distance the Prophet stopped and asked for some water to perform the ablution. So he performed the ablution and the call for the prayer was pronounced and he led the people in prayer. After he finished from the prayer, he saw a man sitting aloof who had not prayed with the people. He asked, "O so and so! What has prevented you from praying with us?" He replied, "I am Junub and there is no water. " The Prophet said, "Perform Tayammum with (clean) earth and that is sufficient for you."

Then the Prophet proceeded on and the people complained to him of thirst. Thereupon he got down and called a person (the narrator 'Auf added that Abu Raja' had named him but he had forgotten) and 'Ali, and ordered them to go and bring water. So they went in search of water and met a woman who was sitting on her camel between two bags of water. They asked, "Where can we find water?" She replied, "I was there (at the place of water) this hour yesterday and my people are behind me." They requested her to accompany them. She asked, "Where?" They said, "To Allah's Apostle ." She said, "Do you mean the man who is called the Sabi, (with a new religion)?" They replied, "Yes, the same person. So come along." They brought her to the Prophet and narrated the whole story. He said, "Help her to dismount." The Prophet asked for a pot, then he opened the mouths of the bags and poured some water into the pot. Then he closed the big openings of the bags and opened the small ones and the people were called upon to drink and water their animals. So they all watered their animals and they (too) all quenched their thirst and also gave water to others and last of all the Prophet gave a pot full of water to the person who was Junub and told him to pour it over his body. The woman was standing and watching all that which they were doing with her water. By Allah, when her water bags were returned the looked like as if they were more full (of water) than they had been before (Miracle of Allah's Apostle) Then the Prophet ordered us to collect something for her; so dates, flour and Sawiq were collected which amounted to a good meal that was put in a piece of cloth. She was helped to ride on her camel and that cloth full of food-stuff was also placed in front of her and then the Prophet said to her, "We have not taken your water but Allah has given water to us." She returned home late. Her relatives asked her, "O so and so what has delayed you?" She said, "A strange thing! Two men met me and took me to the man who is called the Sabi' and he did such and such a thing. By Allah, he is either the greatest magician between this and this (gesturing with her index and middle fingers raising them towards the sky indicating the heaven and the earth) or he is Allah's true Apostle."

Afterwards the Muslims used to attack the pagans around her abode but never touched her village. One day she said to her people, "I think that these people leave you purposely. Have you got any inclination to Islam?" They obeyed her and all of them embraced Islam.

Abu 'Abdullah said, The word Saba'a means "The one who has deserted his old religion and embraced a new religion." Abul 'Ailya said, "The Sabis are a sect of people of the Scripture who recite the Book of Psalms."

Volume 1, Book 7, Number 341,

Narrated Abu Wail,

Abu Muisa said to'Abdullah bin Mas'ud, "If one does not find water (for ablution) can he give up the prayer?" Abdullah replied, "If you give the permission to perform Tayammum they will perform Tayammum even if water was available if one of them found it cold." Abu Musa said, "What about the statement of 'Ammar to 'Umar?" 'Abdullah replied, "Umar was not satisfied by his statement."

Volume 1, Book 7, Number 342.

Narrated Shaqiq bin Salama.

I was with 'Abdullah and Abu Musa; the latter asked the former, "O Abu AbdurRahman! What is your opinion if somebody becomes Junub and no water is available?" 'Abdullah replied, "Do not pray till water is found." Abu Musa said, "What do you say about the statement of 'Ammar (who was ordered by the Prophet to perform Tayammum). The Prophet said to him. "Perform Tayammum and that would be sufficient." 'Abdullah replied, "Don't you see that 'Umar was not satisfied by 'Ammar's statement?" Abu- Musa said, "All right, leave 'Ammalr's statement, but what will you say about this verse (of Tayammum)?" 'Abqiullah kept quiet and then said, "If we allowed it, then they would probably perform Tayammum even if water was available, if one of them found it (water) cold." The narrator added, "I said to Shaqrq, "Then did 'Abdullah dislike to perform Tayammum because of this?" He replied, "Yes."

Volume 1, Book 7, Number 343.

Narrated Al-A'mash.

Shaqiq said, "While I was sitting with 'Abdullah and Abu Musa Al-Ash-'ari, the latter asked the former, 'If a person becomes Junub and does not find water for one month, can he perform Tayammum and offer his prayer?' (He applied in the negative). Abu Musa said, 'What do you say about this verse from Surat "Al-Ma'ida". When you do not find water then perform Tayammum with clean earth? 'Abdullah replied, 'If we allowed it then they would probably perform Tayammum with clean earth even if water were available but cold.' I said to Shaqiq, 'You then disliked to perform Tayammum because of this?' Shaqiq said,'Yes.' (Shaqiq added), "Abu Musa said, 'Haven't you heard the statement of 'Ammar to 'Umar? He said. I was sent out by Allah's Apostle for some job and I became Junub and could not find water so I rolled myself over the dust (clean earth) like an animal does, and when I told the Prophet of that he said, 'Like this would have been sufficient.' The Prophet (saying so) lightly stroked the earth with his hand once and blew it off, then passed his (left) hand over the back of his right hand or his (right) hand over the back of his left hand and then passed them over his face.' So 'Abdullah said to Abu- Musa, 'Don't you know that 'Umar was not satisfied with 'Ammar's statement?' "

Narrated Shaqiq. While I was with 'Abdullah and Abu Musa, the latter said to the former, "Haven't you heard the statement of 'Ammar to 'Umar? He said, "Allah's Apostle sent you and me out and I became Junub and rolled myself in the dust (clean earth) (for Tayammum). When we came to Allah's

Apostle I told him about it and he said, 'This would have been sufficient,' passing his hands over his face and the backs of his hands once only.' "

Volume 1, Book 7, Number 344:

Narrated 'Imran bin Husain Al-Khuza'i:

Allah's Apostle saw a person sitting aloof and not praying with the people. He asked him, "O so and so! What prevented you from offering the prayer with the people?" He replied, "O Allah's Apostle! I am Junub and there is no water." The Prophet said, "Perform Tayammum with clean earth and that will be sufficient for you."

Book 8: Prayers (Salat)

Volume 1, Book 8, Number 345:

Narrated Abu Dhar:

Allah's Apostle said, "While I was at Mecca the roof of my house was opened and Gabriel descended, opened my chest, and washed it with Zam-zam water. Then he brought a golden tray full of wisdom and faith and having poured its contents into my chest, he closed it. Then he took my hand and ascended with me to the nearest heaven, when I reached the nearest heaven, Gabriel said to the gatekeeper of the heaven, 'Open (the gate).' The gatekeeper asked, 'Who is it?' Gabriel answered: 'Gabriel.' He asked, 'Is there anyone with you?' Gabriel replied, 'Yes, Muhammad I is with me.' He asked, 'Has he been called?' Gabriel said, 'Yes.' So the gate was opened and we went over the nearest heaven and there we saw a man sitting with some people on his right and some on his left. When he looked towards his right, he laughed and when he looked toward his left he wept. Then he said, 'Welcome! O pious Prophet and pious son.' I asked Gabriel, 'Who is he?' He replied, 'He is Adam and the people on his right and left are the souls of his offspring. Those on his right are the people of Paradise and those on his left are the people of Hell and when he looks towards his right he laughs and when he looks towards his left he weeps.'

Then he ascended with me till he reached the second heaven and he (Gabriel) said to its gatekeeper, 'Open (the gate).' The gatekeeper said to him the same as the gatekeeper of the first heaven had said and he opened the gate. Anas said: "Abu Dhar added that the Prophet met Adam, Idris, Moses, Jesus and Abraham, he (Abu Dhar) did not mention on which heaven they were but he mentioned that he (the Prophet) met Adam on the nearest heaven and Abraham on the sixth heaven. Anas said, "When Gabriel along with the Prophet passed by Idris, the latter said, 'Welcome! O pious Prophet and pious brother.' The Prophet asked, 'Who is he?' Gabriel replied, 'He is Idris." The Prophet added, "I passed by Moses and he said, 'Welcome! O pious Prophet and pious brother.' I asked Gabriel, 'Who is he?' Gabriel replied, 'He is Moses.' Then I passed by Jesus and he said, 'Welcome! O pious brother and pious Prophet.' I asked, 'Who is he?' Gabriel replied, 'He is Jesus.

Then I passed by Abraham and he said, 'Welcome! O pious Prophet and pious son.' I asked Gabriel, 'Who is he?' Gabriel replied, 'He is Abraham. The Prophet added, 'Then Gabriel ascended with me to a place where I heard the creaking of the pens." Ibn Hazm and Anas bin Malik said: The Prophet said, "Then Allah enjoined fifty prayers on my followers when I returned with this order of Allah, I passed by Moses who asked me, 'What has Allah enjoined on your followers?' I replied, 'He has enjoined fifty prayers on them.' Moses said, 'Go back to your Lord (and appeal for reduction) for your followers will not be able to bear it.' (So I went back to Allah and requested for reduction) and He reduced it to half. When I passed by Moses again and informed him about it, he said, 'Go back to your Lord as your followers will not be able to bear it.' So I returned to Allah and requested for further reduction and half of it was reduced. I again passed by Moses and he said to me: 'Return to your Lord, for your followers will not be able to bear it. So I returned to Allah and He said, 'These are five prayers and they are all (equal to) fifty (in reward) for My Word does not change.' I returned to Moses and he told me to go back once again. I replied, 'Now I feel shy of asking my Lord again.' Then Gabriel took me till we " reached Sidrat-il-Muntaha (Lote tree of; the utmost boundry) which was shrouded in colors, indescribable. Then I was admitted into Paradise where I found small (tents or) walls (made) of pearls and its earth was of musk."

Volume 1, Book 8, Number 346:

Narrated 'Aisha:

the mother of believers: Allah enjoined the prayer when He enjoined it, it was two Rakat only (in every prayer) both when in residence or on journey. Then the prayers offered on journey remained the same, but (the Rakat of) the prayers for non-travellers were increased.

Volume 1, Book 8, Number 347:

Narrated Um 'Atiya:

We were ordered to bring out our menstruating women and veiled women in the religious gatherings and invocation of Muslims on the two 'Id festivals. These menstruating women were to keep away from their Musalla. A woman asked, "O Allah's Apostle ' What about one who does not have a veil?" He said, "Let her share the veil of her companion."

Volume 1, Book 8, Number 348:

Narrated Muhammad bin Al-Munkadir:

Once Jabir prayed with his Izar tied to his back while his clothes were Lying beside him on a wooden peg. Somebody asked him, "Do you offer your prayer in a single Izar?" He replied, "I did so to show it to a fool like you. Had anyone of us two garments in the life-time of the Prophet?"

Volume 1, Book 8, Number 349.

Narrated Muhammad bin Al Munkadir.

I saw Jabir bin 'Abdullah praying in a single garment and he said that he had seen the Prophet praying in a single garment.

Volume 1, Book 8, Number 350.

Narrated 'Umar bin Abi Salama.

The Prophet prayed in one garment and crossed its ends.

Volume 1, Book 8, Number 351.

Narrated 'Umar bin Abi Salama.

I saw the Prophet offering prayers in a single garment in the house of Um-Salama and he had crossed its ends around his shoulders.

Volume 1, Book 8, Number 352.

Narrated 'Umar bin Abi Salama.

In the house of Um-Salama I saw Allah's Apostle offering prayers, wrapped in a single garment around his body with its ends crossed round his shoulders.

Volume 1, Book 8, Number 353.

Narrated Abu Murra.

(the freed slave of Um Hani) Um Hani, the daughter of Abi Talib said, "I went to Allah's Apostle in the year of the conquest of Mecca and found him taking a bath and his daughter Fatima was screening him. I greeted him. He asked, 'Who is she?' I replied, 'I am Um Hani bint Abi Talib.' He said, 'Welcome! O Um Hani.' When he finished his bath he stood up and prayed eight Rak at while wearing a single garment wrapped round his body and when he finished I said, 'O Allah's Apostle ! My brother has told me that he will kill a person whom I gave shelter and that person is so and so the son of Hubaira.' The Prophet said, 'We shelter the person whom you have sheltered.' " Um Ham added, "And that was before noon (Duha)."

Volume 1, Book 8, Number 354:

Narrated Abu Huraira:

A person asked Allah's Apostle about the offering of the prayer in a single garment. Allah's Apostle replied, "Has every one of you got two garments?"

Volume 1, Book 8, Number 355:

Narrated Abu Huraira:

The Prophet said, "None of you should offer prayer in a single garment that does not cover the shoulders."

Volume 1, Book 8, Number 356:

Narrated Abu Huraira:

Allah's Apostle said, "Whoever prays in a single garment must cross its ends (over the shoulders)."

Volume 1, Book 8, Number 357:

Narrated Said bin Al-Harith:

I asked Jabir bin 'Abdullah about praying in a single garment. He said, "I travelled with the Prophet during some of his journeys, and I came to him at night for some purpose and I found him praying. At that time, I was wearing a single garment with which I covered my shoulders and prayed by his side. When he finished the prayer, he asked, 'O Jabir! What has brought you here?' I told him what I wanted. When I finished, he asked, 'O Jabir! What is this garment which I have seen and with which you covered your shoulders?' I replied, 'It is a (tight) garment.' He said, 'If the garment is large enough, wrap it round the body (covering the shoulders) and if it is tight (too short) then use it as an Izar (tie it around your waist only.)' "

Volume 1, Book 8, Number 358:

Narrated Sahl:

The men used to pray with the Prophet with their Izars tied around their necks as boys used to do; therefore the Prophet told the women not to raise their heads till the men sat down straight (while praying).

Volume 1, Book 8, Number 359:

Narrated Mughira bin Shu'ba:

Once I was traveling with the Prophet and he said, "O Mughira! take this container of water." I took it and Allah's Apostle went far away till he disappeared. He answered the call of nature and was wearing a Syrian cloak. He tried to take out his hands from its sleeve but it was very tight so he took out his hands from under it. I poured water and he performed ablution like that for prayers and passed his wet hands over his Khuff (leather socks) and then prayed .

Volume 1, Book 8, Number 360:

Narrated Jabir bin 'Abdullah:

While Allah's Apostle was carrying stones (along) with the people of Mecca for (the building of) the Ka'ba wearing an Izar (waist-sheet cover), his uncle Al-'Abbas said to him, "O my nephew! (It would be better) if you take off your Izar and put it over your shoulders underneath the stones." So he took off his Izar and put it over his shoulders, but he fell unconscious and since then he had never been seen naked.

Volume 1, Book 8, Number 361:

Narrated Abu Huraira:

A man stood up and asked the Prophet about praying in a single garment. The Prophet said, "Has every one of you two garments?" A man put a similar question to 'Umar on which he replied, "When Allah makes you wealthier then you should clothe yourself properly during prayers. Otherwise one can pray with an Izar and a Rida' (a sheet covering the upper part of the body.) Izar and a shirt, Izar and a Qaba', trousers and a Rida, trousers and a shirt or trousers and a Qaba', Tubban and a Qaba' or Tubban and a shirt." (The narrator added, "I think that he also said a Tubban and a Rida. ")

Volume 1, Book 8, Number 362:

Narrated Ibn 'Umar:

A person asked Allah's Apostle, "What should a Muhrim wear?" He replied, "He should not wear shirts, trousers, a burnus (a hooded cloak), or clothes which are stained with saffron or Wars (a kind of perfume). Whoever does not find a sandal to wear can wear Khuffs, but these should be cut short so as not to cover the ankles.

Volume 1, Book 8, Number 363:

Narrated Abu Said Al-Khudri

Allah's Apostle forbade Ishtimal-As-Samma' (wrapping one's body with a garment so that one cannot raise its end or take one's hand out of it). He also forbade Al-Ihtiba' (sitting on buttocks with knees close to abdomen and feet apart with the hands circling the knees) while wrapping oneself with a single garment, without having a part of it over the private parts.

Volume 1, Book 8, Number 364:

Narrated Abu Huraira:

The Prophet forbade two kinds of sales i.e. Al-Limais and An-Nibadh (the former is a kind of sale in which the deal is completed if the buyer touches a thing, without seeing or checking it properly and the latter is a kind of a sale in which the deal is completed when the seller throws a thing towards the buyer giving him no opportunity to see, touch or check it) and (the Prophet forbade) also Ishtimal-As-Samma' and Al-Ihtiba' in a single garment.

Volume 1, Book 8, Number 365:

Narrated Abu Huraira:

On the Day of Nahr (10th of Dhul-Hijja, in the year prior to the last Hajj of the Prophet when Abu Bakr was the leader of the pilgrims in that Hajj) Abu Bakr sent me along with other announcers to Mina to make a public announcement: "No pagan is allowed to perform Hajj after this year and no naked person is allowed to perform the Tawaf around the Ka'ba. Then Allah's Apostle sent 'Ali to read out the Surat Bara'a (At-Tauba) to the people; so he made the announcement along with us on the day of Nahr in Mina: "No pagan is allowed to perform Hajj after this year and no naked person is allowed to perform the Tawaf around the Ka'ba."

Volume 1, Book 8, Number 366:

Narrated Muhammad bin Al-Munkadir:

I went to Jabir bin 'Abdullah and he was praying wrapped in a garment and his Rida was Lying beside him. When he finished the prayers, I said "O 'Abdullah! You pray (in a single garment) while your Rida' is lying beside you." He replied, "Yes, I did it intentionally so that the ignorant ones like you might see me. I saw the Prophet praying like this. "

Volume 1, Book 8, Number 367:

Narrated 'Abdul 'Aziz:

Anas said, 'When Allah's Apostle invaded Khaibar, we offered the Fajr prayer there yearly in the morning) when it was still dark. The Prophet rode and Abu Talha rode too and I was riding behind Abu Talha. The Prophet passed through the lane of Khaibar quickly and my knee was touching the thigh of the Prophet . He uncovered his thigh and I saw the whiteness of the thigh of the Prophet. When he entered the town, he said, 'Allahu Akbar! Khaibar is ruined. Whenever we approach near a (hostile) nation (to fight) then evil will be the morning of those who have been warned.' He repeated this thrice. The people came out for their jobs and some of them said, 'Muhammad (has come).' (Some of our companions added, "With his army.") We conquered Khaibar, took the captives, and the booty was collected. Dihya came and said, 'O Allah's Prophet! Give me a slave girl from the captives.' The Prophet said, 'Go and take any slave girl.' He took Safiya bint Huyai. A man came to the Prophet and said, 'O Allah's Apostles! You gave Safiya bint Huyai to Dihya and she is the chief mistress of the tribes of Quraiza and An-Nadir and she befits none but you.' So the Prophet said, 'Bring him along with her.' So Dihya came with her and when the Prophet saw her, he said to Dihya, 'Take any slave girl other than her from the captives.' Anas added: The Prophet then manumitted her and married her."

Thabit asked Anas, "O Abu Hamza! What did the Prophet pay her (as Mahr)?" He said, "Her self was her Mahr for he manumitted her and then married her." Anas added, "While on the way, Um Sulaim dressed her for marriage (ceremony) and at night she sent her as a bride to the Prophet . So the Prophet was a bridegroom and he said, 'Whoever has anything (food) should bring it.' He spread out a leather sheet (for the food) and some brought dates and others cooking butter. (I think he (Anas) mentioned As-SawTq). So they prepared a dish of Hais (a kind of meal). And that was Walrma (the marriage banquet) of Allah's Apostle ."

Volume 1, Book 8, Number 368:

Narrated 'Aisha:

Allah's Apostle used to offer the Fajr prayer and some believing women covered with their veiling sheets used to attend the Fajr prayer with him and then they would return to their homes unrecognized .

Volume 1, Book 8, Number 369:

Narrated 'Aisha:

the Prophet prayed in a Khamisa (a square garment) having marks. During the prayer, he looked at its marks. So when he finished the prayer he said, "Take this Khamisa of mine to Abu Jahm and get me his Inbijaniya (a woolen garment without marks) as it (the Khamisa) has diverted my attention from the prayer."

Volume 1, Book 8, Number 370:

Narrated 'Aisha:

The Prophet said, 'I was looking at its (Khamisa's) marks during the prayers and I was afraid that it may put me in trial (by taking away my attention).

Volume 1, Book 8, Number 371:

Narrated Anas:

'Aisha had a Qiram (a thin marked woolen curtain) with which he had screened one side of her home. The Prophet said, "Take away this Qiram of yours, as its pictures are still displayed in front of me during my prayer (i.e. they divert my attention from the prayer)."

Volume 1, Book 8, Number 372:

Narrated 'Uqba bin 'Amir:

The Prophet was given a silken Farruj as a present. He wore it while praying. When he had finished his prayer, he took it off violently as if with a strong aversion to it and said, "It is not the dress of Allah-fearing pious people."

Volume 1, Book 8, Number 373:

Narrated Abu Juhaifa:

I saw Allah's Apostle in a red leather tent and I saw Bilal taking the remaining water with which the Prophet had performed ablution. I saw the people taking the utilized water impatiently and whoever got some of it rubbed it on his body and those who could not get any took the moisture from the others' hands. Then I saw Bilal carrying an 'Anza (a spear-headed stick) which he planted in the ground. The Prophet came out tucking up his red cloak, and led the people in prayer and offered two Rakat (facing the Ka'ba) taking 'Anza as a Sutra for his prayer. I saw the people and animals passing in front of him beyond the 'Anza.

Volume 1, Book 8, Number 374:

Narrated Abu Hazim:

Sahl bin Sa'd was asked about the (Prophet's) pulpit as to what thing it was made of? Sahl replied: "None remains alive amongst the people, who knows about it better than I. It was made of tamarisk (wood) of the forest. So and so, the slave of so and so prepared it for Allah's Apostle . When it was constructed and place (in the Mosque), Allah's Apostle stood on it facing the Qibla and said 'Allahu Akbar', and the people stood behind him (and led the people in prayer). He recited and bowed and the people bowed behind him. Then he raised his head and stepped back, got down and prostrated on the ground and then he again ascended the pulpit, recited, bowed, raised his head and stepped back, got down and prostrate on the ground. So, this is what I know about the pulpit."

Ahmad bin Hanbal said, "As the Prophet was at a higher level than the people, there is no harm according to the above-mentioned Hadith if the Imam is at a higher level than his followers during the prayers."

Volume 1, Book 8, Number 375:

Narrated Anas bin Malik:

Once Allah's Apostle fell off a horse and his leg or shoulder got injured. He swore that he would not go to his wives for one month and he stayed in a Mashruba (attic room) having stairs made of date palm trunks. So his companions came to visit him, and he led them in prayer sitting, whereas his companions were standing. When he finished the prayer, he said, "Imam is meant to be followed, so when he says 'Allahu Akbar,' say 'Allahu Akbar' and when he bows, bow and when he prostrates, prostrate and if he prays standing pray, standing. After the 29th day the Prophet came down (from the attic room) and the people asked him, "O Allah's Apostle! You swore that you will not go to your wives for one month." He said, "The month is 29 days."

Volume 1, Book 8, Number 376:

Narrates 'Abdullah bin Shaddad:

Maimuna said, "Allah's Apostle was praying while I was in my menses, sitting beside him and sometimes his clothes would touch me during his prostration." Maimuna added, "He prayed on a Khumra (a small mat sufficient just for the face and the hands while prostrating during prayers).

Volume 1, Book 8, Number 377:

Narrated Ishaq:

Anas bin Malik said, "My grand-mother Mulaika invited Allah's Apostle for a meal which she herself had prepared. He ate from it and said, 'Get up! I will lead you in the prayer.' " Anas added, "I took my Hasir, washed it with water as it had become dark because of long use and Allah's Apostle stood on it. The orphan (Damira or Ruh) and I aligned behind him and the old lady (Mulaika) stood behind us. Allah's Apostle led us in the prayer and offered two Rak'at and then left."

Volume 1, Book 8, Number 378:

Narrated Maimuna:

Allah's Apostle used to pray on Khumra.

Volume 1, Book 8, Number 379:

Narrated Abu Salama:

'Aisha the wife of the Prophet said, "I used to sleep in front of Allah's Apostle and my legs were opposite his Qibla and in prostration he pushed my legs and I withdrew then and when he stood, I stretched them.' 'Aisha added, "In those days the houses were without lights."

Volume 1, Book 8, Number 380:

Narrated 'Aisha:

Allah Apostle prayed while I was lying like a dead body on his family bed between him and his Qibla.

Volume 1, Book 8, Number 381:

Narrated 'Urwa:

The Prophet prayed while 'Aisha was lying between him and his Qibla on the bed on which they used to sleep.

Volume 1, Book 8, Number 382:

Narrated Anas bin Malik:

We used to pray with the Prophet and some of us used to place the ends of their clothes at the place of prostration because of scorching heat.

Volume 1, Book 8, Number 383:

Narrated Abu Maslama:

Said bin Yazid Al-Azdi: I asked Anas bin Malik whether the Prophet had ever, prayed with his shoes on. He replied "Yes."

Volume 1, Book 8, Number 384:

Narrated Ibrahim:

Hammam bin Al-Harith said, "I saw Jarir bin 'Abdullah urinating. Then he performed ablution and passed his (wet) hands over his Khuffs, stood up and prayed. He was asked about it. He replied that he had seen the Prophet doing the same." They approved of this narration as Jarir was one of those who embraced Islam very late.

Volume 1, Book 8, Number 385l:

Narrated Al-Mughira bin Shu'ba:

I helped the Prophet in performing ablution and he passed his wet hands over his Khuffs and prayed.

Volume 1, Book 8, Number 385u.

Narrated 'Abdullah bin Malik.

Ibn Buhaina, "When the Prophet prayed, he used to separate his arms from his body so widely that the whiteness of his armpits was visible."

Volume 1, Book 8, Number 386.

Narrated Anas bin Malik.

Allah's Apostle said, "Whoever prays like us and faces our Quibla and eats our slaughtered animals is a Muslim and is under Allah's and His Apostle's protection. So do not betray Allah by betraying those who are in His protection."

Volume 1, Book 8, Number 387.

Narrated Anas bin Malik.

Allah's Apostle said, "I have been ordered to fight the people till they say: 'None has the right to be worshipped but Allah.' And if they say so, pray like our prayers, face our Qibla and slaughter as we slaughter, then their blood and property will be sacred to us and we will not interfere with them except legally and their reckoning will be with Allah." Narrated Maimun ibn Siyah that he asked Anas bin Malik, "O Abu Hamza! What makes the life and property of a person sacred?" He replied, "Whoever says, 'None has the right to be worshipped but Allah', faces our Qibla during the prayers, prays like us and eats our slaughtered animal, then he is a Muslim, and has got the same rights and obligations as other Muslims have."

Volume 1, Book 8, Number 388.

Narrated Abu Aiyub Al-Ansari.

The Prophet said, "While defecating, neither face nor turn your back to the Qibla but face either east or west." Abu Aiyub added. "When we arrived in Sham we came across some lavatories facing the Qibla; therefore we turned ourselves while using them and asked for Allah's forgiveness."

Volume 1, Book 8, Number 389.

Narrated 'Amr bin Dmar.

I asked Ibn 'Umar, "Can a person who has performed the Tawaf around the Ka'ba for 'Umra but has not performed the (Sa'i) Tawaf of Safa and Marwa, have a sexual relation with his wife?" Ibn 'Umar replied "When the Prophet reached Mecca he performed the Tawaf around the Ka'ba (circumambulated it seven times) and offered a two-Rak'at prayer (at the place) behind the station (of

Abraham) and then performed the Tawaf (Sa'i) of Safa and Marwa, and verily in Allah's Apostle you have a good example." Then we put the same question to Jabir bin 'Abdullah and he too replied, "He should not go near his wife (for sexual relation) till he has finished the Tawaf of Safa and Marwa."

Volume 1, Book 8, Number 390:

Narrated Mujahid:

Someone came to Ibn 'Umar and said, "Here is Allah's Apostle entering the Ka'ba." Ibn 'Umar said, "I went there but the Prophet had come out of the Ka'ba and I found Bilal standing between its two doors. I asked Bilal, 'Did the Prophet pray in the Ka'ba?' Bilal replied, 'Yes, he prayed two Rakat between the two pillars which are to your left on entering the Ka'ba. Then Allah's Apostle came out and offered a two-Rak'at prayer facing the Ka'ba.' "

Volume 1, Book 8, Number 391:

Narrated Ibn Abbas:

When the Prophet entered the Ka'ba, he invoked Allah in each and every side of it and did not pray till he came out of it, and offered a two-Rak'at prayer facing the Ka'ba and said, "This is the Qibla."

Volume 1, Book 8, Number 392:

Narrated Bara' bin 'Azib:

Allah's Apostle prayed facing Baitul-Maqdis for sixteen or seventeen months but he loved to face the Ka'ba (at Mecca) so Allah revealed: "Verily, We have seen the turning of your face to the heaven!" (2.144) So the Prophet faced the Ka'ba and the fools amongst the people namely "the Jews" said, "What has turned them from their Qibla (Bait-ul-Maqdis) which they formerly observed"" (Allah revealed): "Say: 'To Allah belongs the East and the West. He guides whom he will to a straight path'." (2.142) A man prayed with the Prophet (facing the Ka'ba) and went out. He saw some of the Ansar praying the 'Asr prayer with their faces towards Bait-ul-Maqdis, he said, "I bear witness that I prayed with Allah's Apostle facing the Ka'ba." So all the people turned their faces towards the Ka'ba.

Volume 1, Book 8, Number 393:

Narrated Jabir:

Allah's Apostle used to pray (optional, non-obligatory prayer) while riding on his mount (Rahila) wherever it turned, and whenever he wanted to pray the compulsory prayer he dismounted and prayed facing the Qibla.

Volume 1, Book 8, Number 394:

Narrated 'Abdullah:

The Prophet prayed (and the subnarrator Ibrahim said, "I do not know whether he prayed more or less than usual"), and when he had finished the prayers he was asked, "O Allah's Apostle! Has there been any change in the prayers?" He said, "What is it?" The people said, "You have prayed so much and so much." So the Prophet bent his legs, faced the Qibla and performed two prostrations (of Sahu) and finished his prayers with Tasiim (by turning his face to right and left saying: 'As-Sal-amu'Alaikum-Warahmat-ullah'). When he turned his face to us he said, "If there had been anything changed in the prayer, surely I would have informed you but I am a human being like you and liable to forget like you. So if I forget remind me and if anyone of you is doubtful about his prayer, he should follow what he thinks to be correct and complete his prayer accordingly and finish it and do two prostrations (of Sahu)."

Volume 1, Book 8, Number 395:

Narrated 'Umar (bin Al-Khattab):

My Lord agreed with me in three things:

1. I said,"O Allah's Apostle, I wish we took the station of Abraham as our praying place (for some of our prayers). So came the Divine Inspiration: And take you (people) the station of Abraham as a place of prayer (for some of your prayers e.g. two Rakat of Tawaf of Ka'ba)". (2.125)

2. And as regards the (verse of) the veiling of the women, I said, 'O Allah's Apostle! I wish you ordered your wives to cover themselves from the men because good and bad ones talk to them.' So the verse of the veiling of the women was revealed.

3. Once the wives of the Prophet made a united front against the Prophet and I said to them, 'It may be if he (the Prophet) divorced you, (all) that his Lord (Allah) will give him instead of you wives better than you.' So this verse (the same as I had said) was revealed." (66.5).

Volume 1, Book 8, Number 396:

Narrated Anas:

as above (395).

Volume 1, Book 8, Number 397:

Narrated 'Abdullah bin 'Umar:

While the people were offering the Fajr prayer at Quba (near Medina), someone came to them and said: "It has been revealed to Allah's Apostle tonight, and he has been ordered to pray facing the

Ka'ba." So turn your faces to the Ka'ba. Those people were facing Sham (Jerusalem) so they turned their faces towards Ka'ba (at Mecca).

Volume 1, Book 8, Number 398:

Narrated 'Abdullah:

"Once the Prophet offered five Rakat in Zuhr prayer. He was asked, "Is there an increase in the prayer?" The Prophet said, "And what is it?" They said, "You have prayed five Rakat.' So he bent his legs and performed two prostrations (of Sahu).

Volume 1, Book 8, Number 399:

Narrated Anas bin Malik:

The Prophet saw some sputum in the direction of the Qibla (on the wall of the mosque) and he disliked that and the sign of disgust was apparent from his face. So he got up and scraped it off with his hand and said, "Whenever anyone of you stands for the prayer, he is speaking in private to his Lord or his Lord is between him and his Qibla. So, none of you should spit in the direction of the Qibla but one can spit to the left or under his foot." The Prophet then took the corner of his sheet and spat in it and folded it and said, "Or you can do like this. "

Volume 1, Book 8, Number 400:

Narrated 'Abdullah bin 'Umar: Allah's Apostle saw sputum on the wall of the mosque in the direction of the Qibla and scraped it off. He faced the people and said, "Whenever any one of you is praying, he should not spit in front of him because in the prayer Allah is in front of him."

Volume 1, Book 8, Number 401:

Narrated 'Aisha:

(the mother of faithful believers) Allah's Apostle saw some nasal secretions, expectoration or sputum on the wall of the mosque in the direction of the Qibla and scraped it off.

Volume 1, Book 8, Number 402:

Narrated Abd Huraira and Abu Said:

Allah's Apostle saw some expectoration on the wall of the mosque; he took gravel and scraped it off and said, "If anyone of you wanted to spit he should neither spit in front of him nor on his right but he could spit either on his left or under his left foot."

Volume 1, Book 8, Number 403.

Narrated Abd Huraira and Abu Sa'id.

Allah's Apostle saw some expectoration on the wall of the mosque; he took gravel and scraped it off and said, "If anyone of you wanted to spit, he should neither spit in front of him nor on his right but could spit either on his left or under his left foot."

Volume 1, Book 8, Number 404.

Narrated Anas.

The Prophet said, "None of you should spit in front or on his right but he could spit either on his left or under his foot."

Volume 1, Book 8, Number 405.

Narrated Anas bin Malik.

The Prophet said, "A faithful believer while in prayer is speaking in private to his Lord, so he should neither spit in front of him nor to his right side but he could spit either on his left or under his foot."

Volume 1, Book 8, Number 406.

Narrated Abu Said.

The Prophet saw sputum on (the wall of) the mosque in the direction of the Qibla and scraped it off with gravel. Then he forbade Spitting in front or on the right, but allowed it on one's left or under one's left foot.

Volume 1, Book 8, Number 407.

Narrated Anas bin Malik.

The Prophet said, "Spitting in the mosque is a sin and its expiation is to bury it."

Volume 1, Book 8, Number 408.

Narrated Abu Huraira.

Prophet said, "If anyone of you stands for prayer, he should not spit in front of him because in prayer he is speaking in private to Allah and he should not spit on his right as there is an angel, but he can spit either on his left or under his left foot and bury it (i.e. expectoration)."

Volume 1, Book 8, Number 409:

Narrated Anas:

The Prophet saw expectoration (on the wall of the mosque) in the direction of the Qibla and scraped it off with his hand. It seemed that he disliked it and the sign of disgust was apparent from his face. He said, "If anyone of you stands for the prayer, he is speaking in private to his Lord, (or) his Lord is between him and his Qibla, therefore he should not spit towards his Qibla, but he could spit either on his left or under his foot." Then he took the corner of his sheet and spat in it, folded it and said, "Or do like this."

Volume 1, Book 8, Number 410:

Narrated Abu Huraira:

Allah's Apostle said, "Do you consider or see that my face is towards the Qibla? By Allah, neither your submissiveness nor your bowing is hidden from me, surely I see you from my back."

Volume 1, Book 8, Number 411:

Narrated Anas bin Malik:

The Prophet led us in a prayer and then got up on the pulpit and said, "In your prayer and bowing, I certainly see you from my back as I see you (while looking at you.)"

Volume 1, Book 8, Number 412:

Narrated 'Abdullah bin 'Umar:

Allah's Apostle ordered for a horse race; the trained horses were to run from a place called Al-Hafya' to Thaniyat Al-Wada' and the horses which were not trained were to run from Al-Thaniya to the Masjid (mosque of) Bani Zuraiq. The sub narrator added: Ibn Umar was one of those who took part in the race.

Volume 1, Book 8, Number 413:

Narrated Anas:

Some goods came to Allah's Apostle from Bahrain. The Prophet ordered the people to spread them in the mosque --it was the biggest amount of goods Allah's Apostle had ever received. He left for prayer and did not even look at it. After finishing the prayer, he sat by those goods and gave from those to everybody he saw. Al-'Abbas came to him and said, "O Allah's Apostle! give me (something) too, because I gave ransom for myself and 'Aqil" Allah's Apostle told him to take. So he stuffed his garment with it and tried to carry it away but he failed to do so. He said, "O Allah's Apostle! Order someone to help me in lifting it." The Prophet refused. He then said to the Prophet: Will you please help me to lift it?" Allah's Apostle refused. Then Al-'Abbas threw some of it and tried to lift it (but failed). He again said, "O Allah's Apostle Order someone to help me to lift it." He refused. Al-'Abbas then said to the Prophet: "Will you please help me to lift it?" He again refused. Then Al-'Abbas threw some of it, and lifted it on his shoulders and went away. Allah's Apostle kept on watching him till he disappeared from his sight and was astonished at his greediness. Allah's Apostle did not get up till the last coin was distributed.

Volume 1, Book 8, Number 414:

Narrated Anas:

I found the Prophet in the mosque along with some people. He said to me, "Did Abu Talha send you?" I said, "Yes". He said, "For a meal?" I said, "Yes." Then he said to his companions, "Get up." They set out and I was ahead of them.

Volume 1, Book 8, Number 415:

Narrated Sahl bin Sa'd:

A man said, "O Allah's Apostle! If a man finds another man with his wife, (committing adultery) should the husband kill him?" Later on I saw them (the man and his wife) doing Lian in the mosque.

Volume 1, Book 8, Number 416:

Narrated 'Itban bin Malik:

The Prophet came to my house and said, "Where do you like me to pray?" I pointed to a place. The Prophet then said, "Allahu Akbar", and we aligned behind him and he offered a two-Rak'at prayer.

Volume 1, Book 8, Number 417:

Narrated 'Itban bin Malik:

who was one of the companions of Allah's Apostle and one of the Ansar's who took part in the battle of Badr: I came to Allah's Apostle and said, "O Allah's Apostle I have weak eyesight and I lead my people in prayers. When it rains the water flows in the valley between me and my people so I cannot go to their mosque to lead them in prayer. O Allah's Apostle! I wish you would come to my house and pray in it so that I could take that place as a Musalla. Allah's Apostle said. "Allah willing, I will do so." Next day after the sun rose high, Allah's Apostle and Abu Bakr came and Allah's Apostle asked for permission to enter. I gave him permission and he did not sit on entering the house but said to me, "Where do you like me to pray?" I pointed to a place in my house. So Allah's Apostle stood there and said, 'Allahu Akbar', and we all got up and aligned behind him and offered a two-Rak'at prayer and ended it with Taslim. We requested him to stay for a meal called "Khazira" which we had prepared for him. Many members of our family gathered in the house and one of them said, "Where is Malik bin Al-Dukhaishin or Ibn Al-Dukhshun?" One of them replied, "He is a hypocrite and does not love Allah and His Apostle." Hearing that, Allah's Apostle said, "Do not say so. Haven't you seen that he said, 'None has the right to be worshipped but Allah' for Allah's sake only?" He said, "Allah and His Apostle know better. We have seen him helping and advising hypocrites."

Allah's Apostle said, "Allah has forbidden the (Hell) fire for those who say, 'None has the right to be worshipped but Allah' for Allah's sake only."

Volume 1, Book 8, Number 418.

Narrated 'Aisha:

The Prophet used to start every thing from the right (for good things) whenever it was possible in all his affairs; for example: in washing, combing or wearing shoes.

Volume 1, Book 8, Number 419.

Narrated 'Aisha:

Um Habiba and Um Salama mentioned about a church they had seen in Ethiopia in which there were pictures. They told the Prophet about it, on which he said, "If any religious man dies amongst those people they would build a place of worship at his grave and make these pictures in it. They will be the worst creature in the sight of Allah on the Day of Resurrection."

Volume 1, Book 8, Number 420.

Narrated Anas:

When the Prophet arrived Medina he dismounted at 'Awali-i-Medina amongst a tribe called Banu 'Amr bin 'Auf. He stayed there For fourteen nights. Then he sent for Bani An-Najjar and they came armed with their swords. As if I am looking (just now) as the Prophet was sitting over his Rahila (Mount) with Abu Bakr riding behind him and all Banu An-Najjar around him till he dismounted at the courtyard of Abu Aiyub's house. The Prophet loved to pray wherever the time for the prayer was due even at sheep-folds. Later on he ordered that a mosque should be built and sent for some people of Banu-An-Najjar and said, "O Banu An-Najjar! Suggest to me the price of this (walled) piece of land of yours." They replied, "No! By Allah! We do not demand its price except from Allah." Anas added: There were graves of pagans in it and some of it was unleveled and there were some date-palm trees in it. The Prophet ordered that the graves of the pagans be dug out and the unleveled land be level led and the date-palm trees be cut down . (So all that was done). They aligned these cut date-palm trees towards the Qibla of the mosque (as a wall) and they also built two stone side-walls (of the mosque). His companions brought the stones while reciting some poetic verses. The Prophet was with them and he kept on saying, "There is no goodness except that of the Hereafter, O Allah! So please forgive the Ansars and the emigrants. "

Volume 1, Book 8, Number 421,

Narrated Abu Al-Taiyah,

Anas said, "The Prophet prayed in the sheep fold." Later on I heard him saying, "He prayed in the sheep folds before the construction of the, mosque."

Volume 1, Book 8, Number 422,

Narrated Nafi,

"I saw Ibn 'Umar praying while taking his camel as a Sutra in front of him and he said, "I saw the Prophet doing the same."

Volume 1, Book 8, Number 423,

Narrated 'Abdullah bin 'Abbas,

The sun eclipsed and Allah's Apostle offered the eclipse prayer and said, "I have been shown the Hellfire (now) and I never saw a worse and horrible sight than the sight I have seen today."

Volume 1, Book 8, Number 424,

Narrated Ibn 'Umar,

The Prophet had said, "Offer some of your prayers (Nawafil) at home, and do not take your houses as graves."

Volume 1, Book 8, Number 425,

Narrated 'Abdullah bin 'Umar,

Allah's Apostle said, "Do not enter (the places) of these people where Allah's punishment had fallen unless you do so weeping. If you do not weep, do not enter (the places of these people) because Allah's curse and punishment which fell upon them may fall upon you."

Volume 1, Book 8, Number 426,

Narrated 'Aisha,

Um Salama told Allah's Apostle about a church which she had seen in Ethiopia and which was called Mariya. She told him about the pictures which she had seen in it. Allah's Apostle said, "If any righteous pious man dies amongst them, they would build a place of worship at his grave and make these pictures in it; they are the worst creatures in the sight of Allah."

Volume 1, Book 8, Number 427:

Narrated 'Aisha and 'Abdullah bin 'Abbas:

When the last moment of the life of Allah's Apostle came he started putting his 'Khamisa' on his face and when he felt hot and short of breath he took it off his face and said, "May Allah curse the Jews and Christians for they built the places of worship at the graves of their Prophets." The Prophet was warning (Muslims) of what those had done.

Volume 1, Book 8, Number 428:

Narrated Abu Huraira:

Allah's Apostle said, "May Allah's curse be on the Jews for they built the places of worship at the graves of their Prophets."

Volume 1, Book 8, Number 429:

Narrated Jabir bin 'Abdullah:

Allah's Apostle said, "I have been given five things which were not given to any amongst the Prophets before me. These are:

1. Allah made me victorious by awe (by His frightening my enemies) for a distance of one month's journey.

2. The earth has been made for me (and for my followers) a place for praying and a thing to perform Tayammum. Therefore my followers can pray wherever the time of a prayer is due.

3. The booty has been made Halal (lawful) for me (and was not made so for anyone else).

4. Every Prophet used to be sent to his nation exclusively but I have been sent 1o all mankind.

5. I have been given the right of intercession (on the Day of Resurrection.)

Volume 1, Book 8, Number 430:

Narrated 'Aisha:

There was a black slave girl belonging to an 'Arab tribe and they manumitted her but she remained with them. The slave girl said, "Once one of their girls (of that tribe) came out wearing a red leather scarf decorated with precious stones. It fell from her or she placed it somewhere. A kite passed by that place, saw it Lying there and mistaking it for a piece of meat, flew away with it. Those people searched for it but they did not find it. So they accused me of stealing it and started searching me and even searched my private parts." The slave girl further said, "By Allah! while I was standing (in that state) with those people, the same kite passed by them and dropped the red scarf and it fell amongst them. I told them, 'This is what you accused me of and I was innocent and now this is it.' " 'Aisha added: That slave girl came to Allah's Apostle and embraced Islam. She had a tent or a small room with a low roof in the mosque. Whenever she called on me, she had a talk with me and whenever she sat with me, she would recite the following: "The day of the scarf (band) was one of the wonders of our Lord, verily He rescued me from the disbelievers' town. 'Aisha added: "Once I asked her, 'What is the matter with you? Whenever you sit with me, you always recite these poetic verses.' On that she told me the whole story. "

Volume 1, Book 8, Number 431:

Narrated Nafa:

'Abdullah bin 'Umar said: I used to sleep in the mosque of the Prophet while I was young and un-married.

Volume 1, Book 8, Number 432:

Narrated Sahl bin Sa'd:

Allah's Apostle went to Fatima's house but did not find 'Ali there. So he asked, "Where is your cous-in?" She replied, "There was something between us and he got angry with me and went out. He did not sleep (mid-day nap) in the house." Allah's Apostle asked a person to look for him. That person came and said, "O Allah's Apostle! He (Ali) is sleeping in the mosque." Allah's Apostle went there and 'Ali was lying. His upper body cover had fallen down to one side of his body and he was covered with dust. Allah's Apostle started cleaning the dust from him saying: "Get up! O Aba Turab. Get up! O Aba Turab (literally means: O father of dust).

Volume 1, Book 8, Number 433:

Narrated Abu Huraira:

I saw seventy of As-Suffa men and none of them had a Rida' (a garment covering the upper part of the body). They had either Izars (only) or sheets which they tied round their necks. Some of these sheets reached the middle of their legs and some reached their heels and they used to gather them with their hands lest their private parts should become naked.

Volume 1, Book 8, Number 434:

Narrated Jabir bin 'Abdullah:

I went to the Prophet in the mosque (the sub-narrator Mas'ar thought that Jabir had said, "In the forenoon.") He ordered me to pray two Rakat. He owed me some money and he repaid it to me and gave more than what was due to me.

Volume 1, Book 8, Number 435:

Narrated Abu Qatada Al-Aslami:

Allah's Apostle said, "If anyone of you enters a mosque, he should pray two Rakat before sitting."

Volume 1, Book 8, Number 436:

Narrated Abu Huraira:

Allah's Apostle said, "The angels keep on asking Allah's forgiveness for anyone of you, as long as he is at his Mu,salla (praying place) and he does not pass wind (Hadath). They say, 'O Allah! Forgive him, O Allah! be Merciful to him."

Volume 1, Book 8, Number 437:

Narrated 'Abdullah bin 'Umar:

In the life-time of Allah's Apostle the mosque was built of adobes, its roof of the leaves of date-palms and its pillars of the stems of date-palms. Abu Bakr did not alter it. 'Umar expanded it on the same pattern as it was in the lifetime of Allah's Apostle by using adobes, leaves of date-palms and changing the pillars into wooden ones. 'Uthman changed it by expanding it to a great extent and built its walls with engraved stones and lime and made its pillars of engraved stones and its roof of teak wood.

Volume 1, Book 8, Number 438:

Narrated 'Ikrima:

Ibn 'Abbas said to me and to his son 'Ali, "Go to Abu Sa'id and listen to what he narrates." So we went and found him in a garden looking after it. He picked up his Rida', wore it and sat down and started narrating till the topic of the construction of the mosque reached. He said, "We were carrying one adobe at a time while 'Ammar was carrying two. The Prophet saw him and started removing the dust from his body and said, "May Allah be Merciful to 'Ammar. He will be inviting them (i.e. his murderers, the rebellious group) to Paradise and they will invite him to Hell-fire." 'Ammar said, "I seek refuge with Allah from affliction."

Volume 1, Book 8, Number 439:

Narrated Sahl:

Allah's Apostle sent someone to a woman telling her to "Order her slave, carpenter, to prepare a wooden pulpit for him to sit on."

Volume 1, Book 8, Number 440:

Narrated Jabir:

A woman said, "O Allah's Apostle! Shall I get something constructed for you to sit on as I have a slave who is a carpenter?" He replied, "Yes, if you like." So she had that pulpit constructed.

Volume 1, Book 8, Number 441:

Narrated 'Ubdaidullah Al-Khaulani:

I heard 'Uthman bin 'Affan saying, when people argued too much about his intention to reconstruct the mosque of Allah's Apostle, "You have talked too much. I heard the Prophet saying, 'Whoever built a mosque, (Bukair thought that 'Asim, another subnarrator, added, "Intending Allah's Pleasure"), Allah would build for him a similar place in Paradise.' "

Volume 1, Book 8, Number 442:

Narrated 'Amr:

I heard Jabir bin 'Abdullah saying, "A man passed through the mosque carrying arrows. Allah's Apostle said to him, 'Hold them by their heads.' "

Volume 1, Book 8, Number 443:

Narrated Abu Burda bin 'Abdulla:

(on the authority of his father) The Prophet said, "Whoever passes through our mosques or markets with arrows should hold them by their heads lest he should injure a Muslim."

Volume 1, Book 8, Number 444:

Narrated Hassan bin Thabit Al-Ansari:

I asked Abu Huraira "By Allah! Tell me the truth whether you heard the Prophet saying, 'O Hassan! Reply on behalf of Allah's Apostle. O Allah! Help him with the Holy Spirit." Abu Huraira said, "Yes . "

Volume 1, Book 8, Number 445:

Narrated 'Aisha:

Once I saw Allah's Apostle at the door of my house while some Ethiopians were playing in the mosque (displaying their skill with spears). Allah's Apostle was screening me with his Rida' so as to enable me to see their display. ('Urwa said that 'Aisha said, "I saw the Prophet and the Ethiopians were playing with their spears.")

Volume 1, Book 8, Number 446:

Narrated 'Aisha:

Barira came to seek my help regarding her manumission. I told herself you like I would pay your price to your masters but your Al-Wala(1) would be for me." Her masters said, "If you like, you can pay what remains (of the price of her manumission), (Sufyan the sub-narrator once said), or if you like you can manumit her, but her (inheritance) Al-Wala would be for us. "When Allah's Apostle came, I spoke to him about it. He said, "Buy her and manumit her. No doubt Al-Wala(1) is for the manumitted." Then Allah's Apostle stood on the pulpit (or Allah's Apostle ascended the pulpit as Sufyan once said), and said, "What about some people who impose conditions which are not present in Allah's Book (Laws)? Whoever imposes conditions which are not in Allah's Book (Laws), his conditions will be invalid even if he imposed them a hundred times."

Volume 1, Book 8, Number 447:

Narrated Ka'b:

In the mosque I asked Ibn Abi Hadrad to pay the debts which he owed to me and our voices grew louder. Allah's Apostle heard that while he was in his house. So he came to us raising the curtain of his room and said, "O Ka'b!" I replied, "Labaik, O Allah's Apostle!" He said, "O Ka'b! reduce your debt to one half," gesturing with his hand. I said, "O Allah's Apostle! I have done so." Then Allah's Apostle said (to Ibn Abi Hadrad), "Get up and pay the debt to him."

Volume 1, Book 8, Number 448:

Narrated Abu Huraira:

A black man or a black woman used to sweep the mosque and he or she died. The Prophet asked about her (or him). He was told that she (or he) had died. He said, "Why did you not inform me? Show me his grave (or her grave)." So he went to her (his) grave and offered her (his) funeral prayer."

Volume 1, Book 8, Number 449:

Narrated 'Aisha:

When the verses of Surat "Al-Baqara" about the usury Riba were revealed, the Prophet went to the mosque and recited them in front of the people and then banned the trade of alcohol.

Volume 1, Book 8, Number 450f:

Narrated Abu Rafi:

Abu Huraira said, "A man or a woman used to clean the mosque." (A sub-narrator said, 'Most probably a woman..') Then he narrated the Hadith of the Prophet

Volume 1, Book 8, Number 450m:

Narrated Abu Huraira:

"The Prophet said, "Last night a big demon (afreet) from the Jinns came to me and wanted to interrupt my prayers (or said something similar) but Allah enabled me to overpower him. I wanted to fasten him to one of the pillars of the mosque so that all of you could See him in the morning but I remembered the statement of my brother Solomon (as stated in Quran): My Lord! Forgive me and bestow on me a kingdom such as shall not belong to anybody after me (38.35)." The sub narrator Rauh said, "He (the demon) was dismissed humiliated."

Volume 1, Book 8, Number 451:

Narrated Abu Huraira:

The Prophet sent some horsemen to Najd and they brought a man called Thumama bin Uthal from Bani Hanifa. They fastened him to one of the pillars of the mosque. The Prophet came and ordered them to release him. He went to a (garden of) date-palms near the mosque, took a bath and entered the, mosque again and said, "None has the right to be worshipped but Allah an Muhammad is His Apostle (i.e. he embraced Islam)."

Volume 1, Book 8, Number 452:

Narrated 'Aisha:

On the day of Al-Khandaq (battle of the Trench' the medial arm vein of Sa'd bin Mu'ad was injured and the Prophet pitched a tent in the mosque to look after him. There was another tent for Banu Ghaffar in the mosque and the blood started flowing from Sa'd's tent to the tent of Bani Ghaffar. They shouted, "O occupants of the tent! What is coming from you to us?" They found that Sa'd' wound was bleeding profusely and Sa'd died in his tent.

Volume 1, Book 8, Number 453:

Narrated Um Salama:

I complained to Allah's Apostle that I was sick. He told me to perform the Tawaf behind the people while riding. So I did so and Allah's Apostle was praying beside the Ka'ba and reciting the Sura starting with "Wat-tur-wa-Kitabinmastur."

Volume 1, Book 8, Number 454:

Narrated Anas bin Malik:

Two of the companions of the Prophet departed from him on a dark night and were led by two lights like lamps (going in front of them from Allah as a miracle) lighting the way in front of them, and when they parted, each of them was accompanied by one of these lights till he reached their (respective) houses.

Volume 1, Book 8, Number 455:

Narrated Abu Said Al-Khudri:

The Prophet delivered a sermon and said, "Allah gave a choice to one of (His) slaves either to choose this world or what is with Him in the Hereafter. He chose the latter." Abu Bakr wept. I said lo myself, "Why is this Sheikh weeping, if Allah gave choice to one (of His) slaves either to choose this world or what is with Him in the Here after and he chose the latter?" And that slave was Allah's Apostle himself. Abu Bakr knew more than us. The Prophet said, "O Abu Bakr! Don't weep. The Prophet added: Abu- Bakr has favored me much with his property and company. If I were to take a Khalil from mankind I would certainly have taken Abu Bakr but the Islamic brotherhood and friendship is sufficient. Close all the gates in the mosque except that of Abu Bakr.

Volume 1, Book 8, Number 456:

Narrated Ibn 'Abbas:

"Allah's Apostle in his fatal illness came out with a piece of cloth tied round his head and sat on the pulpit. After thanking and praising Allah he said, "There is no one who had done more favor to me with life and property than Abu Bakr bin Abi Quhafa. If I were to take a Khalil, I would certainly have taken Abu- Bakr but the Islamic brotherhood is superior. Close all the small doors in this mosque except that of Abu Bakr."

Volume 1, Book 8, Number 457:

Narrated Nafi:

Ibn 'Umar said, "The Prophet arrived at Mecca and sent for 'Uthman bin Talha. He opened the gate of the Ka'ba and the Prophet, Bilal, Usama bin Zaid and 'Uthman bin Talha entered the Ka'ba and then they closed its door (from inside). They stayed there for an hour, and then came out." Ibn 'Umar added, "I quickly went to Bilal and asked him (whether the Prophet had prayed). Bilal replied, 'He prayed in it.' I asked, 'Where?' He replied, 'Between the two pillars.' "Ibn 'Umar added, "I forgot to ask how many Rakat he (the Prophet) had prayed in the Ka'ba."

Volume 1, Book 8, Number 458:

Narrated Abu Huraira:

Allah's Apostle sent some horse men to Najd and they brought a man called Thumama bin Uthal from Bani Hanifa. They fastened him to one of the pillars of the mosque.

Volume 1, Book 8, Number 459:

Narrated Al-Sa'ib bin Yazid:

I was standing in the mosque and somebody threw a gravel at me. I looked and found that he was 'Umar bin Al-Khattab. He said to me, "Fetch those two men to me." When I did, he said to them, "Who are you? (Or) where do you come from?" They replied, "We are from Ta'if." 'Umar said, "Were you from this city (Medina) I would have punished you for raising your voices in the mosque of Allah's Apostle

Volume 1, Book 8, Number 460:

Narrated 'Kab bin Malik:

During the life-time of Allah's Apostle I asked Ibn Abi Hadrad in the mosque to pay the debts which he owed to me and our voices grew so loud that Allah's Apostle heard them while he was in his house. So he came to us after raising the curtain of his room. The Prophet said, "O Ka'b bin Malik!" I replied, "Labaik, O Allah's Apostle." He gestured with his hand to me to reduce the debt to one half. I said, "O Allah's Apostle have done it." Allah's Apostle said (to Ibn Hadrad), "Get up and pay it."

Volume 1, Book 8, Number 461:

Narrated Nafi':

Ibn 'Umar said, "While the Prophet was on the pulpit, a man asked him how to offer the night prayers. He replied, 'Pray two Rakat at a time and then two and then two and so on, and if you are afraid of the dawn (the approach of the time of the Fajr prayer) pray one Rak'a and that will be the witr for all the Rakat which you have offered." Ibn 'Umar said, "The last Rakat of the night prayer should be odd for the Prophet ordered it to be so.

Volume 1, Book 8, Number 462:

Narrated Ibn 'Umar:

A man came to the Prophet while he was delivering the sermon and asked him how to offer the night prayers. The Prophet replied, 'Pray two Rakat at a time and then two and then two and so on and if you are afraid of dawn (the approach of the time of the Fajr prayer) pray one Rak'a and that will be the with for all the Rakat which you have prayed." Narrated 'Ubaidullah bin 'Abdullah bin 'Umar: A man called the Prophet while he was in the mosque.

Volume 1, Book 8, Number 463:

Narrated Abu Waqid al-Laithi:

While Allah's Apostle was sitting in the mosque (with some people) three men came, two of them came in front of Allah's Apostle and the third one went away, and then one of them found a place in the circle and sat there while the second man sat behind the gathering, and the third one went away. When Allah's Apostle finished his preaching, he said, "Shall I tell you about these three persons? One of them betook himself to Allah and so Allah accepted him and accommodated him; the second felt shy before Allah so Allah did the same for him and sheltered him in His Mercy (and did not punish him), while the third turned his face from Allah, and went away, so Allah turned His face from him likewise.

Volume 1, Book 8, Number 464:

Narrated 'Abbad bin Tamim:

that his uncle said, "I saw Allah's Apostle lying flat (on his back) in the mosque with one leg on the other." Narrated Said bin Al-Musaiyab that 'Umar and 'Uthman used to do the same.

Volume 1, Book 8, Number 465:

Narrated 'Aisha:

(the wife of the Prophet) I had seen my parents following Islam since I attained the age of puberty. Not a day passed but the Prophet visited us, both in the mornings and evenings. My father Abii Bakr thought of building a mosque in the courtyard of his house and he did so. He used to pray and recite the Qur'an in it. The pagan women and their children used to stand by him and look at him with surprise. Abu Bakr was a Softhearted person and could not help weeping while reciting the Quran.

The chiefs of the Quraish pagans became afraid of that (i.e. that their children and women might be affected by the recitation of Quran)."

Volume 1, Book 8, Number 466:

Narrated Abu Huraira:

The Prophet said, "The prayer offered in congregation is twenty five times more superior (in reward) to the prayer offered alone in one's house or in a business center, because if one performs ablution and does it perfectly, and then proceeds to the mosque with the sole intention of praying, then for each step which he takes towards the mosque, Allah upgrades him a degree in reward and (forgives) crosses out one sin till he enters the mosque. When he enters the mosque he is considered in prayer as long as he is waiting for the prayer and the angels keep on asking for Allah's forgiveness for him and they keep on saying, 'O Allah! Be Merciful to him, O Allah! Forgive him, as long as he keeps on sitting at his praying place and does not pass wind. (See Hadith No. 620).

Volume 1, Book 8, Number 467:

Narrated Ibn 'Umar or Ibn 'Amr:

The Prophet clasped his hands, by interlacing his fingers. Narrated 'Abdullah that Allah's Apostle said, "O 'Abdullah bin 'Amr! What will be your condition when you will be left with the sediments of (worst) people?" (They will be in conflict with each other).

Volume 1, Book 8, Number 468:

Narrated Abu Musa:

The Prophet said, "A faithful believer to a faithful believer is like the bricks of a wall, enforcing each other." While (saying that) the Prophet clasped his hands, by interlacing his fingers.

Volume 1, Book 8, Number 469:

Narrates Ibn Sirin:

Abu Huraira said, "Allah's Apostle led us in one of the two 'Isha' prayers (Abu Huraira named that prayer but I forgot it)." Abu Huraira added, "He prayed two Rakat and then finished the prayer with Tasllm. He stood up near a piece of wood Lying across the mosque and leaned on it in such a way as if he was angry. Then he put his right hand over the left and clasped his hands by interlacing his fingers and then put his J right cheek on the back of his left hand. The people who were in haste left the mosque through its gates. They wondered whether the prayer was reduced. And amongst them were Abu Bakr and 'Umar but they hesitated to ask the Prophet. A long-handed man called Dhul-Yadain asked the Prophet, 'O Allah's Apostle! Have you; forgotten or has the prayer been reduced?' The

Prophet replied, 'I have neither forgotten nor has the prayer been reduced' The Prophet added, 'Is what Dhul Yadain has said true?' They (the people) said, 'Yes, it is true.' The Prophet stood up again and led the prayer, completing the remaining prayer, forgotten by him, and performed Talsrm, and then said, 'Allahu Akbar.' And then he did a prostration as he used to prostrate or longer than that. He then raised his head saying, 'Allahu Akbar; he then again said, 'Allahu Akbar', and prostrated as he used to prostrate or longer than that. Then he raised his head and said, 'Allahu Akbar.' " (The sub-narrator added, "I think that they asked (Ibn Sirin) whether the Prophet completed the prayer with Taslim. He replied, "I heard that 'Imran bin Husain had said, 'Then he (the Prophet) did Taslim.")

Volume 1, Book 8, Number 470:

Narrated Fudail bin Sulaiman:

Musa bin 'Uqba said, "I saw Salim bin 'Abdullah looking for some places on the way and prayed there. He narrated that his father used to pray there, and had seen the Prophet praying at those very places."

Narrated Nafi' on the authority of Ibn 'Umar who said, "I used to pray at those places." Musa the narrator added, "I asked Salim on which he said, 'I agree with Nafi' concerning those places, except the mosque situated at the place called Sharaf Ar-Rawha."

Volume 1, Book 8, Number 471:

Narrated Hadith is about the various places on the way from Medina to Mecca where the Prophet prayed and their In locations impossible to translate.

Book 9: Virtues of the Prayer Hall (Sutra of the Musalla)

Volume 1, Book 9, Number 472:

Narrated Ibn 'Abbas:

Once I came riding a she-ass when I had just attained the age of puberty. Allah's Apostle was offering the prayer at Mina with no wall in front of him and I passed in front of some of the row. There I dismounted and let my she-ass loose to graze and entered the row and nobody objected to me about it.

Volume 1, Book 9, Number 473:

Narrated Ibn 'Umar:

Whenever Allah's Apostle came out on 'Id day, he used to order that a Harba (a short spear) to be planted in front of him (as a Sutra for his prayer) and then he used to pray facing it with the people behind him and used to do the same while on a journey. After the Prophet , this practice was adopted by the Muslim rulers (who followed his traditions).

Volume 1, Book 9, Number 474:

Narrated 'Aun bin Abi Juhaifa:

I heard my father saying, "The Prophet led us, and prayed a two-Rak'at Zuhr prayer and then a two-Rak'at 'Asr prayer at Al-Batha' with an 'Anza (planted) in front of him (as a Sutra) while women and donkeys were passing in front of him (beyond that 'Anza)."

Volume 1, Book 9, Number 475:

Narrated Sahl (bin Sa'd):

The distance between the Musalla of Allah's Apostle and the wall was just sufficient for a sheep to pass through .

Volume 1, Book 9, Number 476:

Narrated Salama:

The distance between the wall of the mosque and the pulpit was hardly enough for a sheep to pass through.

Volume 1, Book 9, Number 477.

Narrated 'Abdullah.

The Prophet used to get a Harba planted in front of him (as a Sutra) and pray behind it.

Volume 1, Book 9, Number 478.

Narrated 'Aun bin Abi Juhaifa.

that he had heard his father saying, "Allah's Apostle came to us at mid-day and water was brought for his ablution. He performed ablution and led us in Zuhr and 'Asr prayers with an 'Anza planted in front of him (as a Sutra), while women and donkeys were passing beyond it."

Volume 1, Book 9, Number 479.

Narrated Anas Ibn Malik.

Whenever the Prophet went for answering the call of nature, I and another boy used to go after him with a staff, a stick or an 'Anza and a tumbler of water and when he finished from answering the call of nature we would hand that tumbler of water to him.

Volume 1, Book 9, Number 480.

Narrated Abu Juhaifa.

Allah's Apostle came out at midday and offered a two-Rak'at Zuhr and 'Asr prayers at Al-Batha and an 'Anza was planted in front of him (as a Sutra). He performed ablution and the people took the remaining water left after his ablution and rubbed their bodies with it.

Volume 1, Book 9, Number 481.

Narrated Yazid bin Al 'Ubaid.

I used to accompany Salama bin Al-Akwa' and he used to pray behind the pillar which was near the place where the Quran's were kept I said, "O Abu Muslim! I see you always seeking to pray behind this pillar." He replied, "I saw Allah's Apostle always seeking to pray near that pillar."

Volume 1, Book 9, Number 482.

Narrated Anas.

I saw the most famous people amongst the companions of the Prophet hurrying towards the pillars at the Maghrib prayer before the Prophet came for the prayer.

Volume 1, Book 9, Number 483:

Narrated Ibn 'Umar:

The Prophet entered the Ka'ba along with Usama bin Zaid, 'Uthman bin Talha and Bilal and remained there for a long time. When they came out, I was the first man to enter the Ka'ba. I asked Bilal "Where did the Prophet pray?" Bilal replied, "Between the two front Pillars."

Volume 1, Book 9, Number 484:

Narrated Nafi':

'Abdullah bin 'Umar said, "Allah's Apostle entered the Ka'ba along with Usama bin Zaid, Bilal and 'Uthman bin Talha Al-Hajabi and closed the door and stayed there for some time. I asked Bilal when he came out, 'What did the Prophet do?' He replied, 'He offered prayer with one pillar to his left and one to his right and three behind.' In those days the Ka'ba was supported by six pillars." Malik said: "There were two pillars on his (the Prophet's) right side."

Volume 1, Book 9, Number 485:

Narrated Nafi:

"The Prophet used to make his she-camel sit across and he would pray facing it (as a Sutra)." I asked, "What would the Prophet do if the she camel was provoked and moved?" He said, "He would take its camel-saddle and put it in front of him and pray facing its back part (as a Sutra). And Ibn 'Umar used to do the same." (This indicates that one should not pray except behind a Sutra).

Volume 1, Book 9, Number 486:

Narrated 'Aisha:

Do you make us (women) equal to dogs and donkeys? While I used to lie in my bed, the Prophet would come and pray facing the middle of the bed. I used to consider it not good to stand in front of him in his prayers. So I used to slip away slowly and quietly from the foot of the bed till I got out of my guilt.

Volume 1, Book 9, Number 487:

Narrated Abu Sa'id:

The Prophet said, (what is ascribed to him in the following Hadith 488).

Volume 1, Book 9, Number 488.

Narrated Abu Salih As-Samman,

I saw Abu Said Al-Khudri praying on a Friday, behind something which acted as a Sutra. A young man from Bani Abi Mu'ait, wanted to pass in front of him, but Abu Said repulsed him with a push on his chest. Finding no alternative he again tried to pass but Abu Said pushed him with a greater force. The young man abused Abu Said and went to Marwan and lodged a complaint against Abu Said and Abu Said followed the young man to Marwan who asked him, "O Abu Said! What has happened between you and the son of your brother?" Abu Sa'id said to him, "I heard the Prophet saying, 'If anybody amongst you is praying behind something as a Sutra and somebody tries to pass in front of him, then he should repulse him and if he refuses, he should use force against him for he is a satan.' "

Volume 1, Book 9, Number 489.

Narrated Busr bin Said,

that Zaid bin Khalid sent him to Abi Juhaim to ask him what he had heard from Allah's Apostle about a person passing in front of another person who was praying. Abu Juhaim replied, "Allah's Apostle said, 'If the person who passes in front of another person in prayer knew the magnitude of his sin he would prefer to wait for 40 (days, months or years) rather than to pass in front of him." Abu An-Nadr said, "I do not remember exactly whether he said 40 days, months or years."

Volume 1, Book 9, Number 490.

Narrated 'Aisha,

The things which annul the prayers were mentioned before me. They said, "Prayer is annulled by a dog, a donkey and a woman (if they pass in front of the praying people)." I said, "You have made us (i.e. women) dogs. I saw the Prophet praying while I used to lie in my bed between him and the Qibla. Whenever I was in need of something, I would slip away. for I disliked to face him."

Volume 1, Book 9, Number 491.

Narrated 'Aisha,

The Prophet used to pray while I was sleeping across in his bed in front of him. Whenever he wanted to pray Witr, he would wake me up and I would pray Witr.

Volume 1, Book 9, Number 492:

Narrated 'Aisha:

the wife of the Prophet, "I used to sleep in front of Allah's Apostle with my legs opposite his Qibla (facing him); and whenever he prostrated, he pushed my feet and I withdrew them and whenever he stood, I stretched them." 'Aisha added, "In those days there were no lamps in the houses."

Volume 1, Book 9, Number 493:

Narrated 'Aisha:

The things which annual prayer were mentioned before me (and those were): a dog, a donkey and a woman. I said, "You have compared us (women) to donkeys and dogs. By Allah! I saw the Prophet praying while I used to lie in (my) bed between him and the Qibla. Whenever I was in need of something, I disliked to sit and trouble the Prophet. So, I would slip away by the side of his feet."

Volume 1, Book 9, Number 494:

Narrated 'Aisha:

(the wife of the Prophet) Allah's Apostle used to get up at night and pray while I used to lie across between him and the Qibla on his family's bed.

Volume 1, Book 9, Number 495:

Narrated Abu Qatada Al-Ansari:

Allah's Apostle was praying and he was carrying Umama the daughters of Zainab, the daughter of Allah's Apostle and she was the daughter of 'As bin Rabi'a bin 'AbduShams. When he prostrated, he put her down and when he stood, he carried her (on his neck).

Volume 1, Book 9, Number 496:

Narrated Maimuna bint Al-Harith:

My bed was beside the praying place (Musalla) of the Prophet and sometimes his garment fell on me while I used to lie in my bed.

Volume 1, Book 9, Number 497:

Narrated Maimuna:

The Prophet used to pray while I used to sleep beside him during my periods (menses) and in prostrations his garment used to touch me.

Volume 1, Book 9, Number 498,

Narrated 'Aisha,

It is not good that you people have made us (women) equal to dogs and donkeys. No doubt I saw Allah's Apostle praying while I used to lie between him and the Qibla and when he wanted to prostrate, he pushed my legs and I withdrew them.

Volume 1, Book 9, Number 499,

Narrated 'Amr bin Maimuin,

'Abdullah bin Mas'ud said, "While Allah's Apostle was praying beside the Ka'ba, there were some Quraish people sitting in a gathering. One of them said, 'Don't you see this (who does deeds just to show off)? Who amongst you can go and bring the dung, blood and the abdominal contents (intestines, etc). of the slaughtered camels of the family of so and so and then wait till he prostrates and put that in between his shoulders?' The most unfortunate amongst them ('Uqba bin Abi Mu'ait) went (and brought them) and when Allah's Apostle prostrated, he put them between his shoulders. The Prophet remained in prostration and they laughed so much so that they fell on each other. A passerby went to Fatima, who was a young girl in those days. She came running and the Prophet was still in prostration. She removed them and cursed upon the Quraish on their faces. When Allah's Apostle completed his prayer, he said, 'O Allah! Take revenge on Quraish.' He said so thrice and added, 'O Allah! take revenge on 'Amr bin Hisham, 'Utba bin Rabia, Shaiba bin Rabi'a, Al-Walid bin'Utba, Umaiya bin Khalaf, 'Uqba bin Abi Mu'ait and 'Umar a bin Al-Walid." Abdullah added, "By Allah! I saw all of them dead in the battle field on the day of Badr and they were dragged and thrown in the Qalib (a well) at Badr, Allah's Apostle then said, 'Allah's curse has descended upon the people of the Qalib (well).

Book 10: Times of the Prayers

Volume 1, Book 10, Number 500:

Narrated Ibn Shihab:

Once'Umar bin 'Abdul 'Aziz delayed the prayer and 'Urwa bin Az-Zubair went to him and said, "Once in 'Iraq, Al-MughTra bin Shu'ba delayed his prayers and Abi Mas'ud Al-Ansari went to him and said, 'O Mughira! What is this? Don't you know that once Gabriel came and offered the prayer (Fajr prayer) and Allah's Apostle prayed too, then he prayed again (Zuhr prayer) and so did Allah's Apostle and again he prayed ('Asr prayers and Allah's Apostle did the same; again he prayed (Maghrib-prayer) and so did Allah's Apostle and again prayed ('Isha prayer) and so did Allah's Apostle and (Gabriel) said, 'I was ordered to do so (to demonstrate the prayers prescribed to you)?'" 'Umar (bin 'Abdul 'AzTz) said to 'Urwa, "Be sure of what you Say. Did Gabriel lead Allah's Apostle at the stated times of the prayers?" 'Urwa replied, "Bashir bin Abi Mas'ud narrated like this on the authority of his father." Urwa added, "Aisha told me that Allah's Apostle used to pray 'Asr prayer when the sun-shine was still inside her residence (during the early time of 'Asr)."

Volume 1, Book 10, Number 501:

Narrated Ibn 'Abbas:

"Once a delegation of 'Abdul Qais came to Allah's Apostle and said, "We belong to such and such branch of the tribe of Rab'a and we can only come to you in the sacred months. Order us to do something good so that we may (carry out) take it from you and also invite to it our people whom we have left behind (at home)." The Prophet said, " I order you to do four things and forbid you from four things. (The first four are as follows):

1. To believe in Allah. (And then he: explained it to them i.e.) to testify that none has the right to be worshipped but Allah and (Muhammad) am Allah's Apostle

2. To offer prayers perfectly (at the stated times):

3. To pay Zakat (obligatory charity)

4. To give me Khumus

(The other four things which are forbidden are as follows):

1. Dubba

2. Hantam

3. Muqaiyat

4. Naqir (all these are utensils used for the preparation of alcoholic drinks)."

Volume 1, Book 10, Number 502:

Narrated Jarir bin 'Abdullah:

I gave the pledge of allegiance to Allah's Apostle for to offer prayers perfectly, to pay Zakat regularly, and to give good advice to every Muslim.

Volume 1, Book 10, Number 503:

Narrated Shaqiq:

that he had heard Hudhaifa saying, "Once I was sitting with 'Umar and he said, 'Who amongst you remembers the statement of Allah's Apostle about the afflictions?' I said, 'I know it as the Prophet had said it.' 'Umar said, 'No doubt you are bold.' I said, 'The afflictions caused for a man by his wife, money, children and neighbor are expiated by his prayers, fasting, charity and by enjoining (what is good) and forbidding (what is evil).' 'Umar said, 'I did not mean that but I asked about that affliction which will spread like the waves of the sea.' I (Hudhaifa) said, 'O leader of the faithful believers! You need not be afraid of it as there is a closed door between you and it.' 'Umar asked, Will the door be broken or opened?' I replied, 'It will be broken.' 'Umar said, 'Then it will never be closed again.' I was asked whether 'Umar knew that door. I replied that he knew it as one knows that there will be night before the tomorrow morning. I narrated a Hadith that was free from any mis-statement" The subnarrator added that they deputed Masruq to ask Hudhaifa (about the door). Hudhaifa said, "The door was 'Umar himself."

Volume 1, Book 10, Number 504:

Narrated Ibn Mas'ud:

A man kissed a woman (unlawfully) and then went to the Prophet and informed him. Allah revealed:

And offer prayers perfectly At the two ends of the day And in some hours of the night (i.e. the five compulsory prayers). Verily! good deeds remove (annul) the evil deeds (small sins) (11.114). The man asked Allah's Apostle, "Is it for me?" He said, "It is for all my followers."

Volume 1, Book 10, Number 505:

Narrated 'Abdullah:

I asked the Prophet "Which deed is the dearest to Allah?" He replied, "To offer the prayers at their early stated fixed times." I asked, "What is the next (in goodness)?" He replied, "To be good and dutiful to your parents" I again asked, "What is the next (in goodness)?" He replied, 'To participate in Jihad (religious fighting) in Allah's cause." 'Abdullah added, "I asked only that much and if I had asked more, the Prophet would have told me more."

Volume 1, Book 10, Number 506:

Narrated Abu Huraira:

I heard Allah's Apostle saying, "If there was a river at the door of anyone of you and he took a bath in it five times a day would you notice any dirt on him?" They said, "Not a trace of dirt would be left." The Prophet added, 'That is the example of the five prayers with which Allah blots out (annuls) evil deeds."

Volume 1, Book 10, Number 507:

Narrated Ghailan:

Anas said, "I do not find (now-a-days) things as they were (practiced) at the time of the Prophet." Somebody said "The prayer (is as it was.)" Anas said, "Have you not done in the prayer what you have done?

Narrated Az-Zuhri that he visited Anas bin Malik at Damascus and found him weeping and asked him why he was weeping. He replied, "I do not know anything which I used to know during the lifetime of Allah's Apostle except this prayer which is being lost (not offered as it should be)."

Volume 1, Book 10, Number 508:

Narrated Anas:

The Prophet said, "Whenever anyone of you offers his prayer he is speaking in private to his Lord. So he should not spit to his right but under his left foot." Qatada said, "He should not spit in front of him but to his left or under his feet." And Shu'ba said, "He should not spit in front of him, nor to his right but to his left or under his foot." Anas said: The Prophet said, "He should neither spit in the direction of his Qibla nor to his right but to his left or under his foot."

Volume 1, Book 10, Number 509:

Narrated Anas:

The Prophet said, "Do the prostration properly and do not put your fore-arms flat with elbows touching the ground like a dog. And if you want to spit, do not spit in front, nor to the right for the person in prayer is speaking in private to his Lord."

Volume 1, Book 10, Number 510:

Narrated Abu Huraira and 'Abdullah bin 'Umar:

Allah's Apostle said, "If it is very hot, then pray the Zuhr prayer when it becomes (a bit) cooler, as the severity of the heat is from the raging of the Hell-fire."

Volume 1, Book 10, Number 511:

Narrated Abu Dhar:

The Muadhdhin (call-maker) of the Prophet pronounced the Adhan (call) for the Zuhr prayer but the Prophet said, "Let it be cooler, let it be cooler." Or said, 'Wait, wait, because the severity of heat is from the raging of the Hell-fire. In severe hot weather, pray when it becomes (a bit) cooler and the shadows of hillocks appear."

Volume 1, Book 10, Number 512:

Narrated Abu Huraira:

The Prophet said, "In very hot weather delay the Zuhr prayer till it becomes (a bit) cooler because the severity of heat is from the raging of Hell-fire. The Hell-fire of Hell complained to its Lord saying: O Lord! My parts are eating (destroying) one another. So Allah allowed it to take two breaths, one in the winter and the other in the summer. The breath in the summer is at the time when you feel the severest heat and the breath in the winter is at the time when you feel the severest cold."

Volume 1, Book 10, Number 513:

Narrated Abu Sa'id:

that Allah's Apostle said, "Pray Zuhr prayer when it becomes (a bit) cooler as the severity of heat is from the raging of the Hell-fire."

Volume 1, Book 10, Number 514:

Narrated Abu Dhar Al-Ghifar:

We were with the Prophet on a journey and the Mu'adhdhin (call maker for the prayer) wanted to pronounce the Adhan (call) for the Zuhr prayer. The Prophet said, 'Let it become cooler." He again (after a while) wanted to pronounce the Adhan but the Prophet said to him, "Let it become cooler till we see the shadows of hillocks." The Prophet added, "The severity of heat is from the raging of the Hell-fire, and in very hot weather pray (Zuhr) when it becomes cooler."

Volume 1, Book 10, Number 515:

Narrated Anas bin Malik:

Allah's Apostle came out as the sun declined at mid-day and offered the Zuhr prayer. He then stood on the pulpit and spoke about the Hour (Day of Judgment) and said that in it there would be tremendous things. He then said, "Whoever likes to ask me about anything he can do so and I shall reply as long as I am at this place of mine. Most of the people wept and the Prophet said repeatedly, "Ask me." Abdullah bin Hudhafa As-Sahmi stood up and said, "Who is my father?" The Prophet said, "Your father is Hudhafa." The Prophet repeatedly said, "Ask me." Then Umar knelt before him and said, "We are pleased with Allah as our Lord, Islam as our religion, and Muhammad as our Prophet." The Prophet then became quiet and said, "Paradise and Hell-fire were displayed in front of me on this wall just now and I have never seen a better thing (than the former) and a worse thing (than the latter)."

Volume 1, Book 10, Number 516:

Narrated Abu Al-Minhal:

Abu Barza said, "The Prophet used to offer the Fajr (prayer) when one could recognize the person sitting by him (after the prayer) and he used to recite between 60 to 100 Ayat (verses) of the Qur'an. He used to offer the Zuhr prayer as soon as the sun declined (at noon) and the 'Asr at a time when a man might go and return from the farthest place in Medina and find the sun still hot. (The sub-narrator forgot what was said about the Maghrib). He did not mind delaying the 'Isha prayer to one third of the night or the middle of the night."

Volume 1, Book 10, Number 517:

Narrated Anas bin Malik:

When we offered the Zuhr prayers behind Allah's Apostle we used to prostrate on our clothes to protect ourselves from the heat.

Volume 1, Book 10, Number 518:

Narrated Ibn 'Abbas:

"The Prophet prayed eight Rakat for the Zuhr and 'Asr, and seven for the Maghrib and 'Isha prayers in Medina." Aiyub said, "Perhaps those were rainy nights." Anas said, "May be."

Volume 1, Book 10, Number 519:

Narrated Aisha:

Allah's Apostle used to offer the 'Asr prayer when the sunshine had not disappeared from my chamber.

Volume 1, Book 10, Number 520,

Narrated 'Aisha,

Allah's Apostle used to offer the 'Asr prayers at a time when the sunshine was still inside my chamber and no shadow had yet appeared in it.

Volume 1, Book 10, Number 521,

Narrated Aisha,

The Prophet used to pray the 'Asr prayers at a time when the sunshine was still inside my chamber and no shadow had yet appeared in it.

Volume 1, Book 10, Number 522,

Narrated Saiyar bin Salama,

I along with my father went to Abu- Barza Al-Aslarrni and my father asked him, "How Allah's Apostle used to offer the five compulsory congregational prayers?" Abu- Barza said, "The Prophet used to pray the Zuhr prayer which you (people) call the first one at mid-day when the sun had just declined The Asr prayer at a time when after the prayer, a man could go to the house at the farthest place in Medina (and arrive) while the sun was still hot. (I forgot about the Maghrib prayer). The Prophet Loved to delay the 'Isha which you call Al- Atama and he disliked sleeping before it and speaking after it. After the Fajr prayer he used to leave when a man could recognize the one sitting beside him and he used to recite between 60 to 100 Ayat (in the Fajr prayer) .

Volume 1, Book 10, Number 523,

Narrated Anas bin Malik,

We used to pray the Asr prayer and after that if someone happened to go to the tribe of Bani Amr bin Auf, he would find them still praying the Asr (prayer).

Volume 1, Book 10, Number 524,

Narrated Abu Bakr bin Uthman bin Sahl bin Hunaif,

that he heard Abu Umama saying, We prayed the Zuhr prayer with 'Umar bin Abdul Aziz and then went to Anas bin Malik and found him offering the Asr prayer. I asked him, "O uncle! Which prayer have you offered?" He said 'The Asr and this is (the time of) the prayer of Allah s Apostle which we used to pray with him."

Volume 1, Book 10, Number 525:

Narrated Anas bin Malik:

Allah's Apostle used to offer the 'Asr prayer at a time when the sun was still hot and high and if a person went to Al-'Awali (a place) of Medina, he would reach there when the sun was still high. Some of Al-'Awali of Medina were about four miles or so from the town.

Volume 1, Book 10, Number 526:

Narrated Anas bin Malik:

We used to pray the 'Asr and after that if one of US went to Quba'he would arrive there while the sun was still high.

Volume 1, Book 10, Number 527:

Narrated Ibn 'Umar:

Allah's Apostle said, "Whoever misses the 'Asr prayer (intentionally) then it is as if he lost his family and property."

Volume 1, Book 10, Number 528:

Narrated Abu Al-Mahh:

We were with Buraida in a battle on a cloudy day and he said, "Offer the 'Asr prayer early as the Prophet said, "Whoever leaves the 'Asr prayer, all his (good) deeds will be annulled."

Volume 1, Book 10, Number 529:

Narrated Qais:

Jarir said, "We were with the Prophet and he looked at the moon--full-moon--and said, 'Certainly you will see your Lord as you see this moon and you will have no trouble in seeing Him. So if you can avoid missing (through sleep or business, etc.) a prayer before the sun-rise (Fajr) and a prayer before sunset ('Asr), you must do so.' He then recited Allah's Statement:

And celebrate the praises Of your Lord before The rising of the sun And before (its) setting." (50.39) Isma'il said, "Offer those prayers and do not miss them."

Volume 1, Book 10, Number 530:

Narrated Abu Huraira:

Allah's Apostle said, "Angels come to you in succession by night and day and all of them get together at the time of the Fajr and 'Asr prayers. Those who have passed the night with you (or stayed with you) ascend (to the Heaven) and Allah asks them, though He knows everything about you, well, "In what state did you leave my slaves?" The angels reply: "When we left them they were praying and when we reached them, they were praying."

Volume 1, Book 10, Number 531:

Narrated Abu Huraira:

Allah's Apostle said, "If anyone of you can get one Rak'a of the 'Asr prayer before sunset, he should complete his prayer. If any of you can get one Rak'a of the Fajr prayer before sunrise, he should complete his prayer."

Volume 1, Book 10, Number 532:

Narrated Salim bin 'Abdullah:

My father said, "I heard Allah's Apostle saying, 'The period of your stay as compared to the previous nations is like the period equal to the time between the 'Asr prayer and sunset. The people of the Torah were given the Torah and they acted (upon it) till mid-day then they were exhausted and were given one Qirat (of gold) each. And then the people of the Gospel were given the Gospel and they acted (upon it) till the 'Asr prayer then they were exhausted and were: given one Qirat each. And then we were given the Qur'an and we acted (upon it) till sunset and we were given two Qirats each. On that the people of both the scriptures said, 'O our Lord! You have given them two Qirats and given us one Qirat, though we have worked more than they.' Allah said, 'Have I usurped some of your right?' They said, 'No.' Allah said: "That is my blessing I bestow upon whomsoever I wish."

Volume 1, Book 10, Number 533:

Narrated Abu Musa:

The Prophet said, "The example of Muslims, Jews and Christians is like the example of a man who employed laborers to work for him from morning till night. They worked till mid-day and they said, 'We are not in need of your reward.' SO the man employed another batch and said to them, 'Complete the rest of the day and yours will be the wages I had fixed (for the first batch). They worked Up till the time of the 'Asr prayer and said, 'Whatever we have done is for you.' He employed another batch. They worked for the rest of the day till sunset, and they received the wages of the two former batches."

Volume 1, Book 10, Number 534:

Narrated Rafi' bin Khadij:

We used to offer the Maghrib prayer with the Prophet and after finishing the prayer one of us may go away and could still see as Par as the spots where one's arrow might reach when shot by a bow.

Volume 1, Book 10, Number 535:

Narrated Jabir bin 'Abdullah:

The Prophet used to pray the Zuhr at mid-day, and the 'Asr at a time when the sun was still bright, the Maghrib after sunset (at its stated time) and the Isha at a variable time. Whenever he saw the people assembled (for Isha' prayer) he would pray earlier and if the people delayed, he would delay the prayer. And they or the Prophet used to offer the Fajr Prayers when it still dark.

Volume 1, Book 10, Number 536:

Narrated Salama:

We used to pray the Maghrib prayer with the Prophet when the sun disappeared from the horizon.

Volume 1, Book 10, Number 537:

Narrated Ibn 'Abbas:

The Prophet prayed seven Rakat together and eight Rakat together.

Volume 1, Book 10, Number 538:

Narrated 'Abdullah Al-Muzani:

The Prophet said, "Do not be influenced by bedouins regarding the name of your Maghrib prayer which is called 'Isha' by them."

Volume 1, Book 10, Number 539:

Narrated Abdullah:

"One night Allah's Apostle led us in the 'Isha' prayer and that is the one called Al-'Atma by the people. After the completion of the prayer, he faced us and said, "Do you know the importance of this night? Nobody present on the surface of the earth to-night will be living after one hundred years from this night." (See Hadith No. 575).

Volume 1, Book 10, Number 540,

Narrated Muhammad bin 'Amr,

We asked Jabir bin 'Abdullah about the prayers of the Prophet . He said, "He used to pray Zuhr prayer at mid-day, the 'Asr when the sun was still hot, and the Maghrib after sunset (at its stated time). The 'Isha was offered early if the people gathered, and used to be delayed if their number was less; and the morning prayer was offered when it was still dark. "

Volume 1, Book 10, Number 541,

Narrated 'Aisha,

Allah's Apostle once delayed the 'Isha' prayer and that was during the days when Islam still had not spread. The Prophet did not come out till 'Umar informed him that the women and children had slept. Then he came out and said to the people of the mosque,"None amongst the dwellers of the earth has been waiting for it ('Isha prayer) except you."

Volume 1, Book 10, Number 542,

Narrated Abu Musa,

My companions, who came with me in the boat and I landed at a place called Baqi Buthan. The Prophet was in Medina at that time. One of us used to go to the Prophet by turns every night at the time of the Isha prayer. Once I along with my companions went to the Prophet and he was busy in some of his affairs, so the 'Isha' prayer was delayed to the middle of the night He then came out and led the people (in prayer). After finishing from the prayer, he addressed the people present there saying, "Be patient! Don't go away. Have the glad tiding. It is from the blessing of Allah upon you that none amongst mankind has prayed at this time save you." Or said, "None except you has prayed at this time." Abu Muisa added, 'So we returned happily after what we heard from Alllah's Apostle ."

Volume 1, Book 10, Number 543,

Narrated Abu Barza,

Allah's Apostle disliked to sleep before the 'Isha' prayer and to talk after it.

Volume 1, Book 10, Number 544,

Narrated Ibn Shihab from 'Urwa,

'Aisha said, "Once Allah's Apostle delayed the 'Isha' prayer till 'Umar reminded him by saying, "The prayer!" The women and children have slept. Then the Prophet came out and said, 'None amongst the dwellers of the earth has been waiting for it (the prayer) except you." Urwa said, "Nowhere except in

Medina the prayer used to be offered (in those days)." He further said, "The Prophet used to offer the 'Isha' prayer in the period between the disappearance of the twilight and the end of the first third of the night."

Volume 1, Book 10, Number 545:

Narrated Ibn Juraij from Nafi:

'Abdullah bin 'Umar said, "Once Allah's Apostle was busy (at the time of the 'Isha'), so the prayer was delayed so much so that we slept and woke up and slept and woke up again. The Prophet came out and said, 'None amongst the dwellers of the earth but you have been waiting for the prayer." Ibn 'Umar did not find any harm in praying it earlier or in delaying it unless he was afraid that sleep might overwhelm him and he might miss the prayer, and sometimes he used to sleep before the 'Isha' prayer. Ibn Juraij said, "I said to 'Ata', 'I heard Ibn 'Abbas saying: Once Allah's Apostle delayed the 'Isha' prayer to such an extent that the people slept and got up and slept again and got up again. Then 'Umar bin Al-Khattab I, stood up and reminded the Prophet I of the prayer.' 'Ata' said, 'Ibn 'Abbas said: The Prophet came out as if I was looking at him at this time, and water was trickling from his head and he was putting his hand on his head and then said, 'Hadn't I thought it hard for my followers, I would have ordered them to pray ('Isha' prayer) at this time.' I asked 'Ata' for further information, how the Prophet had kept his hand on his head as he was told by Ibn 'Abbas. 'Ata' separated his fingers slightly and put their tips on the side of the head, brought the fingers downwards approximating them till the thumb touched the lobe of the ear at the side of the temple and the beard on the face. He neither slowed nor hurried in this action but he acted like that. The Prophet said: "Hadn't I thought it hard for my followers I would have ordered them to pray at this time."

Volume 1, Book 10, Number 546:

Narrated Anas:

The Prophet delayed the'Isha' prayer till midnight and then he offered the prayer and said, "The people prayed and slept but you have been in prayer as long as you have been waiting for it (the prayer)." Anas added: As if I am looking now at the glitter of the ring of the Prophet on that night.

Volume 1, Book 10, Number 547:

Narrated Jarir bin 'Abdullah:

We were with the Prophet on a full moon night. He looked at the moon and said, "You will certainly see your Lord as you see this moon, and there will be no trouble in seeing Him. So if you can avoid missing (through sleep, business, etc.) a prayer before the rising of the sun (Fajr) and before its setting ('Asr) you must do so. He (the Prophet) then recited the following verse:

And celebrate the praises Of Your Lord before The rising of the sun And before (its) setting." (50.39)

Volume 1, Book 10, Number 548:

Narrated Abu Bakr bin Abi Musa:

My father said, "Allah's Apostle said, 'Whoever prays the two cool prayers ('Asr and Fajr) will go to Paradise.' "

Volume 1, Book 10, Number 549:

Narrated Anas:

Zaid bin Thabit said, "We took the "Suhur" (the meal taken before dawn while fasting is observed) with the Prophet and then stood up for the (morning) prayer." I asked him how long the interval between the two (Suhur and prayer) was. He replied, 'The interval between the two was just sufficient to recite fifty to Sixth 'Ayat."

Volume 1, Book 10, Number 550:

Narrated Qatada:

Anas bin Malik said, "The Prophet and Zaid bin Thabit took the 'Suhur' together and after finishing the meal, the Prophet stood up and prayed (Fajr prayer)." I asked Anas, "How long was the interval between finishing their 'Suhur' and starting the prayer?" He replied, "The interval between the two was just sufficient to recite fifty 'Ayat." (Verses of the Quran)."

Volume 1, Book 10, Number 551:

Narrated Sahl bin Sa'd:

I used to take the "Suhur" meal with my family and hasten so as to catch the Fajr (morning prayer) with Allah's Apostle

Volume 1, Book 10, Number 552:

Narrated 'Aisha:

The believing women covered with their veiling sheets used to attend the Fajr prayer with Allah's Apostle, and after finishing the prayer they would return to their home and nobody could recognize them because of darkness.

Volume 1, Book 10, Number 553:

Narrated Abu Huraira:

Allah's Apostle said, "Whoever could get one Rak'a (of the Fajr prayer) before sunrise, he has got the (morning) prayer and whoever could get one Rak'a of the'Asr prayer before sunset, he has got the ('Asr) prayer."

Volume 1, Book 10, Number 554:

Narrated Abu Huraira:

Allah's Apostle said, "Whoever could get one Rak'a of a prayer, (in its proper time) he has got the prayer."

Volume 1, Book 10, Number 555:

Narrated 'Umar:

"The Prophet forbade praying after the Fajr prayer till the sun rises and after the 'Asr prayer till the sun sets."

Volume 1, Book 10, Number 556:

Narrated Ibn 'Abbas:

Some people told me the same narration (as above).

Volume 1, Book 10, Number 557:

Narrated Hisham's father:

Ibn 'Umar said, "Allah's Apostle said, 'Do not pray at the time of sunrise and at the time of sunset.' " Ibn 'Umar said, "Allah's Apostle said, 'If the edge of the sun appears (above the horizon) delay the prayer till it becomes high, and if the edge of the sun disappears, delay the prayer till it sets (disappears completely).' "

Volume 1, Book 10, Number 558:

Narrated Abu Huraira:

Allah's Apostle forbade two kinds of sales, two kinds of dresses, and two prayers. He forbade offering prayers after the Fajr prayer till the rising of the sun and after the 'Asr prayer till its setting. He also forbade "Ishtimal-Assama" and "al-Ihtiba" in one garment in such a way that one's private parts are exposed towards the sky. He also forbade the sales called "Munabadha" and "Mulamasa." (See Hadith No. 354 and 355 Vol. 3).

Volume 1, Book 10, Number 559,

Narrated Ibn 'Umar,

Allah's Apostle said, "None of you should try to pray at sunrise or sunset."

Volume 1, Book 10, Number 560,

Narrated Abu Sa'id Al-Khudri,

I heard Allah's Apostle saying, "There is no prayer after the morning prayer till the sun rises, and there is no prayer after the Asr prayer till the sun sets."

Volume 1, Book 10, Number 561,

Narrated Muawiya,

You offer a prayer which I did not see being offered by Allah's Apostle when we were in his company and he certainly had forbidden it (i.e. two Rakat after the Asr prayer).

Volume 1, Book 10, Number 562,

Narrated Abu Huraira,

Allah's Apostle forbade the offering of two prayers,

1. after the morning prayer till the sunrises.

2. after the 'Asr prayer till the sun sets.

Volume 1, Book 10, Number 563,

Narrated Ibn 'Umar,

I pray as I saw my companions praying. I do not forbid praying at any time during the day or night except at sunset and sunrise.

Volume 1, Book 10, Number 564,

Narrated 'Aisha,

By Allah, Who took away the Prophet. The Prophet never missed them (two Rakat) after the 'Asr prayer till he met Allah and he did not meet Allah till it became heavy for him to pray while standing so he used to offer most of the prayers while sitting. (She meant the two Rakat after Asr) He used to pray them in the house and never prayed them in the mosque lest it might be hard for his followers and he loved what was easy for them .

Volume 1, Book 10, Number 565:

Narrated Hisham's father:

'Aisha (addressing me) said, "O son of my sister! The Prophet never missed two prostrations (i.e. Rakat) after the 'Asr prayer in my house."

Volume 1, Book 10, Number 566:

Narrated 'Aisha:

Allah's Apostle never missed two Rakat before the Fajr prayer and after the Asr prayer openly and secretly.

Volume 1, Book 10, Number 567:

Narrated 'Aisha:

Whenever the Prophet come to me after the 'Asr prayer, he always prayed two Rakat.

Volume 1, Book 10, Number 568:

Narrated Ibn Abu Malih:

I was with Buraida on a cloudy day and he said, "Offer the 'Asr prayer earlier as the Prophet said, 'Whoever leaves the 'Asr prayer will have all his (good) deeds annulled." (See Hadith No. 527 and 528)

Volume 1, Book 10, Number 569:

Narrated 'Abdullah bin Abi Qatada:

My father said, "One night we were traveling with the Prophet and some people said, 'We wish that Allah's Apostle would take a rest along with us during the last hours of the night.' He said, 'I am afraid that you will sleep and miss the (Fajr) prayer.' Bilal said, 'I will make you get up.' So all slept and Bilal rested his back against his Rahila and he too was overwhelmed (by sleep) and slept. The Prophet got up when the edge of the sun had risen and said, 'O Bilal! What about your statement?' He replied, 'I have never slept such a sleep.' The Prophet said, 'Allah captured your souls when He wished, and released them when He wished. O Bilal! Get up and pronounce the Adhan for the prayer.' The Prophet performed ablution and when the sun came up and became bright, he stood up and prayed."

Volume 1, Book 10, Number 570:

Narrated Jabir bin 'Abdullah:

On the day of Al-Khandaq (the battle of trench.) 'Umar bin Al-Khattab came cursing the disbelievers of Quraish after the sun had set and said, "O Allah's Apostle I could not offer the 'Asr prayer till the sun had set." The Prophet said, "By Allah! I, too, have not prayed." So we turned towards Buthan, and the Prophet performed ablution and we too performed ablution and offered the 'Asr prayer after the sun had set, and then he offered the Maghrib prayer.

Volume 1, Book 10, Number 571:

Narrated Anas:

The Prophet said, "If anyone forgets a prayer he should pray that prayer when he remembers it. There is no expiation except to pray the same." Then he recited: "Establish prayer for My (i.e. Allah's) remembrance." (20.14).

Volume 1, Book 10, Number 572:

Narrated Jabir:

Umar came cursing the disbelievers (of Quraish) on the day of Al-Khandaq (the battle of Trench) and said, "I could not offer the 'Asr prayer till the sun had set. Then we went to Buthan and he offered the ('Asr) prayer after sunset and then he offered the Maghrib prayer.

Volume 1, Book 10, Number 573:

Narrated Abu-l-Minhal:

My father and I went to Abi Barza Al-Aslami and my father said to him, "Tell us how Allah's Apostle used to offer the compulsory congregational prayers." He said, "He used to pray the Zuhr prayer, which you call the first prayer, as the sun declined at noon, the 'Asr at a time when one of US could go to his family at the farthest place in Medina while the sun was still hot. (The narrator forgot what Abu Barza had said about the Maghrib prayer), and the Prophet preferred to pray the 'Isha' late and disliked to sleep before it or talk after it. And he used to return after finishing the morning prayer at such a time when it was possible for one to recognize the person sitting by his side and he (the Prophet) used to recite 60 to 100 'Ayat' (verses) of the Qur'an in it."

Volume 1, Book 10, Number 574:

Narrated Qurra bin Khalid:

Once he waited for Al-Hasan and he did not show up till it was about the usual time for him to start his speech; then he came and apologized saying, "Our neighbors invited us." Then he added, "Narrated Anas, 'Once we waited for the Prophet till it was midnight or about midnight. He came and led the prayer, and after finishing it, he addressed us and said, 'All the people prayed and then slept and you had been in prayer as long as you were waiting for it." Al-Hasan said, "The people are regarded as performing good deeds as long as they are waiting for doing good deeds." Al-Hasan's statement is a portion of Anas's Hadith from the Prophet .

Volume 1, Book 10, Number 575:

Narrated 'Abdullah bin 'Umar:

The Prophet prayed one of the'Isha' prayer in his last days and after finishing it with Taslim, he stood up and said, "Do you realize (the importance of) this night? Nobody present on the surface of the earth to-night would be living after the completion of one hundred years from this night."

The people made a mistake in grasping the meaning of this statement of Allah's Apostle and they indulged in those things which are said about these narrators (i.e. some said that the Day of Resurrection will be established after 100 years etc.) But the Prophet said, "Nobody present on the surface of earth tonight would be living after the completion of 100 years from this night"; he meant "When that century (people of that century) would pass away."

Volume 1, Book 10, Number 576:

Narrated Abu 'Uthman:

'Abdur Rahman bin Abi Bakr said, "The Suffa Companions were poor people and the Prophet said, 'Whoever has food for two persons should take a third one from them (Suffa companions). And whosoever has food for four persons he should take one or two from them' Abu Bakr took three men and the Prophet took ten of them."

'Abdur Rahman added, my father my mother and I were there (in the house). (The sub-narrator is in doubt whether 'Abdur Rahman also said, 'My wife and our servant who was common for both my house and Abu Bakr's house). Abu Bakr took his supper with the Prophet and remained there till the 'Isha' prayer was offered. Abu Bakr went back and stayed with the Prophet till the Prophet took his meal and then Abu Bakr returned to his house after a long portion of the night had passed. Abu Bakr's wife said, 'What detained you from your guests (or guest)?' He said, 'Have you not served them yet?' She said, 'They refused to eat until you come. The food was served for them but they refused." 'Abdur Rahman added, "I went away and hid myself (being afraid of Abu Bakr) and in the meantime he (Abu Bakr) called me, 'O Ghunthar (a harsh word)!' and also called me bad names and abused me and then said (to his family), 'Eat. No welcome for you.' Then (the supper was served). Abu Bakr took an oath that he would not eat that food. The narrator added: By Allah, whenever any one of us (myself and the guests of Suffa companions) took anything from the food, it increased from underneath. We all ate to our fill and the food was more than it was before its serving.

Abu Bakr looked at it (the food) and found it as it was before serving or even more than that. He addressed his wife (saying) 'O the sister of Bani Firas! What is this?' She said, 'O the pleasure of my eyes! The food is now three times more than it was before.' Abu Bakr ate from it, and said, 'That (oath) was from Satan' meaning his oath (not to eat). Then he again took a morsel (mouthful) from it and then took the rest of it to the Prophet. So that meal was with the Prophet. There was a treaty between us and some people, and when the period of that treaty had elapsed the Prophet divided us into twelve (groups) (the Prophet's companions) each being headed by a man. Allah knows how many men were under the command of each (leader). So all of them (12 groups of men) ate of that meal."

Book 11: Call to Prayers (Adhaan)

Volume 1, Book 11, Number 577:

Narrated Anas:

The people mentioned the fire and the bell (they suggested those as signals to indicate the starting of prayers), and by that they mentioned the Jews and the Christians. Then Bilal was ordered to pronounce Adhan for the prayer by saying its wordings twice, and for the Iqama (the call for the actual standing for the prayers in rows) by saying its wordings once. (Iqama is pronounced when the people are ready for the prayer).

Volume 1, Book 11, Number 578:

Narrated Ibn 'Umar:

When the Muslims arrived at Medina, they used to assemble for the prayer, and used to guess the time for it. During those days, the practice of Adhan for the prayers had not been introduced yet. Once they discussed this problem regarding the call for prayer. Some people suggested the use of a bell like the Christians, others proposed a trumpet like the horn used by the Jews, but 'Umar was the first to suggest that a man should call (the people) for the prayer; so Allah's Apostle ordered Bilal to get up and pronounce the Adhan for prayers.

Volume 1, Book 11, Number 579:

Narrated Anas:

Bilal was ordered to repeat the wording of the Adhan for prayers twice, and to pronounce the wording of the Iqamas once except "Qad-qamat-is-Salat".

Volume 1, Book 11, Number 580:

Narrated Anas bin Malik:

When the number of Muslims increased they discussed the question as to how to know the time for the prayer by some familiar means. Some suggested that a fire be lit (at the time of the prayer) and others put forward the proposal to ring the bell. Bilal was ordered to pronounce the wording of Adhan twice and of the Iqama once only.

Volume 1, Book 11, Number 581:

Narrated Abu Qilaba:

Anas said, "Bilal was ordered to pronounce the wording of Adhan twice and of Iqama once only." The sub narrator Isma'li said, "I mentioned that to Aiyub and he added (to that), "Except Iqama (i.e. Qad-Qamatis-Salat which should be said twice)."

Volume 1, Book 11, Number 582:

Narrated Abu Huraira:

Allah's Apostle said, "When the Adhan is pronounced Satan takes to his heels and passes wind with noise during his flight in order not to hear the Adhan. When the Adhan is completed he comes back and again takes to his heels when the Iqama is pronounced and after its completion he returns again till he whispers into the heart of the person (to divert his attention from his prayer) and makes him remember things which he does not recall to his mind before the prayer and that causes him to forget how much he has prayed."

Volume 1, Book 11, Number 583:

Narrated 'Abdul Rahman:

Abu Sa'id Al-Khudri told my father, "I see you liking sheep and the wilderness. So whenever you are with your sheep or in the wilderness and you want to pronounce Adhan for the prayer raise your voice in doing so, for whoever hears the Adhan, whether a human being, a jinn or any other creature, will be a witness for you on the Day of Resurrection." Abu Said added, "I heard it (this narration) from Allah's Apostle."

Volume 1, Book 11, Number 584:

Narrated Humaid:

Anas bin Malik said, "Whenever the Prophet went out with us to fight (in Allah's cause) against any nation, he never allowed us to attack till morning and he would wait and see: if he heard Adhan he would postpone the attack and if he did not hear Adhan he would attack them." Anas added, "We reached Khaibar at night and in the morning when he did not hear the Adhan for the prayer, he (the Prophet) rode and I rode behind Abi Talha and my foot was touching that of the Prophet.

The inhabitants of Khaibar came out with their baskets and spades and when they saw the Prophet they shouted 'Muhammad! By Allah, Muhammad and his army.' When Allah's Apostle saw them, he said, "Allahu-Akbar! Allahu-Akbar! Khaibar is ruined. Whenever we approach a (hostile) nation (to fight), then evil will be the morning of those who have been warned."

Volume 1, Book 11, Number 585:

Narrated Abu Said Al-Khudri:

Allah's Apostle said, "Whenever you hear the Adhan, say what the Mu'adhdhin is saying."

Volume 1, Book 11, Number 586:

Narrated 'Isa bin Talha:

that he had heard Muawiya repeating the words of Adhan up to "Wa ash-hadu Anna Muhammadan Rasulul-lah (and I testify that Muhammad is Allah's Apostle.)"

Volume 1, Book 11, Number 587:

Narrated Yahya as above (586) and added:

"Some of my companions told me that Hisham had said, "When the Mu'adhdhin said, "Haiya alas-sala(t) (come for the prayer)." Muawiya said, "La hawla wala quwata illa billah (There is neither might nor any power except with Allah)" and added, "We heard your Prophet saying the same."

Volume 1, Book 11, Number 588:

Narrated Jabir bin 'Abdullah:

Allah's Apostle said, "Whoever after listening to the Adhan says, 'Allahumma Rabba hadhihi-d-da' watit-tammati was-salatil qa'imati, ati Muhammadan al-wasilata wal-fadilata, wab' athhu maqa-man mahmudan-il-ladhi wa' adtahu (O Allah! Lord of this perfect call (of not ascribing partners to You) and of the regular prayer which is going to be established! Kindly give Muhammad the right of intercession and superiority and send him (on the Day of Judgment) to the best and the highest place in Paradise which You promised him)', then intercession for me will be permitted for him on the Day of Resurrection").

Volume 1, Book 11, Number 589:

Narrated Abu Huraira:

Allah's Apostle said, "If the people knew the reward for pronouncing the Adhan and for standing in the first row (in congregational prayers) and found no other way to get that except by drawing lots they would draw lots, and if they knew the reward of the Zuhr prayer (in the early moments of its stated time) they would race for it (go early) and if they knew the reward of 'Isha' and Fajr (morning) prayers in congregation, they would come to offer them even if they had to crawl."

Volume 1, Book 11, Number 590:

Narrated 'Abdullah bin Al-Harith:

Once on a rainy muddy day, Ibn 'Abbas delivered a sermon in our presence and when the Mu'ad-hdhin pronounced the Adhan and said, "Haiya ala-s-sala(t) (come for the prayer)" Ibn 'Abbas ordered him to say 'Pray at your homes.' The people began to look at each other (surprisingly). Ibn 'Abbas said. "It was done by one who was much better than I (i.e. the Prophet or his Mu'adhdhin), and it is a license.'

Volume 1, Book 11, Number 591:

Narrated Salim bin Abdullah:

My father said that Allah s Apostle said, "Bilal pronounces 'Adhan at night, so keep on eating and drinking (Suhur) till Ibn Um Maktum pronounces Adhan." Salim added, "He was a blind man who would not pronounce the Adhan unless he was told that the day had dawned."

Volume 1, Book 11, Number 592:

Narrated Hafsa:

When the Muadh-dhin pronounced the Adhan for Fajr prayer and the dawn became evident the Prophet ordered a two Rakat light prayer (Sunna) before the Iqama of the compulsory (congrega-tional) prayer.

Volume 1, Book 11, Number 593:

Narrated 'Aisha:

The Prophet used to offer two light Rakat between the Adhan and the Iqama of the Fajr prayer.

Volume 1, Book 11, Number 594:

Narrated 'Abdullah bin 'Umar:

Allah's Apostle said, "Bilal pronounces the Adhan at night, so keep on eating and drinking (Suhur) till Ibn Um Maktum pronounces the Adhan."

Volume 1, Book 11, Number 595:

Narrated 'Abdullah bin Mas'ud:

The Prophet said, "The Adhan pronounced by Bilal should not stop you from taking Suhur, for he pronounces the Adhan at night, so that the one offering the late night prayer (Tahajjud) from among you might hurry up and the sleeping from among you might wake up. It does not mean that dawn or morning has started." Then he (the Prophet) pointed with his fingers and raised them up (towards the sky) and then lowered them (towards the earth) like this (Ibn Mas'ud imitated the gesture of the Prophet). Az-Zuhri gestured with his two index fingers which he put on each other and then stretched them to the right and left. These gestures illustrate the way real dawn appears. It spreads left and right horizontally. The dawn that appears in the high sky and lowers down is not the real dawn) .

Volume 1, Book 11, Number 596:

Narrated 'Aisha:

The Prophet said, "Bilal pronounces the Adhan at night, so eat and drink (Suhur) till Ibn Um Maktum pronounces the Adhan."

Volume 1, Book 11, Number 597:

Narrated 'Abdullah bin Mughaffal Al-Muzani:

Allah's Apostle said thrice, "There is a prayer between the two Adhans (Adhan and Iqama)," and added, "For the one who wants to pray."

Volume 1, Book 11, Number 598:

Narrated Anas bin Malik:

"When the Mu'adhdhin pronounced the Adhan, some of the companions of the Prophet would proceed to the pillars of the mosque (for the prayer) till the Prophet arrived and in this way they used to pray two Rakat before the Maghrib prayer. There used to be a little time between the Adhan and the Iqama." Shu'ba said, "There used to be a very short interval between the two (Adhan and Iqama)."

Volume 1, Book 11, Number 599:

Narrated 'Aisha:

Allah's Apostle used to pray two light Rakat before the morning (compulsory) prayer after the day dawned and the Mu'adhdhin had finished his Adhan. He then would lie on his right side till the Mu'adhdhin came to pronounce the Iqama.

Volume 1, Book 11, Number 600:

Narrated 'Abdullah bin Mughaffal:

The prophet said, "There is a prayer between the two Adhans (Adhan and Iqama), there is a prayer between the two Adhans." And then while saying it the third time he added, "For the one who wants to (pray)."

Volume 1, Book 11, Number 601:

Narrated Malik bin Huwairth:

I came to the Prophet with some men from my tribe and stayed with him for twenty nights. He was kind and merciful to us. When he realized our longing for our families, he said to us, "Go back and stay with your families and teach them the religion, and offer the prayer and one of you should pronounce the Adhan for the prayer when its time is due and the oldest one amongst you should lead the prayer."

Volume 1, Book 11, Number 602:

Narrated Abu Dhar:

We were in the company of the Prophet on a journey and the Mu'adhdhin wanted to pronounce the Adhan for the (Zuhr) prayer. The Prophet said to him, "Let it become cooler." Then he again wanted to pronounce the Adhan but the Prophet; said to him, "Let it become cooler." The Mu'adh-dhin again wanted to pronounce the Adhan for the prayer but the Prophet said, "Let it become cooler," till the shadows of the hillocks become equal to their sizes. The Prophet added, "The severity of the heat is from the raging of Hell."

Volume 1, Book 11, Number 603:

Narrated Malik bin Huwairth:

Two men came to the Prophet with the intention of a journey. The Prophet said, "When (both of) you set out, pronounce Adhan and then Iqama and the oldest of you should lead the prayer."

Volume 1, Book 11, Number 604:

Narrated Malik:

We came to the Prophet and stayed with him for twenty days and nights. We were all young and of about the same age. The Prophet was very kind and merciful. When he realized our longing for our families, he asked about our homes and the people there and we told him. Then he asked us to go back to our families and stay with them and teach them (the religion) and to order them to do good things. He also mentioned some other things which I have (remembered or) forgotten. The Prophet then added, "Pray as you have seen me praying and when it is the time for the prayer one of you should pronounce the Adhan and the oldest of you should lead the prayer.

Volume 1, Book 11, Number 605:

Narrated Nafi:

Once in a cold night, Ibn 'Umar pronounced the Adhan for the prayer at ,Dajnan (the name of a mountain) and then said, "Pray at your homes", and informed us that Allah's Apostle used to tell the Mu'adhdin to pronounce Adhan and say, "Pray at your homes" at the end of the Adhan on a rainy or a very cold night during the journey."

Volume 1, Book 11, Number 606:

Narrated 'Aun bin Abi Juhaifa:

My father said, "I saw Allah's Apostle at a place called Al-Abtah. Bilal came and informed him about the prayer and then came out with an Anza and planted it in front of Allah's Apostle at Al-Abtah and pronounced the Iqama."

Volume 1, Book 11, Number 607:

Narrated 'Aun bin Abi Juhaifa:

My father said, "I saw Bilal turning his face from side to side while pronouncing the Adhan for the prayer."

Volume 1, Book 11, Number 608:

Narrated 'Abdullah bin Abi Qatada:

My father said, "While we were praying with the Prophet he heard the noise of some people. After the prayer he said, 'What is the matter?' They replied 'We were hurrying for the prayer.' He said, 'Do not make haste for the prayer, and whenever you come for the prayer, you should come with calmness, and pray whatever you get (with the people) and complete the rest which you have missed."

Volume 1, Book 11, Number 609:

Narrated Abu Huraira:

The Prophet said, "When you hear the Iqama, proceed to offer the prayer with calmness and solemnity and do not make haste. And pray whatever you are able to pray and complete whatever you have missed.

Volume 1, Book 11, Number 610.

Narrated 'Abdullah bin Abi Qatada.

My father said. "Allah's Apostle said, 'If the Iqama is pronounced then do not stand for the prayer till you see me (in front of you).' "

Volume 1, Book 11, Number 611.

Narrated 'Abdullah bin Abi.

Qatada, My father said, "Allah's Apostle said, 'If the Iqama is pronounced, then do not stand for the prayer till you see me (in front of you) and do it calmly.' "

Volume 1, Book 11, Number 612.

Narrated Abu Huraira.

Allah's Apostle went out (of the mosque) when the Iqama had been pronounced and the rows straightened. The Prophet stood at his Musalla (praying place) and we waited for the Prophet to begin the prayer with Takbir. He left and asked us to remain in our places. We kept on standing till the Prophet returned and the water was trickling from his head for he had taken a bath (of Janaba).

Volume 1, Book 11, Number 613.

Narrated Abu Huraira.

Once iqama was pronounced and the people had straightened the rows, Allah's Apostle went forward (to lead the prayer) but he was Junub, so he said, "Remain in your places." And he went out, took a bath and returned with water trickling from his head. Then he led the prayer.

Volume 1, Book 11, Number 614.

Narrated Jabir bin 'Abdullah.

On the day of Al-Khandaq (the trench), 'Umar bin Al-Khattab went to the Prophet and said, "O Allah's Apostle! By Allah, I could not pray (the 'Asr) till the sun had set." 'Umar told this to the Prophet at the time when a fasting person had done Iftar (taken his meals). The Prophet then went to Buthan and I was with him. He performed ablution and offered the 'Asr prayer after the sun had set and then the Maghrib prayer.

Volume 1, Book 11, Number 615.

Narrated Anas.

Once the Iqama was pronounced and the Prophet was talking to a man (in a low voice) in a corner of the mosque and he did not lead the prayer till (some of) the people had slept (dozed in a sitting posture) .

Volume 1, Book 11, Number 616:

Narrated Anas bin Malik:

Once Iqama was pronounced a man came to the Prophet and detained him (from the prayer).

Volume 1, Book 11, Number 617:

Narrated Abu Huraira:

Allah's Apostle said, "By Him in Whose Hand my soul is I was about to order for collecting firewood (fuel) and then order Someone to pronounce the Adhan for the prayer and then order someone to lead the prayer then I would go from behind and burn the houses of men who did not present themselves for the (compulsory congregational) prayer. By Him, in Whose Hands my soul is, if anyone of them had known that he would get a bone covered with good meat or two (small) pieces of meat present in between two ribs, he would have turned up for the 'Isha' prayer.'

Volume 1, Book 11, Number 618:

Narrated 'Abdullah bin Umar:

Allah's Apostle said, "The prayer in congregation is twenty seven times superior to the prayer offered by person alone."

Volume 1, Book 11, Number 619:

Narrated Abu Said Al-Khudri:

The Prophet said, "The prayer in congregation is twenty five times superior to the prayer offered by person alone."

Volume 1, Book 11, Number 620:

Narrated Abu Huraira:

Allah's Apostle said, "The reward of the prayer offered by a person in congregation is twenty five times greater than that of the prayer offered in one's house or in the market (alone). And this is because if he performs ablution and does it perfectly and then proceeds to the mosque with the sole intention of praying, then for every step he takes towards the mosque, he is upgraded one degree in reward and his one sin is taken off (crossed out) from his accounts (of deeds). When he offers his prayer, the angels keep on asking Allah's Blessings and Allah's forgiveness for him as long as he is (staying) at his Musalla. They say, 'O Allah! Bestow Your blessings upon him, be Merciful and kind to him.' And one is regarded in prayer as long as one is waiting for the prayer."

Volume 1, Book 11, Number 621.

Narrated Abu Salama bin 'Abdur Rahman.

Abu Huraira said, "I heard Allah's Apostle saying, 'The reward of a prayer in congregation is twenty five times greater than that of a prayer offered by a person alone. The angels of the night and the angels of the day gather at the time of Fajr prayer.' " Abu Huraira then added, "Recite the Holy Book if you wish, for "Indeed, the recitation of the Qur'an in the early dawn (Fajr prayer) is ever witnessed." (17.18).

Narrated 'Abdullah bin 'Umar. The reward of the congregational prayer is twenty seven times greater (than that of the prayer offered by a person alone).

Volume 1, Book 11, Number 622.

Narrated Salim.

I heard Um Ad-Darda' saying, "Abu Ad-Darda' entered the house in an angry mood. I said to him. 'What makes you angry?' He replied, 'By Allah! I do not find the followers of Muhammad doing those good things (which they used to do before) except the offering of congregational prayer." (This happened in the last days of Abu Ad-Darda' during the rule of 'Uthman) .

Volume 1, Book 11, Number 623.

Narrated Abu Musa.

The Prophet said, "The people who get tremendous reward for the prayer are those who are farthest away (from the mosque) and then those who are next farthest and so on. Similarly one who waits to pray with the Imam has greater reward than one who prays and goes to bed. "

Volume 1, Book 11, Number 624.

Narrated Abu Huraira.

Allah's Apostle said, "While a man was going on a way, he saw a thorny branch and removed it from the way and Allah became pleased by his action and forgave him for that." Then the Prophet said, "Five are martyrs. One who dies of plague, one who dies of an abdominal disease, one who dies of drowning, one who is buried alive (and) dies and one who is killed in Allah's cause." (The Prophet further said, "If the people knew the reward for pronouncing the Adhan and for standing in the first row (in the congregational prayer) and found no other way to get it except by drawing lots they would do so, and if they knew the reward of offering the Zuhr prayer early (in its stated time), they would race for it and they knew the reward for 'Isha' and Fajr prayers in congregation, they would attend them even if they were to crawl')

Volume 1, Book 11, Number 625:

Narrated Humaid:

Anas said, "The Prophet said, 'O Bani Salima! Don't you think that for every step of yours (that you take towards the mosque) there is a reward (while coming for prayer)?" Mujahid said: "Regarding Allah's Statement: "We record that which they have sent before (them), and their traces" (36.12). 'Their traces' means 'their steps.' " And Anas said that the people of Bani Salima wanted to shift to a place near the Prophet but Allah's Apostle disliked the idea of leaving their houses uninhabited and said, "Don't you think that you will get the reward for your footprints." Mujahid said, "Their foot prints mean their foot steps and their going on foot."

Volume 1, Book 11, Number 626:

Narrated Abu Huraira:

The Prophet said, "No prayer is harder for the hypocrites than the Fajr and the 'Isha' prayers and if they knew the reward for these prayers at their respective times, they would certainly present themselves (in the mosques) even if they had to c awl." The Prophet added, "Certainly I decided to order the Mu'adh-dhin (call-maker) to pronounce Iqama and order a man to lead the prayer and then take a fire flame to burn all those who had not left their houses so far for the prayer along with their houses."

Volume 1, Book 11, Number 627:

Narrated Malik bin Huwairith:

Prophet said (to two persons), "Whenever the prayer time becomes due, you should pronounce Adhan and then Iqama and the older of you should lead the prayer."

Volume 1, Book 11, Number 628:

Narrated Abu Huraira:

Allah's Apostle said, "The angels keep on asking for Allah's Blessing and Forgiveness for anyone of you as long as he is at his Musalla (praying place) and does not do Hadath (passes wind). The angels say, 'O Allah! Forgive him and be Merciful to him.' Each one of you is in the prayer as long as he is waiting for the prayer and nothing but the prayer detains him from going to his family."

Volume 1, Book 11, Number 629:

Narrated Abu Huraira:

The Prophet said, "Allah will give shade, to seven, on the Day when there will be no shade but His. (These seven persons are) a just ruler, a youth who has been brought up in the worship of Allah (i.e. worships Allah sincerely from childhood), a man whose heart is attached to the mosques (i.e. to pray the compulsory prayers in the mosque in congregation), two persons who love each other only for Allah's sake and they meet and part in Allah's cause only, a man who refuses the call of a charming woman of noble birth for illicit intercourse with her and says: I am afraid of Allah, a man who gives charitable gifts so secretly that his left hand does not know what his right hand has given (i.e. nobody knows how much he has given in charity), and a person who remembers Allah in seclusion and his eyes are then flooded with tears."

Volume 1, Book 11, Number 630:

Narrated Humaid:

Anas was asked, "Did Allah's Apostle wear a ring?" He said, "Yes. Once he delayed the 'Isha' prayer till mid-night and after the prayer, he faced us and said, 'The people prayed and have slept and you remained in prayer as long as you waited for it.' " Anas added, "As if I were just now observing the glitter of his ring."

Volume 1, Book 11, Number 631:

Narrated Abu Huraira:

The Prophet said, "Allah will prepare for him who goes to the mosque (every) morning and in the afternoon (for the congregational prayer) an honorable place in Paradise with good hospitality for (what he has done) every morning and afternoon goings.

Volume 1, Book 11, Number 632:

Narrated Malik Ibn Buhaina:

Allah's Apostle passed by a man praying two Rakat after the Iqama (had been pronounced). When Allah's Apostle completed the prayer, the people gathered around him (the Prophet) or that man and Allah's Apostle said to him (protesting), Are there four Rakat in Fajr prayer? Are there four Rakat in Fajr prayer?"

Volume 1, Book 11, Number 633:

Narrated Al-Aswad:

"We were with 'Aisha discussing the regularity of offering the prayer and dignifying it. She said, 'When Allah's Apostle fell sick with the fatal illness and when the time of prayer became due and Adhan was pronounced, he said, 'Tell Abu Bakr to lead the people in prayer.' He was told that Abu Bakr was a soft-hearted man and would not be able to lead the prayer in his place. The Prophet gave the same order again but he was given the same reply. He gave the order for the third time and said, 'You (women) are the companions of Joseph. Tell Abu Bakr to lead the prayer.' So Abu Bakr came out to lead the prayer. In the meantime the condition of the Prophet improved a bit and he came out with the help of two men one on each side. As if I was observing his legs dragging on the ground owing to the disease. Abu Bakr wanted to retreat but the Prophet beckoned him to remain at his place and the Prophet was brought till he sat beside Abu Bakr." Al-A'mash was asked, "Was the Prophet praying and Abu Bakr following him, and were the people following Abu Bakr in that prayer?" Al-A'mash replied in the affirmative with a nod of his head. Abu Muawiya said, "The Prophet was sitting on the left side of Abu Bakr who was praying while standing."

Volume 1, Book 11, Number 634:

Narrated 'Aisha:

"When the Prophet became seriously ill and his disease became aggravated he asked for permission from his wives to be nursed in my house and he was allowed. He came out with the help of two men and his legs were dragging on the ground. He was between Al-Abbas and another man."

'Ubaid Ullah said, "I told Ibn 'Abbas what 'Aisha had narrated and he said, 'Do you know who was the (second) man whose name 'Aisha did not mention'" I said, 'No.' Ibn 'Abbas said, 'He was 'Ali Ibn Abi Talib.' "

Volume 1, Book 11, Number 635:

Narrated Nafi':

Once on a very cold and stormy night, Ibn 'Umar pronounced the Adhan for the prayer and then said, "Pray in your homes." He (Ibn 'Umar) added. "On very cold and rainy nights Allah's Apostle used to order the Mu'adhdhin to say, 'Pray in your homes.' "

Volume 1, Book 11, Number 636:

Narrated Mahmuid bin Rabi' Al-Ansari:

'Itban bin Malik used to lead his people (tribe) in prayer and was a blind man, he said to Allah's Apostle , "O Allah's Apostle! At times it is dark and flood water is flowing (in the valley) and I am blind man, so please pray at a place in my house so that I can take it as a Musalla (praying place)." So Allah's Apostle went to his house and said, "Where do you like me to pray?" 'Itban pointed to a place in his house and Allah's Apostle, offered the prayer there.

Volume 1, Book 11, Number 637:

Narrated 'Abdullah bin Al-Harith:

Ibn Abbas addressed us on a (rainy and) muddy day and when the Mu'adh-dhin said, "Come for the prayer" Ibn 'Abbas ordered him to say, "Pray in your homes." The people began to look at one another with surprise as if they did not like it. Ibn 'Abbas said, "It seems that you thought ill of it but no doubt it was done by one who was better than I (i.e. the Prophet). It (the prayer) is a strict order and I disliked to bring you out."

Ibn 'Abbas narrated the same as above but he said, "I did not like you to make you sinful (in refraining from coming to the mosque) and to come (to the mosque) covered with mud up to the knees."

Volume 1, Book 11, Number 638:

Narrated Abu Sa'id Al-Khudri:

A cloud came and it rained till the roof started leaking and in those days the roof used to be of the branches of date-palms. Iqama was pronounced and I saw Allah's Apostles prostrating in water and mud and even I saw the mark of mud on his forehead.

Volume 1, Book 11, Number 639:

Narrated Anas bin Sirin:

I heard Anas saying, "A man from Ansar said to the Prophet, 'I cannot pray with you (in congregation).' He was a very fat man and he prepared a meal for the Prophet and invited him to his house. He spread out a mat for the Prophet, and washed one of its sides with water, and the Prophet prayed two Rakat on it." A man from the family of Al-Jaruid asked, "Did the Prophet used to pray the Duha (forenoon) prayer?" Anas said, "I did not see him praying the Duha prayer except on that day."

Volume 1, Book 11, Number 640:

Narrated 'Aisha:

The Prophet said, "If supper is served, and Iqama is pronounced one should start with the supper."

Volume 1, Book 11, Number 641:

Narrated Anas bin Malik:

Allah's Apostle said, "If the supper is served start having it before praying the Maghrib prayer and do not be hasty in finishing it."

Volume 1, Book 11, Number 642:

Narrated Nafi':

Ibn 'Umar said, "Allah's Apostle said, 'If the supper is served for anyone of you and the Iqama is pronounced, start with the supper and don't be in haste (and carry on eating) till you finish it." If food was served for Ibn 'Umar and Iqama was pronounced, he never came to the prayer till he finished it (i.e. food) in spite of the fact that he heard the recitation (of the Qur'an) by the Imam (in the prayer). Narrated Ibn 'Umar: The Prophet said, "If anyone of you is having his meals, he should not hurry up till he is; satisfied even if the prayer has been started."

Volume 1, Book 11, Number 643:

Narrated Ja'far bin 'Amr bin Umaiya:

My father said, "I saw Allah's Apostle eating a piece of meat from the shoulder of a sheep and he was called for the prayer. He stood up, put down the knife and prayed but did not perform ablutilon."

Volume 1, Book 11, Number 644:

Narrated Al-Aswad:

That he asked 'Aisha "What did the Prophet use to do in his house?" She replied, "He used to keep himself busy serving his family and when it was the time for prayer he would go for it."

Volume 1, Book 11, Number 645:

Narrated Aiyub:

Abu Qilaba said, "Malik bin Huwairith came to this Mosque of ours and said, 'I pray in front of you and my aim is not to lead the prayer but to show you the way in which the Prophet used to pray.' " I asked Abu Qilaba,"How did he use to pray?' " He replied, "(The Prophet used to pray) like this Sheikh of ours and the Sheikh used to sit for a while after the prostration, before getting up after the first Rak'a. "

Volume 1, Book 11, Number 646:

Narrated Abu Musa:

"The Prophet became sick and when his disease became aggravated, he said, "Tell Abu Bakr to lead the prayer." 'Aisha said, "He is a soft-hearted man and would not be able to lead the prayer in your place." The Prophet said again, "Tell Abu Bakr to lead the people in prayer." She repeated the same reply but he said, "Tell Abu Bakr to lead the people in prayer. You are the companions of Joseph." So the messenger went to Abu Bakr (with that order) and he led the people in prayer in the lifetime of the Prophet.

Volume 1, Book 11, Number 647:

Narrated 'Aisha:

the mother of the believers: Allah's Apostle in his illness said, "Tell Abu Bakr to lead the people in prayer." I said to him, "If Abu Bakr stands in your place, the people would not hear him owing to his (excessive) weeping. So please order 'Umar to lead the prayer." 'Aisha added I said to Hafsa, "Say to him: If Abu Bakr should lead the people in the prayer in your place, the people would not be able to hear him owing to his weeping; so please, order 'Umar to lead the prayer." Hafsa did so but Allah's Apostle said, "Keep quiet! You are verily the Companions of Joseph. Tell Abu Bakr to lead the people in the prayer. " Hafsa said to 'Aisha, "I never got anything good from you."

Volume 1, Book 11, Number 648:

Narrated Az-Zuhn:

Anas bin Malik Al-Ansari, told me, "Abu Bakr used to lead the people in prayer during the fatal ill-ness of the Prophet till it was Monday. When the people aligned (in rows) for the prayer the Prophet lifted the curtain of his house and started looking at us and was standing at that time. His face was (glittering) like a page of the Qur'an and he smiled cheerfully. We were about to be put to trial for the pleasure of seeing the Prophet, Abu Bakr retreated to join the row as he thought that the Prophet would lead the prayer. The Prophet beckoned us to complete the prayer and he let the curtain fall. On the same day he died."

Volume 1, Book 11, Number 649:

Narrated Anas:

The Prophet did not come out for three days. The people stood for the prayer and Abu Bakr went ahead to lead the prayer. (In the meantime) the Prophet caught hold of the curtain and lifted it. When the face of the Prophet appeared we had never seen a scene more pleasing than the face of the Prophet as it appeared then. The Prophet beckoned to Abu Bakr to lead the people in the prayer and then let the curtain fall. We did not see him (again) till he died.

Volume 1, Book 11, Number 650:

Narrated Hamza bin 'Abdullah:

My father said, "When Allah's Apostle became seriously ill, he was told about the prayer. He said, 'Tell Abu Bakr to lead the people in the prayer.' 'Aisha said, 'Abu Bakr is a soft-hearted man and he would be over-powered by his weeping if he recited the Qur'an.' He said to them, 'Tell him (Abu Bakr) to lead the prayer. The same reply was given to him. He said again, 'Tell him to lead the prayer. You (women) are the companions of Joseph."

Volume 1, Book 11, Number 651:

Narrated 'Urwa's father:

'Aisha said, "Allah's Apostle ordered Abu Bakr to lead the people in the prayer during his illness and so he led them in prayer." 'Urwa, a sub narrator, added, "Allah's Apostle felt a bit relieved and came out and Abu Bakr was leading the people. When Abu Bakr saw the Prophet he retreated but the Prophet beckoned him to remain there. Allah's Apostle sat beside Abu Bakr. Abu Bakr was following the prayer of Allah's Apostle and the people were following the prayer of Abu Bakr."

Volume 1, Book 11, Number 652:

Narrated Sahl bin Sa'd As-Sa'idi:

Allah's Apostle went to establish peace among Bani 'Amr bin 'Auf. In the meantime the time of prayer was due and the Mu'adh-dhin went to Abu Bakr and said, "Will you lead the prayer, so that I may pronounce the Iqama?" Abu Bakr replied in the affirmative and led the prayer. Allah's Apostle came while the people were still praying and he entered the rows of the praying people till he stood in the (first row). The people clapped their hands. Abu Bakr never glanced sideways in his prayer but when the people continued clapping, Abu Bakr looked and saw Allah's Apostle. Allah's Apostle beckoned him to stay at his place. Abu Bakr raised his hands and thanked Allah for that order of Allah's Apostle and then he retreated till he reached the first row. Allah's Apostle went forward and led the prayer. When Allah's Apostle finished the prayer, he said, "O Abu Bakr! What prevented you from staying when I ordered you to do so?"

Abu Bakr replied, "How can Ibn Abi Quhafa (Abu Bakr) dare to lead the prayer in the presence of Allah's Apostle?" Then Allah's Apostle said, "Why did you clap so much? If something happens to anyone during his prayer he should say Subhan Allah. If he says so he will be attended to, for clapping is for women."

Volume 1, Book 11, Number 653:

Narrated Malik bin Huwairth:

We went to the Prophet and we were all young men and stayed with him for about twenty nights. The Prophet was very merciful. He said, "When you return home, impart religious teachings to your families and tell them to offer perfectly such and such a prayer at such and such a time and such and such a prayer at such and such a time. And al the time of the prayer one of you should pronounce the Adhan and the oldest of you should lead the prayer."

Volume 1, Book 11, Number 654:

Narrated Itban bin Malik Al-Ansari:

The Prophet (came to my house and) asked permission for entering and I allowed him. He asked, "Where do you like me to pray in your house?" I pointed to a place which I liked. He stood up for prayer and we aligned behind him and he finished the prayer with Taslim and we did the same.

Volume 1, Book 11, Number 655:

Narrated 'Ubaid-Ullah Ibn 'Abdullah bin 'Utba:

I went to 'Aisha and asked her to describe to me the illness of Allah's Apostle. 'Aisha said, "Yes. The Prophet became seriously ill and asked whether the people had prayed. We replied, 'No. O Allah's Apostle! They are waiting for you.' He added, 'Put water for me in a trough." 'Aisha added, "We did so. He took a bath and tried to get up but fainted. When he recovered, he again asked whether the people had prayed. We said, 'No, they are waiting for you. O Allah's Apostle,' He again said, 'Put water in a trough for me.' He sat down and took a bath and tried to get up but fainted again. Then he recovered and said, 'Have the people prayed?' We replied, 'No, they are waiting for you. O Allah's Apostle.' He said, 'Put water for me in the trough.' Then he sat down and washed himself and tried to get up but he fainted. When he recovered, he asked, 'Have the people prayed?' We said, 'No, they are waiting for you. O Allah's Apostle! The people were in the mosque waiting for the Prophet for the 'Isha prayer. The Prophet sent for Abu Bakr to lead the people in the prayer. The messenger went to Abu Bakr and said, 'Allah's Apostle orders you to lead the people in the prayer.' Abu Bakr was a soft-hearted man, so he asked 'Umar to lead the prayer but 'Umar replied, 'You are more rightful.' So Abu Bakr led the prayer in those days. When the Prophet felt a bit better, he came out for the Zuhr prayer with the help of two persons one of whom was Al-'Abbas. while Abu Bakr was leading the people in the prayer. When Abu Bakr saw him he wanted to retreat but the Prophet beckoned him not to do so and asked them to make him sit beside Abu Bakr and they did so. Abu Bakr was following the Prophet (in the prayer) and the people were following Abu Bakr. The Prophet (prayed) sitting."

'Ubaid-Ullah added "I went to 'Abdullah bin 'Abbas and asked him, Shall I tell you what Aisha has told me about the fatal illness of the Prophet?' Ibn 'Abbas said, 'Go ahead. I told him her narration and he did not deny anything of it but asked whether 'Aisha told me the name of the second person (who helped the Prophet) along with Al-Abbas. I said. 'No.' He said, 'He was 'Ali (Ibn Abi Talib).

Volume 1, Book 11, Number 656:

Narrated Aisha:

the mother of the believers: Allah's Apostle during his illness prayed at his house while sitting whereas some people prayed behind him standing. The Prophet beckoned them to sit down. On completion of the prayer, he said, 'The Imam is to be followed: bow when he bows, raise up your heads (stand erect) when he raises his head and when he says, 'Sami a-l-lahu liman-hamida ' (Allah heard those who sent praises to Him) say then 'Rabbana wa laka-l-hamd' (O our Lord! All the praises are for You), and if he prays sitting then pray sitting."

Volume 1, Book 11, Number 657:

Narrated Anas bin Malik:

Once Allah's Apostle rode a horse and fell down and the right side (of his body) was injured. He offered one of the prayers while sitting and we also prayed behind him sitting. When he completed the prayer, he said, "The Imam is to be followed. Pray standing if he prays standing and bow when he bows; rise when he rises; and if he says, 'Sami a-l-lahu-liman hamida, say then, 'Rabbana wa Lakal-hamd' and pray standing if he prays standing and pray sitting (all of you) if he prays sitting."

Humaid said: The saying of the Prophet "Pray sitting, if he (Imam) prays sitting" was said in his former illness (during his early life) but the Prophet prayed sitting afterwards (in the last illness) and the people were praying standing behind him and the Prophet did not order them to sit. We should follow the latest actions of the Prophet.

Volume 1, Book 11, Number 658:

Narrated Al-Bara:

(and he was not a liar) When Allah's Apostle said, "Sami a-l-lahu Liman hamida " none of us bent his back (for prostrations) till the Prophet prostrated and then we would prostrate after him.

Volume 1, Book 11, Number 659:

Narrated Abu Ishaq:

as above.

Volume 1, Book 11, Number 660:

Narrated Abu Huraira:

The Prophet said, "Isn't he who raises his head before the Imam afraid that Allah may transform his head into that of a donkey or his figure (face) into that of a donkey?"

Volume 1, Book 11, Number 661:

Narrated Ibn 'Umar:

When the earliest emigrants came to Al-'Usba a place in Quba', before the arrival of the Prophet-Salim, the slave of Abu Hudhaifa, who knew the Qur'an more than the others used to lead them in prayer.

Volume 1, Book 11, Number 662,

Narrated Anas,

The Prophet said, "Listen and obey (your chief) even if an Ethiopian whose head is like a raisin were made your chief."

Volume 1, Book 11, Number 663,

Narrated Abu Huraira,

Allah's Apostle said, "If the Imam leads the prayer correctly then he and you will receive the rewards but if he makes a mistake (in the prayer) then you will receive the reward for the prayer and the sin will be his."

Volume 1, Book 11, Number 664,

Narrated Anas bin Malik,

The Prophet said to Abu-Dhar, "Listen and obey (your chief) even if he is an Ethiopian with a head like a raisin."

Volume 1, Book 11, Number 665,

Narrated Ibn 'Abbas,

Once I passed the night in the house of my aunt Maimuna. Allah's Apostle offered the 'Isha' prayer and then came to the house and offered four Rakat an slept. Later on, he woke up and stood for the prayer and I stood on his left side. He drew me to his right and prayed five Rakat and then two. He then slept till I heard him snoring (or heard his breath sounds). Afterwards he went out for the morning prayer.

Volume 1, Book 11, Number 666,

Narrated Ibn 'Abbas,

One night I slept at the house of (my aunt) Maimuna and the Prophet was there on that night. He performed ablution and stood up for the prayer. I joined him and stood on his left side but he drew me to his right and prayed thirteen Rakat and then slept till I heard his breath sounds. And whenever he slept, he used to breathe with audible sounds. The Mu'adhdhin came to the Prophet and he went out and prayed the morning prayer) without repeating the ablution.

Volume 1, Book 11, Number 667:

Narrated Ibn 'Abbas:

Once I passed the night in the house of my aunt Maimuna. The Prophet stood for the night prayer and I joined him and stood on his left side but he drew me to his right by holding me by the head.

Volume 1, Book 11, Number 668:

Narrated Mu'adh bin Jabal:

I used to pray the 'Isha prayer with the Prophet and then go to lead my people in the prayer.

Volume 1, Book 11, Number 669:

Narrated 'Amr:

Jabir bin 'Abdullah said, "Mu'adh bin Jabal used to pray with the Prophet and then go to lead his people in prayer Once he led the 'Isha' prayer and recited Surat "Al-Baqra." Somebody left the prayer and Mu'adh criticized him. The news reached the Prophet and he said to Mu'adh, 'You are putting the people to trial,' and repeated it thrice (or said something similar) and ordered him to recite two medium Suras of Mufassal." ('Amr said that he had forgotten the names of those Suras).

Volume 1, Book 11, Number 670:

Narrated Abu Mas'ud:

A man came and said, "O Allah's Apostle! By Allah, I keep away from the morning prayer only because So and so prolongs the prayer when he leads us in it." The narrator said, "I never saw Allah's Apostle more furious in giving advice than he was at that time. He then said, "Some of you make people dislike good deeds (the prayer). So whoever among you leads the people in prayer should shorten it because among them are the weak, the old and the needy."

Volume 1, Book 11, Number 671:

Narrated Abu Huraira:

Allah's Apostle said, "If anyone of you leads the people in the prayer, he should shorten it for amongst them are the weak, the sick and the old; and if anyone among your prays alone then he may prolong (the prayer) as much as he wishes. "

Volume 1, Book 11, Number 672:

Narrated Abu Mas'ud:

A man came and said, "O Allah's Apostle! I keep away from the morning prayer because so-and-so (Imam) prolongs it too much." Allah's Apostle became furious and I had never seen him more furious than he was on that day. The Prophet said, "O people! Some of you make others dislike the prayer, so whoever becomes an Imam he should shorten the prayer, as behind him are the weak, the old and the needy."

Volume 1, Book 11, Number 673:

Narrated Jabir bin 'Abdullah Al-Ansari:

Once a man was driving two Nadihas (camels used for agricultural purposes) and night had fallen. He found Mu'adh praying so he made his camel kneel and joined Mu'adh in the prayer. The latter recited Surat 'AlBaqara" or Surat "An-Nisa", (so) the man left the prayer and went away. When he came to know that Mu'adh had criticized him, he went to the Prophet, and complained against Mu'adh. The Prophet said thrice, "O Mu'adh ! Are you putting the people to trial?" It would have been better if you had recited "Sabbih Isma Rabbika-l-a-la (87)", Wash-Shamsi wadu-haha (91)", or "Wal-laili Idha yaghsha (92)", for the old, the weak and the needy pray behind you." Jabir said that Mu'adh recited Sura Al-Baqara in the 'Isha' prayer.

Volume 1, Book 11, Number 674:

Narrated Anas:

The Prophet used to pray a short prayer (in congregation) but used to offer it in a perfect manner.

Volume 1, Book 11, Number 675:

Narrated 'Abdullah bin 'Abi Qatada:

My father said, "The Prophet said, 'When I stand for prayer, I intend to prolong it but on hearing the cries of a child, I cut it short, as I dislike to trouble the child's mother.' "

Volume 1, Book 11, Number 676:

Narrated Anas bin Malik:

I never prayed behind any Imam a prayer lighter and more perfect than that behind the Prophet and he used to cut short the prayer whenever he heard the cries of a child lest he should put the child's mother to trial.

Volume 1, Book 11, Number 677:

Narrated Anas bin Malik:

The Prophet said, "When I start the prayer I intend to prolong it, but on hearing the cries of a child, I cut short the prayer because I know that the cries of the child will incite its mother's passions."

Volume 1, Book 11, Number 678:

Narrated Anas bin Malik:

The Prophet, said, "Whenever I start the prayer I intend to prolong it, but on hearing the cries of a child, I cut short the prayer because I know that the cries of the child will incite its mother's passions."

Volume 1, Book 11, Number 679:

Narrated Jabir bin 'Abdullah:

Mu'adh used to pray with the Prophet and then go and lead his people (tribe) in the prayer.

Volume 1, Book 11, Number 680:

Narrated 'Aisha:

When the Prophet, became ill in his fatal illness, Someone came to inform him about the prayer, and the Prophet told him to tell Abu Bakr to lead the people in the prayer. I said, "Abu Bakr is a soft-hearted man and if he stands for the prayer in your place, he would weep and would not be able to recite the Qur'an." The Prophet said, "Tell Abu Bakr to lead the prayer." I said the same as before. He (repeated the same order and) on the third or the fourth time he said, "You are the companions of Joseph. Tell Abu Bakr to lead the prayer." So Abu Bakr led the prayer and meanwhile the Prophet felt better and came out with the help of two men; as if I see him just now dragging his feet on the ground. When Abu Bakr saw him, he tried to retreat but the Prophet beckoned him to carry on. Abu Bakr retreated a bit and the Prophet sat on his (left) side. Abu Bakr was repeating the Takbir (Allahu Akbar) of Allah's Apostle for the people to hear.

Volume 1, Book 11, Number 681:

Narrated 'Aisha:

When Allah's Apostle became seriously ill, Bilal came to him for the prayer. He said, "Tell Abu Bakr to lead the people in the prayer." I said, "O Allah's Apostle! Abu Bakr is a soft-hearted man and if he stands in your place, he would not be able to make the people hear him. Will you order 'Umar (to lead the prayer)?" The Prophet said, "Tell Abu Bakr to lead the people in the prayer." Then I said to Hafsa, "Tell him, Abu i Bakr is a soft-hearted man and if he stands in his place, he would not be able to make the people hear him. Would you order 'Umar to lead the prayer?' " Hafsa did so. The Prophet said, "Verily you are the companions of Joseph. Tell Abu Bakr to lead the people in the prayer." So Abu- Bakr stood for the prayer. In the meantime Allah's Apostle felt better and came out with the help of two persons and both of his legs were dragging on the ground till he entered the mosque. When Abu Bakr heard him coming, he tried to retreat but Allah's Apostle beckoned him to carry on. The Prophet sat on his left side. Abu Bakr was praying while standing and Allah's Apostle was leading the prayer while sitting. Abu Bakr was following the Prophet and the people were following Abu Bakr (in the prayer).

Volume 1, Book 11, Number 682.

Narrated Abu Huraira.

Once Allah's Apostle prayed two Rakat (instead of four) and finished his prayer. Dhu-l-yadain asked him whether the prayer had been reduced or whether he had forgotten. Allah's Apostle asked the people whether Dhu-l-yadain was telling the truth. The people replied in the affirmative. Then Allah's Apostle stood up, offered the remaining two Rakat and then finished his prayer with Taslim and then said, "Allahu Akbar." He followed it with two prostrations like ordinary prostrations or a bit longer.

Volume 1, Book 11, Number 683.

Narrated Abu Huraira.

The Prophet prayed two Rakat of Zuhr prayer (instead of four) and he was told that he had prayed two Rakat only. Then he prayed two more Rakat and finished them with the Taslim followed by two prostrations.

Volume 1, Book 11, Number 684.

Narrated 'Aisha.

the mother of the faithful believers. Allah's Apostle in his last illness said, "Tell Abu Bakr to lead the people in the prayer." I said, "If Abu Bakr stood in your place, he would not be able to make the people hear him owing to his weeping. So please order 'Umar to lead the prayer." He said, "Tell Abu Bakr to lead the people in the prayer." I said to Hafsa, "Say to him, 'Abu Bakr is a softhearted man and if he stood in your place he would not be able to make the people hear him owing to his weeping. So order 'Umar to lead the people in the prayer.' " Hafsa did so but Allah's Apostle said, "Keep quiet. Verily you are the companions of (Prophet) Joseph. Tell Abu Bakr to lead the people in the prayer." Hafsa said to me, "I never got any good from you."

Volume 1, Book 11, Number 685:

Narrated An-Nu'man bin 'Bashir:

The Prophet said, "Straighten your rows or Allah will alter your faces."

Volume 1, Book 11, Number 686:

Narrated Anas:

The Prophet said, "Straighten your rows, for I see you from behind my back.'

Volume 1, Book 11, Number 687:

Narrated Anas bin Malik:

Once the Iqama was pronounced and Allah's Apostle faced us and said, "Straighten your rows and stand closer together, for I see you from behind my back.'

Volume 1, Book 11, Number 688:

Narrated Abu Huraira:

The Prophet said, "Martyrs are those who die because of drowning, plague, an abdominal disease, or of being buried alive by a falling building." And then he added, "If the people knew the Reward for the Zuhr prayer in its early time, they would race for it. If they knew the reward for the 'Isha' and the Fajr prayers in congregation, they would join them even if they had to crawl. If they knew the reward for the first row, they would draw lots for it."

Volume 1, Book 11, Number 689:

Narrated Abu Huraira:

The Prophet said, "The Imam is (appointed) to be followed. So do not differ from him, bow when he bows, and say, "Rabbana-lakal hamd" if he says "Sami'a-l-lahu Liman hamida"; and if he prostrates, prostrate (after him), and if he prays sitting, pray sitting all together, and straighten the rows for the prayer, as the straightening of the rows is amongst those things which make your prayer a correct and perfect one. (See Hadith No. 657).

Volume 1, Book 11, Number 690:

Narrated Anas bin Malik:

The Prophet said, "Straighten your rows as the straightening of rows is essential for a perfect and correct prayer. "

Volume 1, Book 11, Number 691:

Narrated Anas bin Malik:

I arrived at Medina and was asked whether I found any change since the days of Allah's Apostle. I said, "I have not found any change except that you do not stand in alignment in your prayers."

Volume 1, Book 11, Number 692:

Narrated Anas bin Malik:

The Prophet said, "Straighten your rows for I see you from behind my back." Anas added, "Everyone of us used to put his shoulder with the shoulder of his companion and his foot with the foot of his companion."

Volume 1, Book 11, Number 693:

Narrated Ibn 'Abbas:

I prayed with the Prophet one night and stood on his left side. Allah's Apostle caught hold of my head from behind and drew me to his right and then offered the prayer and slept. Later the Mu'adhdhin came and the Prophet stood up for prayer without performing ablution.

Volume 1, Book 11, Number 694:

Narrated Anas bin Malik:

One night an orphan and I offered the prayers behind the Prophet in my house and my mother (Um Sulaim) was standing behind us (by herself forming a row).

Volume 1, Book 11, Number 695:

Narrated Ibn 'Abbas:

One night I stood to the left of the Prophet in the prayer but he caught hold of me by the hand or by the shoulder (arm) till he made me stand on his right and beckoned with his hand (for me) to go from behind (him). (Al-Kashmaihani-Fateh al-Bari).

Volume 1, Book 11, Number 696:

Narrated 'Aisha:

Allah's Apostle used to pray in his room at night. As the wall of the room was LOW, the people saw him and some of them stood up to follow him in the prayer. In the morning they spread the news. The following night the Prophet stood for the prayer and the people followed him. This went on for two or three nights. Thereupon Allah's Apostle did not stand for the prayer the following night, and did not come out. In the morning, the people asked him about it. He replied, that he way afraid that the night prayer might become compulsory.

Volume 1, Book 11, Number 697:

Narrated 'Aisha:

The Prophet had a mat which he used to spread during the day and use as a curtain at night. So a number of people gathered at night facing it and prayed behind him.

Volume 1, Book 11, Number 698:

Narrated Zaid bin Thabit:

Allah's Apostle made a small room in the month of Ramadan (Sa'id said, "I think that Zaid bin Thabit said that it was made of a mat") and he prayed there for a few nights, and so some of his companions prayed behind him. When he came to know about it, he kept on sitting. In the morning, he went out to them and said, "I have seen and understood what you did. You should pray in your houses, for the best prayer of a person is that which he prays in his house except the compulsory prayers."

Book 12: Characteristics of Prayer

Volume 1, Book 12, Number 699:

Narrated Anas bin Malik Al-Ansari:

Allah's Apostle rode a horse and fell down and the right side of his body was injured. On that day he prayed one of the prayers sitting and we also prayed behind him sitting. When the Prophet finished the prayer with Taslim, he said, "The Imam is to be followed and if he prays standing then pray standing, and bow when he bows, and raise your heads when he raises his head; prostrate when he prostrates; and if he says "Sami'a-l-lahu Liman hamida", you should say, "Rabbana wa-laka-l hamd.:

Volume 1, Book 12, Number 700:

Narrated Anas bin Malik:

Allah's Apostle fell from a horse and got injured so he led the prayer sitting and we also prayed sitting. When he completed the prayer he said, "The Imam is to be followed; if he says Takbir then say Takbir, bow if he bows; raise your heads when he raises his head, when he says, 'Sami' a-l-lahu Liman hamida say, 'Rabbana laka-l-hamd', and prostrate when he prostrates."

Volume 1, Book 12, Number 701:

Narrated Abu Huraira:

The Prophet said, "The Imam is to be followed. Say the Takbir when he says it; bow if he bows; if he says 'Sami a-l-lahu Liman hamida', say, ' Rabbana wa-laka-l-hamd', prostrate if he prostrates and pray sitting altogether if he prays sitting."

Volume 1, Book 12, Number 702:

Narrated Salim bin 'Abdullah:

My father said, "Allah's Apostle used to raise both his hands up to the level of his shoulders when opening the prayer; and on saying the Takbir for bowing. And on raising his head from bowing he used to do the same and then say "Sami a-l-lahu Liman hamida, Rabbana walaka-l-hamd." And he did not do that (i.e. raising his hands) in prostrations.

Volume 1, Book 12, Number 703:

Narrated 'Abdullah bin 'Umar:

I saw that whenever Allah's Apostle stood for the prayer, he used to raise both his hands up to the shoulders, and used to do the same on saying the Takbir for bowing and on raising his head from it and used to say, "Sami a-1-lahu Liman hamida". But he did not do that (i.e. raising his hands) in prostrations.

Volume 1, Book 12, Number 704:

Narrated Abu Qilaba:

I saw Malik bin Huwairith saying Takbir and raising both his hands (on starting the prayers and raising his hands on bowing and also on raising his head after bowing. Malik bin Huwairith said, "Allah's Apostle did the same."

Volume 1, Book 12, Number 705:

Narrated 'Abdullah bin 'Umar:

I saw Allah's Apostle opening the prayer with the Takbir and raising his hands to the level of his shoulders at the time of saying the Takbir, and on saying the Takbir for bowing he did the same; and when he said, "Sami a-1-lahu Liman hamida ", he did the same and then said, "Rabbana wa laka-1-hamd." But he did not do the same on prostrating and on lifting the head from it."

Volume 1, Book 12, Number 706:

Narrated Nafi':

Whenever Ibn 'Umar started the prayer with Takbir, he used to raise his hands: whenever he bowed, he used to raise his hands (before bowing) and also used to raise his hands on saying, "Sami a-1-lahu Liman hamida", and he used to do the same on rising from the second Rak'a (for the 3rd Rak'a). Ibn 'Umar said: "The Prophet used to do the same."

Volume 1, Book 12, Number 707:

Narrated Sahl bin Sa'd:

The people were ordered to place the right hand on the left forearm in the prayer. Abu Hazim said, "I knew that the order was from the Prophet ."

Volume 1, Book 12, Number 708:

Narrated Abu Huraira:

Allah's Apostle said, "You see me facing the Qibla; but, by Allah, nothing is hidden from me regarding your bowing and submissiveness and I see you from behind my back."

Volume 1, Book 12, Number 709:

Narrated Anas bin Malik:

The Prophet said, "Perform the bowing and the prostrations properly. By Allah, I see you from behind me (or from behind my back) when you bow or prostrate."

Volume 1, Book 12, Number 710:

Narrated Anas bin Malik:

The Prophet, Abu Bakr and 'Umar used to start the prayer with "Al-hamdu lil-lahi Rabbil-'ala-min (All praises are for Allah the Lord of the Worlds)."

Volume 1, Book 12, Number 711:

Narrated Abu Huraira:

Allah's Apostle used to keep silent between the Takbir and the recitation of Qur'an and that interval of silence used to be a short one. I said to the Prophet "May my parents be sacrificed for you! What do you say in the pause between Takbir and recitation?" The Prophet said, "I say, 'Allahumma, ba'id baini wa baina khatayaya kama ba'adta baina-1-mashriqi wa-1-maghrib. Allahumma, naqqim min khatayaya kama yunaqqa-ththawbu-1-abyadu mina-ddanas. Allahumma, ighsil khatayaya bil-ma'i wa-th-thalji wal-barad (O Allah! Set me apart from my sins (faults) as the East and West are set apart from each other and clean me from sins as a white garment is cleaned of dirt (after thorough washing). O Allah! Wash off my sins with water, snow and hail.)"

Volume 1, Book 12, Number 712:

Narrated Asma' bint Abi Bakr:

The Prophet once offered the eclipse prayer. He stood for a long time and then did a prolonged bowing. He stood up straight again and kept on standing for a long time, then bowed a long bowing and then stood up straight and then prostrated a prolonged prostration and then lifted his head and prostrated a prolonged prostration. And then he stood up for a long time and then did a prolonged bowing and then stood up straight again and kept on standing for a long time. Then he bowed a long bowing and then stood up straight and then prostrated a prolonged prostration and then lifted his head and went for a prolonged prostration. On completion o the prayer, he said, "Paradise became s near to me that if I had dared, I would have plucked one of its bunches for you and Hell became so near to me that said, 'O my Lord will I be among those people?' Then suddenly I saw a woman and a cat was lacerating her with it claws. On inquiring, it was said that the woman had imprisoned the cat till it died of starvation and she neither fed it no freed it so that it could feed itself."

Volume 1, Book 12, Number 713:

Narrated Abu Ma'mar:

We asked Khabbab whether Allah's Apostle used to recite (the Qur'an) in the Zuhr and the 'Asr prayers. He replied in the affirmative. We said, "How did you come to know about it?" He said, "By the movement of his beard."

Volume 1, Book 12, Number 714:

Narrated Al-Bara:

(And Al-Bara was not a liar) Whenever we offered prayer with the Prophet and he raised his head from the bowing, we used to remain standing till we saw him prostrating .

Volume 1, Book 12, Number 715:

Narrated 'Abdullah bin 'Abbas:

Once solar eclipse occurred during the lifetime of Allah's Apostle. He offered the eclipse prayer. His companions asked, "O Allah's Apostle! We saw you trying to take something while standing at your place and then we saw you retreating." The Prophet said, "I was shown Paradise and wanted to have a bunch of fruit from it. Had I taken it, you would have eaten from it as long as the world re-mains."

Volume 1, Book 12, Number 716:

Narrated Anas bin Malik:

The Prophet led us in prayer and then went up to the pulpit and beckoned with both hands to-wards the Qibla of the mosque and then said, "When I started leading you in prayer, I saw the dis-play of Paradise and Hell on the wall of the mosque (facing the Qibla). I never saw good and bad as I have seen today." He repeated the last statement thrice.

Volume 1, Book 12, Number 717:

Narrated Anas bin Malik:

The Prophet said, "What is wrong with those people who look towards the sky during the prayer?" His talk grew stern while delivering this speech and he said, "They should stop (looking towards the sky during the prayer); otherwise their eye-sight would be taken away."

Volume 1, Book 12, Number 718:

Narrated 'Aisha:

I asked Allah's Apostle about looking hither and thither in prayer. He replied, "It is a way of stealing by which Satan takes away (a portion) from the prayer of a person."

Volume 1, Book 12, Number 719:

Narrated 'Aisha:

Once the Prophet prayed on a Khamisa with marks on it and said, "The marks on it diverted my attention, take this Khamisa to Abu Jahm and bring an Inbijaniya (from him.)"

Volume 1, Book 12, Number 720:

Narrated Ibn 'Umar:

The Prophet saw expectoration in the direction of the Qibla of the mosque while he was leading the prayer, and scratched it off. After finishing the prayer, he said, "Whenever any of you is in prayer he should know that Allah is in front of him. So none should spit in front of him in the prayer."

Volume 1, Book 12, Number 721:

Narrated Anas:

While the Muslims were offering the Fajr prayer, Allah's Apostle suddenly appeared before them by living the curtain of the dwelling place of 'Aisha, looked towards the Muslims who were standing in rows. He smiled with pleasure. Abu Bakr started retreating to join the row on the assumption that the Prophet wanted to come out for the prayer The Muslims intended to leave the prayer (and were on the verge of being put to trial), but the Prophet beckoned them to complete their prayer and then he let the curtain fall. He died in the last hours of that day.

Volume 1, Book 12, Number 722:

Narrated Jabir bin Samura:

The People of Kufa complained against Sa'd to 'Umar and the latter dismissed him and appointed 'Ammar as their chief . They lodged many complaints against Sa'd and even they alleged that he did not pray properly. 'Umar sent for him and said, "O Aba Ishaq! These people claim that you do not pray properly." Abu Ishaq said, "By Allah, I used to pray with them a prayer similar to that of Allah's Apostle and I never reduced anything of it. I used to prolong the first two Rakat of 'Isha prayer and shorten the last two Rakat." 'Umar said, "O Aba Ishaq, this was what I thought about you." And then he sent one or more persons with him to Kufa so as to ask the people about him. So they went there and did not leave any mosque without asking about him. All the people praised him till they came to the mosque of the tribe of Bani 'Abs; one of the men called Usama bin Qatada with a surname of Aba Sa'da stood up and said, "As you have put us under an oath; I am bound to tell you that Sa'd never went himself with the army and never distributed (the war booty) equally and never did justice in legal verdicts." (On hearing it) Sa'd said, "I pray to Allah for three things. O Allah! If this slave of yours is a liar and got up for showing off, give him a long life, increase his poverty and put him to trials." (And so it happened). Later on when that person was asked how he was, he used to reply that he was an old man in trial as the result of Sa'd's curse. 'Abdul Malik, the sub narrator, said that he had seen him afterwards and his eyebrows were over-hanging his eyes owing to old age and he used to tease and assault the small girls in the way.

Volume 1, Book 12, Number 723:

Narrated 'Ubada bin As-Samit:

Allah's Apostle said, "Whoever does not recite Al-Fatiha in his prayer, his prayer is invalid."

Volume 1, Book 12, Number 724:

Narrated Abu Huraira:

Allah's Apostle entered the mosque and a person followed him. The man prayed and went to the Prophet and greeted him. The Prophet returned the greeting and said to him, "Go back and pray, for you have not prayed." The man went back prayed in the same way as before, returned and greeted the Prophet who said, "Go back and pray, for you have not prayed." This happened thrice. The man said, "By Him Who sent you with the Truth, I cannot offer the prayer in a better way than this. Please, teach me how to pray." The Prophet said, "When you stand for Prayer say Takbir and then recite from the Holy Qur'an (of what you know by heart) and then bow till you feel at ease. Then raise your head and stand up straight, then prostrate till you feel at ease during your prostration, then sit with calmness till you feel at ease (do not hurry) and do the same in all your prayers

Volume 1, Book 12, Number 725:

Narrated Jabir bin Samura:

Sa'd said, "I used to pray with them a prayer similar to that of Allah's Apostle (the prayer of Zuhr and 'Asr) reducing nothing from them. I used to prolong the first two Rakat and shorten the last two Rak'at." 'Umar said to Sa'd "This was what we thought about you."

Volume 1, Book 12, Number 726:

Narrated 'Abdullah bin Abi Qatada:

My father said, "The Prophet in Zuhr prayers used to recite Al-Fatiha along with two other Suras in the first two Rakat: a long one in the first Rak'a and a shorter (Sura) in the second, and at times the verses were audible. In the 'Asr prayer the Prophet used to recite Al-Fatiha and two more Suras in the first two Rakat and used to prolong the first Rak'a. And he used to prolong the first Rak'a of the Fajr prayer and shorten the second.

Volume 1, Book 12, Number 727:

Narrated Abu Ma'mar:

I asked Khabbab whether the Prophet used to recite the Qur'an in the Zuhr and the 'Asr prayers. He replied in the affirmative. We said, "How did you come to know that?" He said, "From the movement of his beard."

Volume 1, Book 12, Number 728:

Narrated Abu Ma'mar:

I asked Khabbab bin Al-Art whether the Prophet used to recite the Qur'an in the Zuhr and the 'Asr prayers. He replied in the affirmative. I said, "How did you come to know that?" He replied, "From the movement of his beard."

Volume 1, Book 12, Number 729:

Narrated 'Abdullah bin Abi Qatada:

My father said, "The Prophet used to recite Al-Fatiha along with another Sura in the first two Rakat of the Zuhr and the 'Asr prayers and at times a t verse or so was audible to us."

Volume 1, Book 12, Number 730:

Narrated Ibn 'Abbas:

(My mother) Umu-l-Fadl heard me reciting "Wal Mursalati 'Urfan" (77) and said, "O my son! By Allah, your recitation made me remember that it was the last Sura I heard from Allah's Apostle. He recited it in the Maghrib prayer. "

Volume 1, Book 12, Number 731:

Narrated Marwan bin Al-Hakam:

Zaid bin Thabit said to me, "Why do you recite very short S&ras in the Maghrib prayer while I heard the Prophet reciting the longer of the two long Suras?"

Volume 1, Book 12, Number 732:

Narrated Jubair bin Mut'im:

My father said, "I heard Allah's Apostle reciting "At-Tur" (52) in the Maghrib prayer."

Volume 1, Book 12, Number 733:

Narrated Abu Rafi:

I offered the 'Isha' prayer behind Abu Huraira and he recited, "Idha-s-Sama'u-n-Shaqqat" (84) and prostrated. On my inquiring, he said, "I prostrated behind Abu-l-Qasim (the Prophet) (when he recited that Sura) and I will go on doing it till I meet him."

Volume 1, Book 12, Number 734:

Narrated Al-Bara:

The Prophet was on a journey and recited in one of the first two Rakat of the 'Isha' prayer "Wat-tini waz-zaituni." (95)

Volume 1, Book 12, Number 735:

Narrated Abu Rafi':

Once I prayed the 'Isha' prayer with Abu Huraira and he recited, "Idha-s-Sama' u-nShaqqat" (84) and prostrated. I said, "What is that?" He said, "I prostrated behind Abu-l-Qasim, (the Prophet) (when he recited that Sura) and I will go on doing it till I meet him."

Volume 1, Book 12, Number 736:

Narrated Al-Bara:

I heard the Prophet reciting wat-tini wazzaituni" (95) in the 'Isha' prayer, and I never heard a sweeter voice or a better way of recitation than that of the Prophet.

Volume 1, Book 12, Number 737:

Narrated Jabir bin Samura:

'Umar said to Sa'd, "The people complained against you in everything, even in prayer." Sa'd replied, "Really I used to prolong the first two Rakat and shorten the last two and I will never shorten the prayer in which I follow Allah's Apostle." 'Umar said, "You are telling the truth and that is what I think a tout you."

Volume 1, Book 12, Number 738:

Narrated Saiyar bin Salama:

My father and I went to Abu Barza-al-Aslami to ask him about the stated times for the prayers. He replied, "The Prophet used to offer the Zuhr prayer when the sun just declined from its highest position at noon; the 'Asr at a time when if a man went to the farthest place in Medina (after praying) he would find the sun still hot (bright). (The sub narrator said: I have forgotten what Abu Barza said about the Maghrib prayer). The Prophet never found any harm in delaying the 'Isha' prayer to the first third of the night and he never liked to sleep before it and to talk after it. He used to offer the morning prayer at a time when after finishing it one could recognize the person sitting beside him and used to recite between 60 to 100 verses in one or both the Rakat."

Volume 1, Book 12, Number 739:

Narrated Abu Huraira:

The Qur'an is recited in every prayer and in those prayers in which Allah's Apostle recited aloud for us, we recite aloud in the same prayers for you; and the prayers in which the Prophet recited quietly, we recite quietly. If you recite "Al-Fatiha" only it is sufficient but if you recite something else in addition, it is better.

Volume 1, Book 12, Number 740:

Narrated Ibn 'Abbas:

The Prophet set out with the intention of going to Suq 'Ukaz (market of 'Ukaz) along with some of his companions. At the same time, a barrier was put between the devils and the news of heaven. Fire commenced to be thrown at them. The Devils went to their people, who asked them, "What is wrong with you?" They said, "A barrier has been placed between us and the news of heaven. And fire has been thrown at us." They said, "The thing which has put a barrier between you and the news of heaven must be something which has happened recently. Go eastward and westward and see what has put a barrier between you and the news of heaven." Those who went towards Tuhama came across the Prophet at a place called Nakhla and it was on the way to Suq 'Ukaz and the Prophet was offering the Fajr prayer with his companions. When they heard the Qur'an they listened to it and said, "By Allah, this is the thing which has put a barrier between us and the news of heaven." They went to their people and said, "O our people; verily we have heard a wonderful recital (Qur'an) which shows the true path; we believed in it and would not ascribe partners to our Lord." Allah revealed the following verses to his Prophet (Sura 'Jinn') (72): "Say: It has been revealed to me." And what was revealed to him was the conversation of the Jinns.

Volume 1, Book 12, Number 741:

Narrated Ibn 'Abbas:

The Prophet recited aloud in the prayers in which he was ordered to do so and quietly in the prayers in which he was ordered to do so. "And your Lord is not forgetful." "Verily there was a good example for you in the ways of the Prophet."

Volume 1, Book 12, Number 742:

Narrated Abu Wa'il:

A man came to Ibn Mas'ud and said, "I recited the Mufassal (Suras) at night in one Rak'a." Ibn Mas'ud said, "This recitation is (too quick) like the recitation of poetry. I know the identical Suras which the Prophet used to recite in pairs." Ibn Mas'ud then mentioned 20 Mufassal Suras including two Suras from the family of (i.e. those verses which begin with) AL, HA, MIM (which the Prophet used to recite) in each Rak'a.

Volume 1, Book 12, Number 743:

Narrated 'Abdullah bin Abi Qatada:

My father said, "The Prophet uses to recite Al-Fatiha followed by another Sura in the first two Rakat of the prayer and used to recite only Al-Fatiha in the last two Rakat of the Zuhr prayer. Sometimes a verse or so was audible and he used to prolong the first Rak'a more than the second and used to do the same in the 'Asr and Fajr prayers."

Volume 1, Book 12, Number 744:

Narrated Abu Ma'mar:

We said to Khabbab "Did Allah's Apostle used to recite in Zuhr and 'Asr prayers?" He replied in the affirmative. We said, "How did you come to know about it?" He said, "By the movement of his beard."

Volume 1, Book 12, Number 745:

Narrated 'Abdullah bin Abi Qatada:

My father said, "The Prophet used to recite Al-Fatiha along with another Sura in the first two Rakat of the Zuhr and 'Asr prayers. A verse or so was audible at times and he used to prolong the first Rak'a."

Volume 1, Book 12, Number 746:

Narrated 'Abdullah bin Abi Qatada:

My father said, "The Prophet used to prolong the first Rak'a of the Zuhr prayer and shorten the second one and used to do the same in the Fajr prayer."

Volume 1, Book 12, Number 747:

Narrated Abu Huraira:

The Prophet said, "Say Amin" when the Imam says it and if the Amin of any one of you coincides with that of the angels then all his past sins will be forgiven." Ibn Shihab said, "Allah's Apostle used to Say "Amin."

Volume 1, Book 12, Number 748:

Narrated Abu Huraira:

Allah's Apostle said, "If any one of you says, "Amin" and the angels in the heavens say "Amin" and the former coincides with the latter, all his past sins will be forgiven."

Volume 1, Book 12, Number 749:

Narrated Abu Huraira:

Allah's Apostle said, "Say Amen' when the Imam says "Ghair-il-maghdubi 'alaihim wala-ddal-lin; not the path of those who earn Your Anger (such as Jews) nor of those who go astray (such as Christians); all the past sins of the person whose saying (of Amin) coincides with that of the angels, will be forgiven.

Volume 1, Book 12, Number 750:

Narrated Abu Bakra:

I reached the Prophet in the mosque while he was bowing in prayer and I too bowed before joining the row mentioned it to the Prophet and he said to me, "May Allah increase your love for the good. But do not repeat it again (bowing in that way)."

Volume 1, Book 12, Number 751:

Narrated Imran bin Husain:

I offered the prayer with 'Ali in Basra and he made us remember the prayer which we used to pray with Allah's Apostle. 'Ali said Takbir on each rising and bowing.

Volume 1, Book 12, Number 752:

Narrated Abu Salama:

When Abu Huraira led us in prayer he used to say Takbir on each bowing and rising. On the completion of the prayer he used to say, "My prayer is more similar to the prayer of Allah's Apostle than that of anyone of you."

Volume 1, Book 12, Number 753:

Narrated Mutarrif bin 'Abdullah:

'Imran bin Husain and I offered the prayer behind Ali bin Abi Talib. When 'Ali prostrated, he said the Takbir, when he raised his head, he said the Takbir and when he got up for the third Rak'a he said the Takbir. On completion of the prayer Imran took my hand and said, "This (i.e. 'Ali) made me remember the prayer of Muhammad" Or he said, "He led us in a prayer like that of Muhammad."

Volume 1, Book 12, Number 754:

Narrated 'Ikrima:

I saw a person praying at Muqam-Ibrahim (the place of Abraham by the Ka'ba) and he was saying Takbir on every bowing, rising, standing and sitting. I asked Ibn 'Abbas (about this prayer). He admonished me saying: "Isn't that the prayer of the Prophet?"

Volume 1, Book 12, Number 755:

Narrated 'Ikrima:

I prayed behind a Sheikh at Mecca and he said twenty two Takbirs (during the prayer). I told Ibn 'Abbas that he (i.e. that Sheikh) was foolish. Ibn 'Abbas admonished me and said, "This is the tradition of Abu-l-Qasim." And narrated Abu Huraira: Whenever Allah's Apostle stood for the prayer, he said Takbir on starting the prayer and then on bowing. On rising from bowing he said, "Sami' a-l-lahu li-man hamida," and then while standing straight he used to say, "Rabbana laka-l hamd" (Al-Laith said, "(The Prophet said), 'Walaka-l-hamd'." He used to say Takbir on prostrating and on raising his head from prostration; again he would Say Takbir on prostrating and raising his head. He would then do the same in the whole of the prayer till it was completed. On rising from the second Rak'a (after sitting for At-Tahiyyat), he used to say Takbir.

Volume 1, Book 12, Number 756:

Narrated Mus'ab bin Sa'd:

I offered prayer beside my father and approximated both my hands and placed them in between the knees. My father told me not to do so and said, "We used to do the same but we were forbidden (by the Prophet) to do it and were ordered to place the hands on the knees."

Volume 1, Book 12, Number 757:

Narrated Zaid binWahb:

Hudhaifa saw a person who was not performing the bowing and prostrations perfectly. He said to him, "You have not prayed and if you should die you would die on a religion other than that of Muhammad."

Volume 1, Book 12, Number 758:

Narrated Al-Bara:

The bowing, the prostration the sitting in between the two prostrations and the standing after the bowing of the Prophet but not Qiyam (standing in the prayer) and Qu'ud (sitting in the prayer) used to be approximately equal (in duration).

Volume 1, Book 12, Number 759:

Narrated Abu Huraira:

Once the Prophet entered the mosque, a man came in, offered the prayer and greeted the Prophet. The Prophet returned his greeting and said to him, "Go back and pray again for you have not prayed." The man offered the prayer again, came back and greeted the Prophet. He said to him thrice, "Go back and pray again for you have not prayed." The man said, "By Him Who has sent you with the truth! I do not know a better way of praying. Kindly teach Me how to pray." He said, "When you stand for the prayer, say Takbir and then recite from the Qur'an what you know and then bow with calmness till you feel at ease, then rise from bowing till you stand straight. Afterwards prostrate calmly till you feel at ease and then raise (your head) and sit with Calmness till you feel at ease and then prostrate with calmness till you feel at ease in prostration and do the same in the whole of your prayer."

Volume 1, Book 12, Number 760:

Narrated 'Aisha:

The Prophet used to say in his bowing and prostrations, "Subhanaka-Allahumma Rabbana wa-bi-hamdika Allahumma-ighfirli.' (I honor Allah from all what (unsuitable things) is ascribed to Him. O Allah Our Lord! And all the praises are for You. O Allah! Forgive me)."

Volume 1, Book 12, Number 761:

Narrated Abu Huraira:

When the Prophet said, "Sami' a-l-lahu Liman hamida," (Allah heard those who sent praises to Him), he would say, "Rabbana wa-laka-l-hamd." On bowing and raising his head from it the Prophet used to say Takbir. He also used to say Takbir on rising after the two prostrations. (See Hadith No. 656).

Volume 1, Book 12, Number 762:

Narrated Abu Huraira:

Allah's Apostle said, "When the Imam says, "Sami' a-l-lahu Liman hamida," you should say, "Allahumma Rabbana laka-l-hamd." And if the saying of any one of you coincides with that of the angels, all his past sins will be forgiven."

Volume 1, Book 12, Number 763:

Narrated Anas:

The Qunut used to be recited in the Maghrib and the Fajr prayers.

Volume 1, Book 12, Number 764:

Narrated Rifa'a bin Rafi AzZuraqi:

One day we were praying behind the Prophet. When he raised his head from bowing, he said, "Sami'a-l-lahu Liman hamida." A man behind him said, "Rabbana walaka-l hamd hamdan Kathiran taiyiban mubarakan fihi" (O our Lord! All the praises are for You, many good and blessed praises). When the Prophet completed the prayer, he asked, "Who has said these words?" The man replied, "I." The Prophet said, "I saw over thirty angels competing to write it first." Prophet rose (from bowing) and stood straight till all the vertebrae of his spinal column came to a natural position.

Volume 1, Book 12, Number 765:

Narrated Thabit:

Anas used to demonstrate to us the prayer of the Prophet and while demonstrating, he used to raise his head from bowing and stand so long that we would say that he had forgotten (the prostration).

Volume 1, Book 12, Number 766:

Narrated Al-Bara':

The bowing, the prostrations, the period of standing after bowing and the interval between the two prostrations of the Prophet used to be equal in duration .

Volume 1, Book 12, Number 767:

Narrated Aiyub:

Abu Qilaba said, "Malik bin Huwairith used to demonstrate to us the prayer of the Prophet at times other than that of the compulsory prayers. So (once) he stood up for prayer and performed a perfect Qiyam (standing and reciting from the Holy Qur'an) and then bowed and performed bowing perfectly; then he raised his head and stood straight for a while." Abu Qilaba added, "Malik bin Huwairith in that demonstration prayed like this Sheikh of ours, Abu Yazid." Abu, Yazid used to sit (for a while) on raising his head from the second prostration before getting up.

Volume 1, Book 12, Number 768:

Narrated Abu Bakr bin 'Abdur Rahman Ibn Harith bin Hisham and Abu Salama bin 'Abdur Rahman:

Abu Huraira used to say Takbir in all the prayers, compulsory and optional -- in the month of Ramadan or other months. He used to say Takbir on standing for prayer and on bowing; then he would say, "Salmi'a-l-lahu Liman hamida," and before prostrating he would say "Rabbana walaka-l-hamd." Then he would say Takbir on prostrating and on raising his head from the prostration, then another Takbir on prostrating (for the second time), and on raising his head from the prostration. He also would say the Takbir on standing from the second Rak'a. He used to do the same in every Rak'a till he completed the prayer. On completion of the prayer, he would say, "By Him in Whose Hands my soul is! No doubt my prayer is closer to that of Allah's Apostle than yours, and this was His prayer till he left this world." And Abu Huraira said, "When Allah's Apostle raised his head from (bowing) he used to say "Sami a-l-lahu Liman hamida, Rabbana walakal-hamd." He Would invoke Allah for some people by naming them: "O Allah! Save Al-Walid bin Al-Walid and Salama bin Hisham and 'Aiyash bin Abi Rabi'a and the weak and the helpless people among the faithful believers O Allah! Be hard on the tribe of Mudar and let them suffer from famine years like that of the time of Joseph." In those days the Eastern section of the tribe of Mudar was against the Prophet.

Volume 1, Book 12, Number 769:

Narrated Anas bin Malik:

Allah's Apostle fell from a horse and the right side of his body was injured. We went to enquire about his health meanwhile it was time for the prayer and he led the prayer sitting and we also prayed while sitting. On completion of the prayer he said, "The Imam is to be followed; say Takbir when he says it; bow when he bows; rise when he rises and when he says "Sami'a-1-lahu Liman hamida," say, "Rabbana walaka-lhamd", and prostrate if he prostrates." Sufyan narrated the same from Ma'mar. Ibn Juraij said that his (the Prophet's) right leg had been injured.

Volume 1, Book 12, Number 770:

Narrated Abu Huraira:

The people said, "O Allah's Apostle! Shall we see our Lord on the Day of Resurrection?" He replied, "Do you have any doubt in seeing the full moon on a clear (not cloudy) night?" They replied, "No, O Allah's Apostle!" He said, "Do you have any doubt in seeing the sun when there are no clouds?" They replied in the negative. He said, "You will see Allah (your Lord) in the same way. On the Day of Resurrection, people will be gathered and He will order the people to follow what they used to worship. So some of them will follow the sun, some will follow the moon, and some will follow other deities; and only this nation (Muslims) will be left with its hypocrites. Allah will come to them and say, 'I am Your Lord.' They will say, 'We shall stay in this place till our Lord comes to us and when our Lord will come, we will recognize Him. Then Allah will come to them again and say, 'I am your Lord.' They will say, 'You are our Lord.' Allah will call them, and As-Sirat (a bridge) will be laid across Hell and I (Muhammad) shall be the first amongst the Apostles to cross it with my followers. Nobody except the Apostles will then be able to speak and they will be saying then, 'O Allah! Save us. O Allah Save us.'

There will be hooks like the thorns of Sa'dan in Hell. Have you seen the thorns of Sa'dan?" The people said, "Yes." He said, "These hooks will be like the thorns of Sa'dan but nobody except Allah knows their greatness in size and these will entangle the people according to their deeds; some of them will fall and stay in Hell forever; others will receive punishment (torn into small pieces) and will get out of Hell, till when Allah intends mercy on whomever He likes amongst the people of Hell, He will order the angels to take out of Hell those who worshipped none but Him alone. The angels will take them out by recognizing them from the traces of prostrations, for Allah has forbidden the (Hell) fire to eat away those traces. So they will come out of the Fire, it will eat away from the whole of the human body except the marks of the prostrations. At that time they will come out of the Fire as mere skeletons. The Water of Life will be poured on them and as a result they will grow like the seeds growing on the bank of flowing water. Then when Allah had finished from the Judgments amongst his creations, one man will be left between Hell and Paradise and he will be the last man from the people of Hell to enter paradise. He will be facing Hell, and will say, 'O Allah! Turn my face from the fire as its wind has dried me and its steam has burnt me.' Allah will ask him, "Will you ask for anything more in case this favor is granted to you?' He will say, "No by Your (Honor) Power!" And he will give to his Lord (Allah) what he will of the pledges and the covenants. Allah will then turn his face from the Fire. When he will face Paradise and will see its charm, he will remain quiet as long as Allah will. He then will say, 'O my Lord! Let me go to the gate of Paradise.' Allah will ask him, 'Didn't you give pledges and make covenants (to the effect) that you would not ask for anything more than what you requested at first?' He will say, 'O my Lord! Do not make me the most wretched, amongst Your creatures.' Allah will say, 'If this request is granted, will you then ask for anything else?' He will say, 'No! By Your Power! I shall not ask for anything else.' Then he will give to his Lord what He will of the pledges and the covenants. Allah will then let him go to the gate of Paradise. On reaching then and seeing its life, charm, and pleasure, he will remain quiet as long as Allah wills and then will say, 'O my Lord ! Let me enter Paradise.' Allah will say, May Allah be merciful unto you, O son of Adam! How treacherous you are! Haven't you made covenants and given pledges that you will not ask for anything more that what you have been given?' He will say, 'O my Lord! Do not make me the most wretched amongst Your creatures.' So Allah will laugh and allow him to enter Paradise and will ask him to request as much as he likes. He will do so till all his desires have been fulfilled . Then Allah will say, 'Request more of such and such things.' Allah will remind him and when all his desires and wishes; have been fulfilled, Allah will say "All this is granted to you and a similar amount besides." Abu Said Al-Khudri, said to Abu Huraira, 'Allah's Apostle said, "Allah said, 'That is for you and ten times more like it.' "Abu Huraira said, "I do not remember from Allah's Apostle except (his saying), 'All this is granted to you and a similar amount besides." Abu Sahd said, "I heard him saying, 'That is for you and ten times more the like of it."

Volume 1, Book 12, Number 771:

Narrated 'Abdullah bin Malik bin Buhaina:

Whenever the Prophet used to offer prayer he used to keep arms away (from the body) so that the whiteness of his armpits was visible.

Volume 1, Book 12, Number 772:

Narrated Abu Wail:

Hudhaifa said, "I saw a person not performing his bowing and prostrations perfectly. When he completed the prayer, I told him that he had not prayed." I think that Hudhaifa added (i.e. said to the man), "Had you died, you would have died on a tradition other than that of the Prophet Muhammad."

Volume 1, Book 12, Number 773:

Narrated Ibn 'Abbas:

The Prophet was ordered (by Allah) to prostrate on seven parts and not to tuck up the clothes or hair (while praying). Those parts are: the forehead (along with the tip of nose), both hands, both knees, and (toes of) both feet.

Volume 1, Book 12, Number 774:

Narrated Ibn 'Abbas:

The Prophet said, "We have been ordered to prostrates on seven bones and not to tuck up the clothes or hair."

Volume 1, Book 12, Number 775:

Narrated Al-Bara' bin 'Azib:

(and he was not a liar) We used to pray behind the Prophet and when he said, "Sami' a-l-lahu Li-man hamida", none of us would bend his back (to go for prostration) till the Prophet had placed his, forehead on the ground.

Volume 1, Book 12, Number 776:

Narrated Ibn 'Abbas:

The Prophet said, "I have been ordered to prostrate on seven bones i.e. on the forehead along with the tip of the nose and the Prophet pointed towards his nose, both hands, both knees and the toes of both feet and not to gather the clothes or the hair."

Volume 1, Book 12, Number 777:

Narrated Abu Salama:

Once I went to Abu- Sa'id Al-Khudri and asked him, "Won't you come with us to the date-palm trees to have a talk?" So Abu Said went out and I asked him, "Tell me what you heard from the Prophet about the Night of Qadr." Abu Said replied, "Once Allah's Apostle performed I'tikaf (seclusion) on the first ten days of the month of Ramadan and we did the same with him. Gabriel came to him and said, 'The night you are looking for is ahead of you.' So the Prophet performed the I'tikaf in the middle (second) ten days of the month of Ramadan and we too performed I'tikaf with him. Gabriel came to him and said, 'The night which you are looking for is ahead of you.' In the morning of the 20th of Ramadan the Prophet delivered a sermon saying, 'Whoever has performed I'tikaf with me should continue it. I have been shown the Night of "Qadr", but have forgotten its date, but it is in the odd nights of the last ten nights. I saw in my dream that I was prostrating in mud and water.' In those days the roof of the mosque was made of branches of date-palm trees. At that time the sky was clear and no cloud was visible, but suddenly a cloud came and it rained. The Prophet led us in the prayer and I saw the traces of mud on the forehead and on the nose of Allah's Apostle. So it was the confirmation of that dream."

Volume 1, Book 12, Number 778:

Narrated Sahl bin Sa'd:

The people used to pray with the Prophet tying their Izars around their necks because of their small sizes and the women were directed that they should not raise their heads from the prostrations till the men had sat straight.

Volume 1, Book 12, Number 779:

Narrated Ibn 'Abbas:

The Prophet was ordered to prostrate on seven bony parts and not to tuck up his clothes or hair.

Volume 1, Book 12, Number 780:

Narrated Ibn 'Abbas:

The Prophet said, "I have been ordered to prostrate on seven (bones) and not to tuck up the hair or garment."

Volume 1, Book 12, Number 781:

Narrated 'Aisha:

The Prophet used to say frequently in his bowing and prostrations "Subhanaka-Allahumma Rabbana Wabihamdika, Allahumma Ighfir-li" (I honor Allah from all what (unsuitable things) is ascribed to Him, O Allah! Our Lord! All praises are for You. O Allah! Forgive me). In this way he was acting on what was explained to him in the Holy Qur'an.

Volume 1, Book 12, Number 782:

Narrated Abu Qilaba:

Once Malik bin Huwairith said to his friends, "Shall I show you how Allah's Apostle used to offer his prayers?" And it was not the time for any of the compulsory congregational prayers. So he stood up (for the prayer) bowed and said the Takbir, then he raised his head and remained standing for a while and then prostrated and raised his head for a while (sat up for a while). He prayed like our Sheikh 'Amr Ibn Salama. (Aiyub said, "The latter used to do a thing which I did not see the people doing i.e. he used to sit between the third and the fourth Rak'a). IMalik bin Huwairith said, "We came to the Prophet (after embracing Islam) and stayed with him. He said to us, 'When you go back to your families, pray such and such a prayer at such and such a time, pray such and such a prayer at such and such a time, and when there is the time for the prayer then only of you should pronounce the Adhan for the prayer and the oldest of you should lead the prayer."

Volume 1, Book 12, Number 783:

Narrated Al-Bara':

The time taken by the Prophet in prostrations, bowing, and the sitting interval between the two prostrations was about the same.

Volume 1, Book 12, Number 784:

Narrated Thabit:

Anas said, "I will leave no stone unturned in making you offer the prayer as I have seen the Prophet making us offer it." Anas used to do a thing which I have not seen you doing. He used to stand after the bowing for such a long time that one would think that he had forgotten (the prostrations) and he used to sit in-between the prostrations so long that one would think that he had forgotten the second prostration.

Volume 1, Book 12, Number 785:

Narrated Anas bin Malik:

The Prophet said, "Be straight in the prostrations and none of you should put his forearms on the ground (in the prostration) like a dog."

Volume 1, Book 12, Number 786:

Narrated Malik bin Huwairith Al-Laithi:

I saw the Prophet praying and in the odd Rakat, he used to sit for a moment before getting up.

Volume 1, Book 12, Number 787:

Narrated Aiyub:

Abu Qilaba said, "Malik bin Huwairith came to us and led us in the prayer in this mosque of ours and said, 'I lead you in prayer but I do not want to offer the prayer but just to show you how Allah's Apostle performed his prayers." I asked Abu Qilaba, "How was the prayer of Malik bin Huwairith?" He replied, "Like the prayer of this Sheikh of ours-- i.e. 'Amr bin Salima." That Sheikh used to pronounce the Takbir perfectly and when he raised his head from the second prostration he would sit for a while and then support himself on the ground and get up.

Volume 1, Book 12, Number 788:

Narrated Said bin Al-Harith:

Abu Said led us in the prayer and said the Takbir aloud on arising from the prostration, and on prostrating, on rising again, and on getting up from the second Rak'a. Abu Said said, "I saw the Prophet doing the same."

Volume 1, Book 12, Number 789:

Narrated Mutarrif:

'Imran and I prayed behind 'Ali bin Abi Talib and he said Takbir on prostrating, on rising and on getting up after the two Rakat (i.e. after the second Rak'a). When the prayer was finished, 'Imran took me by the hand and said, "He ('Ali) has prayed the prayer of Muhammad" (or said, "He made us remember the prayer of Muhammad)."

Volume 1, Book 12, Number 790:

Narrated 'Abdullah bin 'Abdullah:

I saw 'Abdullah bin 'Umar crossing his legs while sitting in the prayer and I, a mere youngster in those days, did the same. Ibn 'Umar forbade me to do so, and said, "The proper way is to keep the right foot propped up and bend the left in the prayer." I said questioningly, "But you are doing so (crossing the legs)." He said, "My feet cannot bear my weight."

Volume 1, Book 12, Number 791:

Narrated Muhammad bin 'Amr bin 'Ata':

I was sitting with some of the companions of Allah's Apostle and we were discussing about the way of praying of the Prophet. Abu Humaid As-Saidi said, "I remember the prayer of Allah's Apostle better than any one of you. I saw him raising both his hands up to the level of the shoulders on saying the Takbir; and on bowing he placed his hands on both knees and bent his back straight, then he stood up straight from bowing till all the vertebrate took their normal positions. In prostrations, he placed both his hands on the ground with the forearms away from the ground and away from his body, and his toes were facing the Qibla. On sitting In the second Rak'a he sat on his left foot and propped up the right one; and in the last Rak'a he pushed his left foot forward and kept the other foot propped up and sat over the buttocks "

Volume 1, Book 12, Number 792:

Narrated 'Abdullah bin Buhaina:

(he was from the tribe of Uzd Shan'u'a and was the ally of the tribe of 'Abdul-Manaf and was one of the companions of the Prophet): Once the Prophet led us in the Zuhr prayer and stood up after the second Rak'a and did not sit down. The people stood up with him. When the prayer was about to end and the people were waiting for him to say the Taslim, he said Takbir while sitting and prostrated twice before saying the Taslim and then he said the Taslim."

Volume 1, Book 12, Number 793:

Narrated 'Abdullah bin Malik bin Buhaina:

Once Allah's Apostle led us in the Zuhr prayer and got up (after the prostrations of the second Rak'a) although he should have sat (for the Tashah-hud). So at the end of the prayer, he prostrated twice while sitting (prostrations of Sahu).

Volume 1, Book 12, Number 794:

Narrated Shaqlq bin Salama:

'Abdullah said, "Whenever we prayed behind the Prophet we used to recite (in sitting) 'Peace be on Gabriel, Michael, peace be on so and so. Once Allah's Apostle looked back at us and said, 'Allah Himself is As-Salam (Peace), and if anyone of you prays then he should say, At-Tahiyatu lil-lahi was-salawatu wat-taiyibatu. AsSalamu 'alalika aiyuha-n-Nabiyu wa rahmatu-l-lahi wa barakatuhu. As-Salam alaina wa ala ibadil-lah is-salihin. (All the compliments, prayers and good things are due to Allah: peace be on you, O Prophet and Allah's mercy and blessings be on you. Peace be on us an on the true pious slaves of Allah). (If you say that, it will be for all the slaves in the heaven and the earth). Ash-hadu an la-ilaha illa-l-lahu wa ash-hadu anna Muhammadan 'abduhu wa Rasuluhu. (I testify that none has the right to be worshipped but Allah and I also testify that Muhammad is His slave and His Apostle)."

Volume 1, Book 12, Number 795:

Narrated 'Aisha:

(the wife of the Prophet) Allah's Apostle used to invoke Allah in the prayer saying "Allahumma inni a'udhu bika min adhabil-qabri, wa a'udhu bika min fitnatil-masihid-dajjal, wa a'udhu bika min fit-natil-mahya wa fitnatil-mamati. Allahumma inni a'udhu bika minal-ma thami wal-maghrami. (O Allah, I seek refuge with You from the punishment of the grave and from the afflictions of Masi,h Ad-Dajjal and from the afflictions of life and death. O Allah, I seek refuge with You from the sins and from being in debt)." Somebody said to him, "Why do you so frequently seek refuge with Allah from being in debt?" The Prophet replied, "A person in debt tells lies whenever he speaks, and breaks promises whenever he makes (them)." 'Aisha also narrated: I heard Allah's Apostle in his prayer seeking refuge with Allah from the afflictions of Ad-dajjal.

Volume 1, Book 12, Number 796:

Narrated Abu Bakr As-Siddiq:

I asked Allah's Apostle to teach me an invocation so that I may invoke Allah with it in my prayer. He told me to say, "Allahumma inni zalumtu nafsi zulman kathiran, Wala yaghfirudhdhunuba illa anta faghfirli maghfiratan min 'Indika, war-hamni innaka antal-ghafururrahim (O Allah! I have done great injustice to myself and none except You forgives sins, so please forgive me and be Merciful to me as You are the Forgiver, the Merciful)."

Volume 1, Book 12, Number 797:

Narrated 'Abdullah:

When we prayed with the Prophet we used to say, "Peace be on Allah from His slaves and peace be on so and so." The Prophet said, "Don't say As-Salam be on Allah, for He Himself is As-Salam, but say, 'At-tahiyatu lil-lahi was-salawatu wat-taiyibatu. As-salamu 'Alaika aiyuhan-Nabiyu warahmatu-l-lahi wa barakatuhu. As-salamu 'alaina wa 'ala ibadillahis-salihin. (If you say this then it will be for all the slaves in heaven or between heaven and earth). Ashhadu an la-ilaha illallahu wa ashhadu anna Muhammadan 'Abduhu wa Rasuluhu.' Then select the invocation you like best and recite it." (See Hadith No. 794, 795 & 796).

Volume 1, Book 12, Number 798:

Narrated Abu Said Al-Khudri:

I saw Allah's Apostle prostrating in mud and water and saw the mark of mud on his forehead.

Volume 1, Book 12, Number 799:

Narrated Um Salama:

Whenever Allah's Apostle finished his prayers with Taslim, the women would get up and he would stay on for a while in his place before getting up. Ibn Shihab said, "I think (and Allah knows better), that the purpose of his stay was that the women might leave before the men who had finished their prayer. "

Volume 1, Book 12, Number 800:

Narrated 'Itban bin Malik:

We prayed with the Prophet and used to finish our prayer with the Taslim along with him.

Volume 1, Book 12, Number 801:

Narrated Mahmud bin Ar-Rabi':

I remember Allah's Apostle and also the mouthful of water which he took from a bucket in our house and ejected (on me). I heard from Itban bin Malik Al-Ansari, who was one from Bani Salim, saying, "I used to lead my tribe of Bani Salim in prayer. Once I went to the Prophet and said to him, 'I have weak eye-sight and at times the rainwater flood intervenes between me and the mosque of my tribe and I wish that you would come to my house and pray at some place so that I could take that place as a place for praying (mosque). He said, "Allah willing, I shall do that." Next day Allah's Apostle along with Abu Bakr, came to my house after the sun had risen high and he asked permission to enter. I gave him permission, but he didn't sit till he said to me, "Where do you want me to pray in your house?" I pointed to a place in the house where I wanted him to pray. So he stood up for the prayer and we aligned behind him. He completed the prayer with Taslim and we did the same simultaneously."

Volume 1, Book 12, Number 802:

Narrated Abu Ma'bad:

(the freed slave of Ibn 'Abbas) Ibn 'Abbas told me, "In the lifetime of the Prophet it was the custom to celebrate Allah's praises aloud after the compulsory congregational prayers." Ibn 'Abbas further said, "When I heard the Dhikr, I would learn that the compulsory congregational prayer had ended."

Volume 1, Book 12, Number 803:

Narrated Ibn 'Abbas:

I used to recognize the completion of the prayer of the Prophet by hearing Takbir.

Volume 1, Book 12, Number 804:

Narrated Abu Huraira:

Some poor people came to the Prophet and said, "The wealthy people will get higher grades and will have permanent enjoyment and they pray like us and fast as we do. They have more money by which they perform the Hajj, and 'Umra; fight and struggle in Allah's Cause and give in charity." The Prophet said, "Shall I not tell you a thing upon which if you acted you would catch up with those who have surpassed you? Nobody would overtake you and you would be better than the people amongst whom you live except those who would do the same. Say "Sub-han-al-lah", "Alhamdu-lil-lah" and "Allahu Akbar" thirty three times each after every (compulsory) prayer." We differed and some of us said that we should say, "Subhan-al-lah" thirty three times and "Alhamdu lillah" thirty three times and "Allahu Akbar" thirty four times. I went to the Prophet who said, "Say, "Subhan-allah" and "Alhamdu lillah" and "Allahu Akbar" all together for thirty three times."

Volume 1, Book 12, Number 805:

Narrated Warrad:

(the clerk of Al-Mughira bin Shu'ba) Once Al-Mughira dictated to me in a letter addressed to Mu'awiya that the Prophet used to say after every compulsory prayer, "La ilaha ilallah wahdahu la sharika lahu, lahul-mulku wa-lahul-hamdu, wahuwa ala kulli shai in qadir. Allahumma la mani 'a lima a'taita, wa la mu'tiya lima mana'ta, wa la yanfa'u dhal-jaddi minka-l-jadd. (None has the right to be worshipped but Allah and He has no partner in Lordship or in worship or in the Names and the Qualities, and for Him is the Kingdom and all the praises are for Him and He is omnipotent. O Allah! Nobody can hold back what you give and nobody can give what You hold back. Hard (efforts by anyone for anything cannot benefit one against Your Will)." And Al-Hasan said, "Al-jadd' means prosperity."

Volume 1, Book 12, Number 806:

Narrated Samura bin Jundab:

The Prophet used to face us on completion of the prayer.

Volume 1, Book 12, Number 807:

Narrated Zaid bin Khalid Al-Juhani:

The Prophet led us in the Fajr prayer at Hudaibiya after a rainy night. On completion of the prayer, he faced the people and said, "Do you know what your Lord has said (revealed)?" The people replied, "Allah and His Apostle know better." He said, "Allah has said, 'In this morning some of my slaves remained as true believers and some became non-believers; whoever said that the rain was due to the Blessings and the Mercy of Allah had belief in Me and he disbelieves in the stars, and whoever said that it rained because of a particular star had no belief in Me but believes in that star.' "

Volume 1, Book 12, Number 808:

Narrated Anas bin Malik:

Once the Prophet delayed the 'Isha' prayer until midnight and then came to us. Having prayed he faced us and said, "The people had prayed and slept but you were in the prayer as long as you were waiting for it."

Volume 1, Book 12, Number 809:

Narrated Um Salama:

"The Prophet after finishing the prayer with Taslim used to stay at his place for a while." Ibn Shihab said, "I think (and Allah knows better), that he used to wait for the departure of the women who had prayed." Ibn Shihab wrote that he had heard it from Hind bint Al-Harith Al-Firasiya from Um Salama, the wife of the Prophet (Hind was from the companions of Um Salama) who said, "When the Prophet finished the prayer with Taslim, the women would depart and enter their houses before Allah's Apostle departed."

Volume 1, Book 12, Number 810:

Narrated 'Uqba:

I offered the 'Asr prayer behind the Prophet at Medina. When he had finished the prayer with Taslim, he got up hurriedly and went out by crossing the rows of the people to one of the dwellings of his wives. The people got scared at his speed . The Prophet came back and found the people surprised at his haste and said to them, "I remembered a piece of gold Lying in my house and I did not like it to divert my attention from Allah's worship, so I have ordered it to be distributed (in charity)."

Volume 1, Book 12, Number 811:

Narrated 'Abdullah:

You should not give away a part of your prayer to Satan by thinking that it is necessary to depart (after finishing the prayer) from one's right side only; I have seen the Prophet often leave from the left side.

Volume 1, Book 12, Number 812:

Narrated Ibn 'Umar:

During the holy battle of Khaibar the Prophet said, "Whoever ate from this plant (i.e. garlic) should not enter our mosque."

Volume 1, Book 12, Number 813:

Narrated 'Ata':

I heard Jabir bin 'Abdullah saying, "The Prophet said, 'Whoever eats (from) this plant (he meant garlic) should keep away from our mosque." I said, "What does he mean by that?" He replied, "I think he means only raw garlic."

Volume 1, Book 12, Number 814:

Narrated Jabir bin 'Abdullah:

The Prophet said, "Whoever eats garlic or onion should keep away from our mosque or should remain in his house." (Jabir bin 'Abdullah, in another narration said, "Once a big pot containing cooked vegetables was brought. On finding unpleasant smell coming from it, the Prophet asked, 'What is in it?' He was told all the names of the vegetables that were in it. The Prophet ordered that it should be brought near to some of his companions who were with him. When the Prophet saw it he disliked to eat it and said, 'Eat. (I don't eat) for I converse with those whom you don't converse with (i.e. the angels)."

Volume 1, Book 12, Number 815:

Narrated 'Abdul 'Aziz:

A man asked Anas, "What did you hear from the Prophet about garlic?" He said, "The Prophet said, 'Whoever has eaten this plant should neither come near us nor pray with us."

Volume 1, Book 12, Number 816:

Narrated Sulaiman Ash-Shaibam:

I heard Ash-Sha'bi saying, "A person who was accompanying the Prophet passed by a grave that was separated from the other graves told me that the Prophet once led the people in the (funeral) prayer and the people had aligned behind him. I said, "O Aba 'Amr! Who told you about it?" He said, "Ibn Abbas."

Volume 1, Book 12, Number 817:

Narrated Abu Said Al-Khudri:

The Prophet said, "Ghusl (taking a bath) on Friday is compulsory for every Muslim reaching the age of puberty."

Volume 1, Book 12, Number 818:

Narrated Ibn 'Abbas:

One night I slept at the house of my aunt Maimuna and the Prophet slept (too). He got up (for prayer) in the last hours of the night and performed a light ablution from a hanging leather skin. ('Amr, the sub-narrator described that the ablution was very light). Then he stood up for prayer and I got up too and performed the ablution in the same way and joined him on his left side. He pulled me to the right and prayed as much as Allah will. Then he lay down and slept and I heard his breath sounds till the Mu'adh-dhin came to him to inform him about the (Fajr) prayer. He left with him for the prayer and prayed without repeating the ablution. (Sufyan the subnarrator said: We said to 'Amr, "Some people say, 'The eyes of the Prophet sleep but his heart never sleeps.' " 'Amr said, "'Ubai bin 'Umar said, 'The dreams of the Prophets are Divine Inspirations. Then he recited, '(O my son), I have seen in dream that I was slaughtering you (offering you in sacrifice).") (37.102)

Volume 1, Book 12, Number 819:

Narrated Anas bin Malik:

My grandmother Mulaika invited Allah's Apostle for a meal which she had prepared specially for him. He ate some of it and said, "Get up. I shall lead you in the prayer." I brought a mat that had become black owing to excessive use and I sprinkled water on it. Allah's Apostle stood on it and prayed two Rakat; and the orphan was with me (in the first row), and the old lady stood behind us.

Volume 1, Book 12, Number 820:

Narrated Ibn 'Abbas:

Once I came riding a she-ass and I, then, had just attained the age of puberty. Allah's Apostle was leading the people in prayer at Mina facing no wall. I passed in front of the row and let loose the she-ass for grazing and joined the row and no one objected to my deed.

Volume 1, Book 12, Number 821:

Narrated 'Aisha:

Once Allah's Apostle delayed the 'Isha' prayer till 'Umar informed him that the women and children had slept. Then Allah's Apostle came out and said: "None from amongst the dwellers of earth have prayed this prayer except you." In those days none but the people of Medina prayed.

Volume 1, Book 12, Number 822:

Narrated 'Abdur Rahman bin 'Abis:

A person asked Ibn Abbas, "Have you ever presented yourself at the ('Id) prayer with Allah's Apostle?" He replied, "Yes." And had it not been for my kinship (position) with the Prophet it would not have been possible for me to do so (for he was too young). The Prophet went to the mark near the house of Kathir bin As-Salt and delivered a sermon. He then went towards the women. He advised and reminded them and asked them to give alms. So the woman would bring her hand near her neck and take off her necklace and put it in the garment of Bilal. Then the Prophet and Bilal came to the house."

Volume 1, Book 12, Number 823:

Narrated 'Aisha:

Once Allah's Apostle delayed the 'Isha' prayer till 'Umar informed him that the women and children had slept. The Prophet came out and said, "None except you from amongst the dwellers of earth is waiting for this prayer." In those days, there was no prayer except in Medina and they used to pray the 'Isha' prayer between the disappearance of the twilight and the first third of the night.

Volume 1, Book 12, Number 824:

Narrated Ibn 'Umar:

The Prophet said, "If your women ask permission to go to the mosque at night, allow them."

Volume 1, Book 12, Number 825:

Narrated Um Salama:

(the wife of the Prophet) In the lifetime of Allah's Apostle the women used to get up when they finished their compulsory prayers with Taslim. The Prophet and the men would stay on at their places as long as Allah will. When the Prophet got up, the men would then get up.

Volume 1, Book 12, Number 826:

Narrated 'Aisha:

When Allah's Apostle finished the Fajr prayer, the women would leave covered in their sheets and were not recognized owing to the darkness.

Volume 1, Book 12, Number 827:

Narrated 'Abdullah bin Abi Qatada Al-Ansari:

My father said, "Allah's Apostle said, "Whenever I stand for prayer, I want to prolong it but on hearing the cries of a child, I would shorten it as I dislike to put its mother in trouble."

Volume 1, Book 12, Number 828:

Narrated 'Aisha:

Had Allah's Apostle known what the women were doing, he would have forbidden them from going to the mosque as the women of Bani Israel had been forbidden. Yahya bin Said (a sub-narrator) asked 'Amra (another sub-narrator), "Were the women of Bani Israel forbidden?" She replied "Yes."

Volume 1, Book 12, Number 829:

Narrated Um Salama:

Whenever Allah's Apostle completed the prayer with Taslim, the women used to get up immediately and Allah's Apostle would remain at his place for someone before getting up. (The sub-narrator (Az-Zuhri) said, "We think, and Allah knows better, that he did so, so that the women might leave before men could get in touch with them)."

Volume 1, Book 12, Number 830:

Narrated Anas:

The Prophet prayed in the house of Um Sulaim; and I, along with an orphan stood behind him while Um Sulaim (stood) behind us.

Volume 1, Book 12, Number 831:

Narrated 'Aisha:

Allah's Apostle used to offer the Fajr prayer when it was still dark and the believing women used to return (after finishing their prayer) and nobody could recognize them owing to darkness, or they could not recognize one another.

Volume 1, Book 12, Number 832:

Narrated Salim bin 'Abdullah:

My father said, "The Prophet said, 'If the wife of any one of you asks permission (to go to the mosque) do not forbid her."

www.ingramcontent.com/pod-product-compliance
Lightning Source LLC
Chambersburg PA
CBHW062010090426
42811CB00005B/809